0 304 936 790 01

AIR-GUNS AND AIR-PISTOLS

AIR-GUNS
AND
AIR-PISTOLS

by L. WESLEY

Revised and enlarged edition

CASSELL
LONDON

CASSELL LTD.
35 Red Lion Square, London WC1R 4SG
and at Sydney, Auckland, Toronto, Johannesburg,
an affiliate of
Macmillan Publishing Co., Inc.,
New York.

First published November 1955
Second edition January 1957
Third (revised and enlarged) edition 1961
Fourth (revised) edition August 1964
Fifth edition October 1965
Sixth (revised and enlarged) edition July 1971
Sixth edition, second impression February 1974
Sixth edition, third impression October 1976
Sixth edition, fourth impression July 1978

ISBN 0 304 93679 0

Printed in Great Britain by
Fletcher & Son Ltd, Norwich

TO MY WIFE

without whose encouragement this book would probably never have been written.

ACKNOWLEDGEMENTS

For supplying many of the photographs published in this book, and also for their kind co-operation in other ways, grateful acknowledgement is due to the following: Webley and Scott Ltd., Birmingham; B.S.A. Guns Ltd., Birmingham; W. W. Greener Ltd., Birmingham; Accles and Shelvoke Ltd., Birmingham; A. and A. Brown and Sons, Birmingham; Westley Richards and Co. Ltd., London; Frank Dyke and Co., Ltd.; Sheridan Products Inc., Wisconsin, U.S.A.; Crosman Arms Corporation, New York, U.S.A.; Gustav Genschow and Co., Hamburg; Daisy and Heddon, Arkansas, U.S.A.

CONTENTS

SOME DO'S AND DON'TS

Do take adequate precautions when handling or using an air-gun or pistol.

Do remember to buy a gun licence if you intend to carry or use your weapon away from your own house or grounds.

Do make certain your weapon is not cocked or loaded before putting it aside.

Do use only slugs or pellets of a well-known and reliable brand. These will ensure consistently accurate shooting, whereas cheap, poorly-formed ammunition will not.

Do give your weapon a little regular attention to preserve its finish and maintain its velocity at the maximum.

Do be careful to use the correct internal lubricant if the makers specially recommend one; and use only genuine spare parts obtainable through a recognized dealer or direct from the manufacturers.

Don't lend your air weapon to anyone unless you are positive they can be safely trusted with it.

Don't load a pellet into the breech tap of an underlever air-rifle unless you have first cocked it, or a partial vacuum may be formed in front of the piston, and the weapon will not develop its full power.

Don't cock a spring-operated air-rifle or air-pistol until you are ready to shoot it. Mainsprings become rapidly weakened by being kept compressed for long periods.

Don't discharge a spring-operated air weapon without first loading it with a pellet, or serious internal damage may result.

Don't try to improve your weapon's performance by fitting an extra-powerful mainspring. You may obtain a slight increase in velocity but will create excessive wear on all the working parts.

Don't allow the local handyman to dismantle or repair your weapon—take it to a reliable dealer who can be relied on to execute the work in a professional manner.

Don't forget to raise the backsight of your air-rifle for long-range shots and to lower it again for short distances or you will not hit your target.

ILLUSTRATIONS

INTRODUCTION

THIS book has been written to satisfy the many requests I have had for information about air-guns. I do not pretend that it covers the subject comprehensively, as to do full justice to such a vast subject would need far more space than is at my disposal and, indeed, would take up far more time than I could devote to its writing. It would not, in fact, be an exaggeration to say that a whole book of this size could be written about any one type of air weapon mentioned within these pages.

During the past twenty years I have made an extensive study of firearms in general and of air-guns in particular, and it has been my privilege to set down in the following pages a part of this experience in the hope that this book will be both instructive and interesting.

I must stress, however, that this is not intended to be a technical work, but has been compiled to give information that should interest everyone from the schoolboy owning a Junior air-gun, to the adult, interested in high-power pneumatic rifles.

I think most men have an inborn love of weapons. Certainly, most schoolboys long for an air-rifle, and happy are their proud possessors, who delight in showing their prowess at target practice or at shooting vermin and small game.

Usually these youngsters graduate to better and more powerful air-rifles, and eventually to the ownership of a ·22 cartridge rifle or a shotgun. Many, however, still retain their old favourites, and time has shown that, however many weapons a man may possess, he will get far more sport from a good air-rifle than he will from all the rest of his guns together.

Nor is it only the young generation who succumb to the peculiar charm of the air-rifle. Adults find that a good air-rifle is capable of giving an excellent account of itself, both in accuracy and power, and that it also has many other advantages that render it an extremely desirable weapon to possess.

For example, it can be shot and laid aside without the need for elaborate cleaning, as there are no powder residues liable to rust or corrode the barrel. It calls for no special attention other than an occasional drop of oil, and, provided it is treated with ordinary care, will virtually last a lifetime.

The cost of shooting with an air-rifle is modest in the extreme, and the trifling cost of pellets is many times less than that of ·22 cartridges.

Other advantages are that air-rifles can be purchased and used without the need for obtaining a firearm certificate, and that they can be used in one's house, cellar, or garden, provided reasonable safety precautions are taken, where a ·22 cartridge rifle would be quite out of the question.

Air-rifles, particularly the pneumatic or 'pump-up' types, are extremely pleasant to shoot, have no noticeable recoil, and, moreover, make practically no noise.

The absence of noise is important to the tyro, as it eliminates 'flinching', one of the commonest faults of bad marksmanship with the powder rifle. Furthermore, when used for sporting purposes, the disturbance to game (and to one's neighbours) is entirely eliminated.

These are some of the factors that have led to the ever-increasing popularity of the air-rifle throughout the years. To-day, an extremely high standard of reliability and efficiency has been attained whilst accuracy at moderate ranges is equal to that of a first-class cartridge rifle.

May I make three requests to everyone reading this book?

Firstly, please do not shoot at cats, dogs, or other domestic animals. Painful injuries resulting in much unnecessary suffering can be caused in this way.

Secondly, please do not shoot our song birds. Try your hand at shooting pigeons or rabbits by all means, and enjoy a tasty meal as a reward for your skill. Rats, mice, grey squirrels and starlings are pests that should be shot, and provide excellent sport for the 'air-gunner', whilst one enthusiast of my acquaintance considers that snail shooting is the finest sport of all!

Lastly, please treat the air-rifle with the respect you would accord to a firearm, and regard every one as a loaded weapon until you have satisfied yourself that it is not. Even the feeblest toy air-gun, if wantonly discharged, can cause the loss of an eye or other injury.

During the three years ending 28th February 1934, all Chief Constables in Great Britain were requested to furnish reports of all cases of accidents involving personal injury, caused by certain types of weapons.

A total of 302 persons were injured by air-guns, air-rifles and air-pistols, and in 63 of these cases the injuries were of a serious nature. In only two instances were the accidents due to any mechanical fault with the weapon itself.

It cannot be too strongly stressed that weapons should never be pointed at anyone, even in fun, and if you see this being done, do not hesitate to stop it at once.

CHAPTER I

THE CLASSIFICATION OF AIR WEAPONS

ALTHOUGH there are hundreds of thousands of air-rifles in use to-day, the great majority of 'air-gunners' are familiar only with those whose makers' names are so well known as to be almost household words. There are, however, in existence large numbers of unusual air weapons of different types and designs, which are extremely interesting and well worthy of their place in the gun rack of the collector or the shooting enthusiast.

Many of the types I shall mention are comparatively rare, and some extremely so; which, of course, from the collector's point of view, makes them all the more desirable to possess.

It would be almost impossible for anyone to have a specimen of every kind of air weapon, as their numbers are legion. Many years ago I began seriously to collect air-guns, thinking that I should eventually have every known type. I acquired some four hundred air-guns and still the end was nowhere in sight. I then decided to narrow the field by collecting air-pistols, thinking that I should certainly be able to obtain a specimen of every different type of air-pistol. Once again I had to call a halt when I had collected a mere 280 and it seemed as if I could go on for ever. Just when I thought I had seen every possible type, several more quite different ones would turn up and make me revise my previous convictions.

For example, who would think of an air-gun as having more than one barrel? Yet types exist having two, three, four, and five barrels and I have even had an air-operated goose-gun with seven barrels.

Air-gun collecting can be an expensive hobby if one covets the rare specimens that are in existence, yet there is no reason at all why the enthusiast should not be able to acquire at least a fair selection of different types that he can proudly display and shoot with. The essentials of collecting consist in being able to recognize all the different types, in having sufficient space to house and display your collection under suitable conditions, and above all in 'biding your time'. Remember, it is nearly always the person who is in a hurry to buy who pays the price. Obviously, there is more to air-gun collecting than can be put in a few sentences and further advice to collectors will be found in another chapter.

It would be as well at this stage to explain exactly what is meant by an air-gun, air-rifle, or air-pistol. I sometimes meet people who think that an air-gun is a gun for shooting into the air with! Others have told me that they always think of an air-gun as a machine-gun used for aerial combat in war. Most members of the fair sex frankly have not the slightest idea what an air-gun is, but we can cheerfully excuse them as, after all, why should they bother their pretty heads over such things?

AIR-GUNS. The term 'air-guns' is loosely used (as in the title of this book) to mean any and every long arm in which the bullets or missiles are projected by compressed air. Properly applied, however, the term air-gun means a gun *with a smooth, non-rifled barrel* in which the propellant is compressed air. A gun, incidentally, is intended to be held with both hands, but not necessarily shot from the shoulder.

AIR-RIFLES. An 'air-*rifle*' can be described in the same way as an air-gun, except that to be a 'rifle' the barrel *must* contain internal helical lines or grooves running through its length. The number of these grooves may vary from as few as two to as many as thirty. The purpose of this twist is to cause the pellet or bullet to spin on its axis, which makes it fly much straighter and truer than it would do if fired from a smooth-bore gun.

Rifling is such a pronounced improvement that all air weapons of to-day are so rifled with the exception of a few cheap air-guns and pistols mainly of foreign manufacture, which are mere toys and not intended for serious shooting. Such weapons are primarily designed to shoot the coloured tufted air-gun darts and provide much harmless fun for the young shooter.

AIR-PISTOLS. An air-pistol is a weapon designed to be aimed and discharged with one hand, and can have either a rifled or a smooth-bore barrel.

Throughout this book the various air weapons will be referred to by their correct designations. The two main classifications of all air weapons are 'spring-operated' and 'pneumatic', the latter type often being known as 'pump-up'. For the sake of clarity, I think it would be as well, before going any further, to explain exactly what is meant by these terms, 'Spring-Operated' and 'Pneumatic'.

SPRING-OPERATED WEAPONS. A spring-operated air weapon is one in which the air is compressed at the moment of discharging the arm. Nearly all such weapons, irrespective of whether they are guns, rifles, or pistols, consist essentially of a smooth-walled cylinder containing a well-fitting piston, driven by a powerful spring. Provision is made by suitably arranged levers to push or draw this piston backward thus compressing the spring where it is held by the sear. When the trigger is pressed, the sear is disengaged from the piston, which is driven forward violently. This results in the air which is contained in the cylinder in front of the piston being compressed and escaping down the barrel of the arm, thus projecting the pellet, slug, or dart with great force.

It must be borne in mind that many hundreds of different spring-operated air weapons have been produced and each maker has had his own particular ideas of design. Consequently, such guns, rifles, and pistols appear to be all quite distinctly different from one another, but the basic principles remain the same.

The two main classifications of spring-operated and pneumatic weapons can be sub-divided into many different headings, according to the ways and means employed in their mechanical operation.

SPRING-OPERATED AIR-RIFLES. Spring-operated weapons can, as we have seen, be in the form of guns, rifles, or pistols. Those coming under the heading of rifles with rifled barrels can be divided again into two types:

1. Those whose spring is compressed or cocked by 'breaking the gun', or in other words using the barrel itself as a lever. These are commonly referred to as 'breakdown air-rifles'.
2. Those whose barrels are fixed rigidly and the cocking performed by a separate lever or levers. These are known as underlever air-rifles. Many forms of spring-operated repeating rifles have been made at different times, these being mainly of continental manufacture.

SPRING-OPERATED AIR-GUNS. Modern spring-operated air-guns with smooth-bore barrels are all of the breakdown variety, but there are many vintage air-guns in existence which used other means of cocking. The most notable were those using the 'bellows' system; and those cocked by turning a crank handle. Several repeating air-guns were available, too, many years ago.

SPRING-OPERATED AIR-PISTOLS. Spring air-pistols take numerous forms, among which are those cocked by means of using the pistol barrel as a lever, those cocked by pulling the barrel outwards, and those in which the barrel is pushed inwards to compress the spring. Other pistols make use of the pistol butt as a lever, to cock the weapon. There have also been many other mechanical arrangements used at different times by both English and continental makers.

One such cocking system used a lever pivoted at the muzzle end of the weapon and fitted along the side of the spring chamber. Another pistol had a rod which fitted into a groove at the rear end of the butt. This rod was pivoted at the breech of the weapon and could be lifted up until it came into line with the spring chamber and then pushed inwards to compress the mainspring.

There are, in existence, many forms of repeating air-pistols of the spring-operated variety, mostly of German make, although an American repeater is being produced at the present time.

PNEUMATIC WEAPONS. Pneumatic or 'pump-up' weapons operate on an entirely different system. It is true that they make use of compressed air as a propellant for the bullet or slug, but in this case the air is *first* compressed or condensed into a reservoir or chamber and is retained there under compression until the arm is discharged. This is usually accomplished by pumping air into the air-chamber or reservoir by means of a single-stage air pump, the air-chamber being fitted with either one or two valves.

Pneumatic weapons take the form of rifles, guns and pistols, and each of these three main divisions can be divided again into two headings.

1. Those charged by means of a self-contained air pump arranged as an integral part of the weapon itself.
2. Those in which an entirely separate pump is employed.

The former include all the modern pneumatics, while the latter embrace mainly the older types.

The further sub-division of the different types of pneumatic weapons is a far more complex matter than in the case of the spring varieties.

There are, for instance, both single-shot and repeating pneumatic guns and rifles; and also single-barrelled and multi-barrelled weapons.

Some of these weapons had their air reservoir contained in the stock or butt, or in a cylinder underneath the barrel, while other air storage containers consisted of a hollow metal ball which was usually fixed to the underside of the gun. Specimens also exist where this air-ball is located in the centre of the stock or on the top of the gunlock, set slightly to one side in order to keep it clear of the sights. Some of the more cunningly designed ones had the air container built like a hollow shell round the barrel. Many of these different pneumatic weapons exist in single and multi-barrelled forms and with either breech-loading or muzzle-loading systems.

Pneumatic pistols were always single-barrelled although some early ones were constructed as repeaters and were fitted with a bullet magazine.

It will be convenient not to take the classification of pneumatic weapons too far, as there are other variations of construction far too numerous to deal with at length. Many different systems were employed, for example, in releasing the highly compressed air, whilst loading and cocking were also arranged in a number of original ways.

GAS-OPERATED WEAPONS. There are other types of rifles and pistols which do not strictly fall within the two main classifications described above, the most notable being the gas-rifle. This type substitutes liquified carbon-dioxide gas for compressed air. Originally, such gas-rifles were provided with a small detachable gas cyclinder, generally located underneath and parallel to the barrel. These cylinders when empty were intended to be exchanged by the makers or their agents for full ones, but modern American-made gas-rifles now have the gas cylinder as an integral part of the rifle and a small supply cylinder sold with the rifle contains sufficient gas for many complete charges. The supply cylinder must, of course, be exchanged when exhausted, for a full one.

Rifles and pistols operating on this system are a standard product in the U.S.A. at the present time.

Gas-operated weapons are usually repeaters in that one charging of gas will fire many shots, but normally the pellets or bullets have to be loaded one at a time, by hand. Modern rifles using gas instead of air have a gas container running underneath the barrel and usually about as long as the barrel, and this container is filled by screwing the gas supply cylinder directly to it.

Some pistols operating on compressed gas use the same system for filling, but others have a small gas bulb or cartridge which is put into the pistol and removed when exhausted. These gas bulbs provide twenty-five to thirty shots on those pistols not having a power adjustment device and usually up to fifty shots at lower power, if a power controller is provided.

BLOWPIPES. Another type of air-gun that is technically a pneumatic, but is not embraced by either of the two main groups, is the very simple blow-tube or blowpipe, through which a dart is blown by the mouth. This is an air-gun reduced to its simplest form, yet it is a very deadly weapon indeed, and in skilful hands is capable of astonishing accuracy. So interesting are these blowpipes that I have thought them worthy of a short chapter to themselves (see Chapter 3).

MISCELLANEOUS WEAPONS. Very early air-guns that I have handled and shot with include those in which a flat spring, when released, compressed a pair of bellows that blew the bullet out of the barrel. Some such specimens exist in museums and private collections and are rare enough to command a high price.

Others of a later date were wound up by means of a crank which operated a rack and pinion arrangement to cock the springs. Still another system of cocking was by means of a long lever terminating in a knob which acted directly on the mainspring.

One of the most extraordinary weapons that I have ever seen was apparently designed to operate in a most peculiar way. A cylinder located underneath the weapon's barrel was fitted with a percussion nipple which was struck by a hammer in the same way as with the old muzzle-loading firearms. In this case, however, the explosion of the cap fired a charge of loose gunpowder, the burning of which created a gas pressure in the cylinder, and this pressure, released by means of a second hammer, was utilized to project the bullet from the barrel. Unfortunately, the valve and parts of the mechanism were missing, which made it difficult to understand how such an arrangement could be made to function satisfactorily.

It serves to show, however, that the most 'weird and wonderful' systems have been devised and utilized at different times in the construction of air weapons.

In fact, so much could be written about the subject that one might well quote the story of the learned professor, who, when asked if he would give a lecture on fish, replied that it was impossible, but he would be prepared to give a course of lectures on a fish scale!

CHAPTER 2

A BRIEF HISTORY

THE invention of the air-gun is often ascribed to that celebrated inventor and painter Leonardo da Vinci. That da Vinci was an outstanding genius in mechanical matters no one will deny, nor is anyone likely to dispute the many inventions which were without doubt products of his fertile brain. Nevertheless there is no proof that he invented the air-gun, nor are there any grounds for supposition that this was the case.

The earliest known record of any such weapon was of a 'Windbüchse' made by Guter of Nuremberg in 1530, and it is therefore probable that Guter could be named as the true inventor.

Various improvements were made by German, French, Polish, Dutch, Swiss, and English gunmakers. Among those who played their part in producing and improving the air-gun were Sars of Berlin, Contriner of Vienna, Muller of Warsaw, Bouillet of France, Speyer of Holland, and Bate of England.

Guter's air-gun was constructed with a hollow stock in which the air was contained. Such hollow stocks were usually flask shaped and were brazed down their length and riveted. They were of crude workmanship as would be expected at such an early period, but they were enormously strong. An odd 'air-stock' which had at some time belonged to a very ancient air-gun of around 1600 vintage, was recently tested to the point of destruction by means of a gradually increasing air pressure.

This air-stock withstood the enormous pressure of six

thousand pounds per square inch, before it eventually gave way, and even at this pressure the stock did not explode but merely leaked at one of the rivet holes.

Air-guns were made also by Lobsinger of Nuremberg and other German gunmakers around 1550, while in 1600 Marin of Lisieux constructed a 'repeating' air-gun. This was a repeating weapon only in that the air-chamber contained enough air to fire several shots. It was not a true repeater because it had no bullet magazine. This gun was of the type known as a wheel-lock in which the spring operating the air release was wound up by means of a key or spanner, and the action was similar to the rapid opening and closing of a tap. When the trigger was pressed, the spring expanded and a tap was revolved, causing it to open momentarily and then close and remain in the closed position. It is recorded that Marin presented one of his air-guns to Henry IV of France.

In 1607, another Nuremberg gunsmith named Dumbler made an air-gun that according to contemporary records 'shot through a thumb-thick plank'. The Town Council, however, refused to allow him to market it because it was held to be a 'murderous weapon with which a man might be killed and yet not know what had hit him'.

About 1655 George Fehr of Dresden was making air-guns in which the air reservoir was constructed in a jacket or shell arranged round the barrel.

These weapons had an external hammer that was located underneath the gun and this hammer struck the valve pin and released the air. The air pumps were not separate units, but were built into the stocks of the weapons and were arranged so that the pump was not visible when in the closed position at the end of its stroke. Calibres varied from ·375 to ·500.

Fehr also made air-pistols on the same principle and, as far as I am aware, these are the earliest known pistols operated by compressed air.

Between 1700 and 1750 air-guns were being made by very many gunmakers in North Germany. A peculiarity of construction appeared to become popular at this period whereby the lock mechanism (hammer springs, etc.) was built on the *outside* of the lock-plate.

There appears to be no explanation for this, as it was unsightly to say the least, and was in my opinion a step backwards rather than forwards. It had the doubtful advantage that the mechanism was self-explanatory and, being exposed, could be repaired by the replacement of any of the working parts without dismantling the whole gun. It is possible that this may have been the real reason behind such an arrangement, as air-guns were no longer a rarity and obviously repairs must have been carried out by gun-makers who did not themselves actually make air-guns.

It has since occurred to me that a reason for the outside lock construction may have been to allow the air to pass straight through the space usually occupied by the mechanism without resorting to the provision of a separate tube for this purpose. The air would therefore pass from stock to barrel without any restriction.

Among the many German makers of this period were Hauschka of Wolfenbuttel, and Schlatter of Rostock. Calibres varied from ·250 to ·500 although a few guns were made with calibres up to ·750, but these were the exceptions rather than the rule.

About 1720 the 'flintlock' air-gun was invented and it is recorded that Franck of Hanover was a maker of this type of gun.

These 'flintlock' air-guns were very peculiar weapons. Externally they looked exactly like the flintlock gunpowder guns of the period, and had an external cock or hammer and a pan and frizzen. On many of these air-guns the pan could be primed with gunpowder and then by pulling back the cock, the pan of powder could be fired. The powder, however, did not in any way affect the bullet as there was no communication between the barrel of the gun and the pan. The bullet was propelled solely by compressed air although the flash from the pan gave the impression that the weapon was a firearm.

Some guns were constructed in which the 'flintlock' part was only a dummy and the cock and the pan cover were immovable, but mostly the external cock and pan were made to be used. The reason behind all this is subject to conjecture and many arguments have been put forward in support of various theories.

At this time, arms operated by compressed air were regarded as being the weapons of assassins, poachers, and other persons of ill-repute, and this would explain quite satisfactorily the reason for gunmakers cunningly designing air-guns and camouflaging them so that they looked exactly like firearms.

On the other hand it is quite as likely that it may have been done purely for novelty, in much the same way as, for example, some modern air-pistols are designed to look like automatics. Some of these flintlock air-guns were so expertly made that it was only by a very careful scrutiny that they could be distinguished from the flint-guns of the period. These air-guns and rifles were almost silent and very deadly weapons, and were frequently used for shooting deer and other large game.

'Flintlock' air-guns were still being made in 1740, although a few years before this a new type of air-gun had been introduced. This was the 'bellows' air-gun. These were all made with smooth-bore barrels and were not powerful. They were used mainly for target shooting in shooting galleries and their advantage for such purposes was that no laborious pumping was needed. Wax bullets were frequently shot from these guns, although lead bullets were also used.

These weapons were operated by a pair of leather bellows concealed in a cavity in the stock. A strong, flat spring was compressed by means of a key or lever which was inserted into a hole in the side of the stock. The key was fitted to the squared end of a spigot just below the surface.

In these bellows guns the key was removed after cocking and the hole was closed by a small metal disc which was hinged or pivoted to form a cover for the keyhole. When the trigger was pressed, the spring was released and this caused the bellows to be suddenly compressed. The air contained in the bellows rushed up the barrel and blew out the bullet. A few pistols were constructed on the bellows principle, but they are very rare weapons to-day. Such bellows guns were made by A. Bell of Linz, Spatzirer of Vienna, Bosler of Darmstadt, Volkman of Vienna, Hinz of Prague and several others, mostly in Germany and Austria. Calibres were usually ·250 or thereabouts but specimens exist both with larger and smaller bore barrels.

Another pneumatic weapon now appeared. This kind, usually referred to as the 'ball type', had the air stored in a large metal ball which was at first placed on the top of the gun or rifle and later underneath the barrel.

The usual place for the ball was just in front of the trigger guard, but specimens of the 'ball on top' have the ball set slightly farther back, with the ball arranged a little off centre to allow an uninterrupted sight line.

Many of these early pneumatics had 'hair' or 'set' triggers by which means great accuracy could be obtained.

The usual method of operating a hair-trigger was by pressing the trigger forwards. This set a system of delicately arranged levers and springs so that the smallest touch on the trigger caused the weapon to be discharged. Some had an adjustment by which such hair-triggers could be regulated so that the pressure required to fire the gun was little more than the weight of a hair and this is why they were so called. These looked exactly like ordinary triggers and could be used if desired without setting, by using a normal pressure. I have known collectors who have owned air weapons for many years, which had such hair-triggers, without being aware that these triggers could be 'set' by a slight forward pressure.

Another type of 'set' trigger which was of even finer construction and was fitted to only the very best weapons consisted of two separate triggers, both contained within the trigger guard. One trigger could be used in the usual way with normal pressure, but it could be immediately used as a hair-trigger by pressing the second one. The advantage obtained when shooting a hair-triggered weapon is obvious. It eliminates all the usual slow squeezing, and directly the sights are aligned correctly, the merest touch with the tip of the finger will discharge the arm.

Ball-type air-guns and rifles were in vogue from about 1730 to 1810. German makers included Gerlach of Berlin, and there were many English makers of which the best-known were Bate, Utting, Martin, and Davidson. The ball was screwed to the gun, and was detached in order to charge it with air. Separate pumps were always used with these ball air-guns. Some of the weapons were supplied with an extra ball by which means a great number of shots could be fired without the need for carrying the pump. Usually each air-ball would contain enough air for between ten and twenty shots, according to the size of the ball. Some I have seen were as small as an orange, whereas I have also come across others with a ball nearly the size of a bowling 'wood'. These ball air reservoirs were made of copper, brass, or steel, the oldest usually being of copper.

Guns having the air-ball underneath the arm are very comfortable to shoot. If the air-ball is rested in the palm of the left hand it will be found that the left elbow can be pressed against the shooter's body and thus the weapon can be supported easily and held remarkably steady whilst shooting.

Many ball-type air-guns had bullet magazines which ensured a really rapid rate of fire, often far in excess of the firearms of the period.

A few air-pistols were made with air-balls positioned underneath the barrel, and sometimes such pistols had attachable extension stocks so that the weapon could be used either as a pistol or as a rifle. Several pistols of this type were made by Davidson.

About 1760, the original flask-butt air-guns and rifles were again made, but they had what are known as box-locks with only the hammer or cocking-piece visible.

Kolbe was at this time making air-rifles with a shell air-chamber around the barrel. Many of his rifles had bullet magazines positioned inside the wooden fore-end.

Another type of rifle was made by Johan Leur about 1760. These were breechloaders and had a detachable breech-chamber which could be removed for loading. They do not appear to have been very successful as they took longer to load than those having the tube magazine parallel to the barrel.

The next type of importance were the repeating air-rifles made by Giradoni of Vienna in 1780. So successful and powerful were these weapons that they were used by the Austrian Army in war, and their deadliness accounted for large numbers of their enemy's casualties.

These rifles were 48½ inches long and weighed 9½ lb. Their calibre was ·44 and they had rifled barrels containing twelve grooves with a twist of one and a quarter turns in their length. In 1780 four men from each company were equipped with these air-rifles and were known as The Croat Sharpshooters. In 1790 a complete corps of 1,300 men were so equipped and the air-rifle remained their especial weapon until 1815.

The following extract from Thornton's *Sporting Tour Through France* (London, 1806) will give the reader some idea of the power of these deadly weapons:

> One day in particular, General Mortier, in speaking of air-guns, recalled to the recollection of some officers in company a circumstance which happened after the retreat of the enemy, but where I cannot call precisely to mind. He said, 'Do you not remember when I ordered the cannon to cease firing, that an orderly sergeant who was standing close to us, leaped very high in the air and

then fell down? We supposed, at first, that he was in a fit, and we were greatly astonished to find him dead, as nothing had been seen or heard, to injure him. On his being undressed, however, a ball was found to have struck him, which must have been shot from an air-gun in the adjoining field, and aimed at some of us.' 'Yes,' replied one of the officers, 'I remember it well, and I think we had a fortunate escape.'

They then stated that on account of this treachery they hung up all of that corps that fell into their hands, considering them not as soldiers, but as assassins, and never gave them any quarter.

These Austrian Service air-rifles were not only extremely powerful and accurate, but their rate of fire was remarkably high and easily exceeded the maximum rate of discharge of the firearms of the period. The Army air-rifle could fire about twenty shots with great rapidity using the air contained in a previously charged 'air-stock', while the practice of carrying an extra reservoir immediately doubled the capacity. They were fitted with a tubular bullet magazine holding twenty balls and located parallel to the barrel.

A few air-pistols were made at this time but were still comparatively rare and at no time in the early days were more than a very few constructed.

Other makers of weapons similar to the Army air-rifle included Rutta of Boem-Lippa, Goellner of Suhl, J. Lowenz, Ridiger of Copenhagen, and Staudenmayer of Austria. The last-named gunmaker came to London and had a shop in Cockspur Street where he made guns for many important personages, including the Duke of York, the Commander-in-Chief, who died in 1827. Staudenmayer remained in business until about 1832.

The next important phase was the introduction of the air-cane or walking-stick air-gun about 1840.

The 'stocked air-cane' was also introduced about this time. I have never seen or even heard of any foreign walking-stick air-guns or 'stocked air-canes' and undoubtedly their manufacture was confined exclusively to British makers.

The difficulty of deciding the country of origin of many such weapons is made greater by the fact that only the best-grade weapons were named by their makers, and there were few special points of interest peculiar to any one maker.

Air-rifles with air-stocks were made in many countries at this period and they were far neater than the earlier types. The stocks were shaped exactly like ordinary gun stocks and were often covered with black calf leather, black pigskin or sharkskin. This sharkskin was particularly durable, having a very hard, glazed surface which did not easily become damaged. It was wetted and stretched over the hollow steel stocks and glued in position with the joint running lengthwise along the underside of the stock. Such work appears to be a lost art nowadays and if a stock covered in this manner becomes damaged, it is almost impossible to have it recovered with sharkskin. The next best material would be a good quality leather, and sometimes a real old craftsman saddler can be located who will do this work in a worthy manner.

In passing, it is interesting to note that air-guns were prohibited weapons in France in 1857 according to a French scientific dictionary of this date.

Another type of air-gun and rifle now appeared. These were known as 'crank-wound' weapons and were the first air-guns to use the true spring, piston, and cylinder arrangement that we use to-day.

The general outlines of these crank-wound guns was somewhat similar to our modern air-rifles and both breech- and muzzle-loading guns and rifles were made. As usual, pistols were rare, but I have seen a few which operated on this system.

To cock, or compress the mainspring, it was necessary to fit the crank into an aperture in the body of the weapon and turn or wind the handle several times. What actually happened was as follows. The crank terminated in a small cogwheel or pinion, and this engaged with a toothed strip or rack which passed through the centre of the spring and was attached to the piston.

When the handle was turned, the rack was pulled backwards, carrying the piston with it and compressing the spring. After cocking such guns the crank was removed before discharging the arm. Calibres were small, compared to the larger bores of the pneumatics, the usual calibre for crank guns being ·250.

The mainsprings of all weapons of this type were made not from round wire but from flat steel strip, coiled up in spiral form. Usually the springs were fitted with the smallest coils of the spirals facing one another and having a washer interposed between them.

Crank-wound guns were never powerful and cannot be made so, because the spring chamber is not long enough to take a modern coil spring of more than about 4½ inches in length. They were used mainly for indoor shooting galleries and were never a great success, probably because of their lack of power.

The Giffard gas-gun created much interest when it first appeared on the English market. Paul Giffard was a civil engineer living in Paris and he had many inventions to his credit. In 1862 he patented a single-shot pneumatic air-gun having a long-stroke piston air-pump located underneath the barrel. These guns were made with 6 mm. and 8 mm. smooth-bore barrels and were powerful enough to flatten out a lead bullet shot at a steel plate.

I have had several of these Giffard pump-guns and found them quite effective used as shotguns, but not accurate with a single bullet.

They were designed with a springless valve which was held closed by the trigger-sear. Directly the trigger was pressed, the valve was blown open by the compressed air and all the air was immediately released. This instantaneous air release caused quite a loud report, in some cases enough to make one's ears ring.

Provision was made in his patent covering pistols using this arrangement, and I know of the existence of two or three such pistols, but very few indeed were made. Giffard pump-up weapons of this type were mostly breech-loading, using a breech-tap similar to our modern air-rifles.

Giffard next patented in 1872 a system whereby variously shaped air weapons could be operated by using an 'air-cartridge'. In other words, cartridges containing compressed air were used in weapons constructed to use them, each cartridge firing one shot. This was a very ingenious idea, but it did not pass the experimental stage and none were commercially produced. Provision was made in the patent to include walking-sticks, rifles, and pistols, but I have only come across one weapon using a compressed-air cartridge and that was a rifle which is now on display in the Milwaukee Museum, U.S.A.

I made up several cartridges to fit this air-rifle and it performed very well and was quite powerful. Its calibre, as I recall it, was 8 mm. Several cartridges could be placed in a tube with one end closed, and by connecting the other end to an air pump, all the cartridges could be charged at once.

A further patent was taken out in 1886 relating to an improved form of air-cartridge, but as before, none appeared to have been commercially produced.

In 1889 Giffard filed a provisional patent which was completed in the same year, outlining the system of rifles and pistols operated by liquefied carbonic acid gas (carbon-dioxide). These were commercially produced, but not in any great quantity. They were made in 6 mm. and 8 mm. calibres only and had an external hammer gas-release.

Provision was made for adjusting the power by means of a screw which regulated the fall of the hammer. Very few pistols were made. Further improvements followed and later a London company, called the Giffard Gun Company, was formed. This concern manufactured the Giffard gas-rifle, and appeared to have had a certain measure of success. Much was said and written about these rifles at the time, but they died a natural death within a few years.

The rifles made by the Giffard Gun Company were beautifully designed and constructed, and were hammerless. The calibre was ·295 and the weapons were extremely powerful and accurate. Comparatively few of these rifles are in existence to-day but the hammerless London model is far commoner than the earlier Giffards with the visible hammer.

The Giffard guns and rifles bring us more or less up to the time when pneumatic weapons were fast losing favour and were being replaced by the newer spring-operated rifles which were the forerunners of our modern air weapons.

I have endeavoured within the brief space of a chapter, to give some account of air-gun history, and I would like to thank my good friend, Mr. F. C. Bewsey, for much information regarding dates of early gunmakers. Many such dates can only be approximate, as there were, of course, periods in which considerable overlapping occurred. For example, air weapons of one type were in many instances being constructed while an earlier type was still being made. Also many developments were pioneered simultaneously by different makers in different countries. The Germans, however, were the real pioneers of the air-gun, whilst gunmakers of many nationalities were equally responsible for its transformation into the weapon that we know to-day.

CHAPTER 3

BLOWPIPES

THE blowpipe is the very simplest form of air weapon and has been in use from the earliest times. No one knows when the first blowpipe was invented, or by whom, but we have good reason to believe that it was invented simultaneously in several countries and that its development proceeded as the skill of the users increased, and the ingenuity of man came to his aid in utilizing local material to the best advantage.

Blowpipes are technically pneumatic weapons, as they depend on the storage of a volume of air in the mouth and lungs and the sudden release of this air under compression. They are used, chiefly with poisoned darts, for killing small animals and birds of the forest, but are also used for shooting fish, large animals, and sometimes against human beings.

Such weapons are common in South America, Southern India, Borneo, Assam, Madagascar, Java, and other parts of South-east Asia. Those used by the various tribes show marked differences in dimensions and in their method of construction. They vary in length from the short tube about two feet long used by the natives of Assam for shooting rats, to others nearly twenty feet in length. The usual length, however, varies between six and ten feet.

The projectiles are tiny, light darts of cane or other wood, to which is affixed at one end a piece of pith, a tuft of raw cotton, a cone formed of a rolled up leaf, or some similar substance, in order to provide a close fit between dart and pipe. Sometimes a separate head may be fitted to the dart, but it is more usual for the whole thing to be constructed from a single piece of wood.

The tips of these darts or arrows are sharpened to a needle point and are usually dipped in some type of vegetable or animal poison. Snake venom is commonly used in Africa for this purpose, and darts in this region are constructed in such a way that any attempt to pull one out of a wound causes the tip to break off, and be left embedded, thus giving the poison plenty of time to work. Cutting a small nick across the point of the dart near the extreme tip renders the tip so fragile that, on impact, the weight of the dart itself will cause the missile to fall to the ground, leaving the tip in the wound.

Where separate barbs or points are fixed to blowpipe darts, they are generally stuck to the dart by means of the poison itself, which is heated until it has a glue-like consistency.

Another poison employed is compounded from the juices of poisonous plants mixed with snake and spider venom. This is a particularly deadly concoction, although the quickest acting and most lethal poison used for arrows and darts in Central Africa is obtained from a small grub. In South America the substance most frequently used is curare which is obtained from the wourali vine, although certain kinds of venomous ants also provide another deadly poison.

In every case, the tiniest scratch or prick from a poisoned arrow causes a rapid and often extremely painful death.

Blowpipes can be classified into several types, all distinctly different in construction, and there have even been instances on record of multi-barrelled weapons, although their use has never been satisfactorily explained. It is possible however, that such peculiar types were made either for experimental use or for some obscure ceremonial purpose, and we must confine our attention to the types in common use.

The simplest type is used by the most primitive tribes in Southern India and in North and South America. It consists merely of the hollowed-out stem of a reed, although sometimes a mouthpiece is fitted and the reed ornamented. It is used in India chiefly for shooting fish by means of a small dart which has a tiny steel point provided with barbs.

One type of blowpipe consists of two long pieces of wood grooved along their entire length in much the same way as the wood of a pencil is grooved to receive the lead. Into this groove is laid a long hollow reed which has a smooth and natural polish and the whole is either cemented together with wax or bound externally. Often a mouthpiece is made by extra binding at one end and the opposite end sometimes has a crude foresight made by fixing a nutshell or other similar protuberance to it.

Another kind is similar in construction but does not have the inner reed tube. Often these grooved pieces of wood, made from bamboo or other wood growing in the locality, are bound together with fibres from plants or trees, or sometimes they are secured together by drawing over them the intestinal tubes of an animal. This makes a particularly strong blowpipe as these intestines, when dried, form an extremely hard, tough covering.

Yet another type of blowpipe, and one moreover calling for the highest degree of skill in its manufacture, is bored out of a solid piece of wood. These are peculiar to the Punans and Kenyah-Kayan tribes of Borneo, and are known as Sumpitans. They are made from hard, straight-grained woods, the best being made from the wood of the Jagang tree and of beautiful workmanship.

The method of boring these is ingenious, though necessarily slow and laborious.

First the tree is selected and felled, and cut into lengths of seven or eight feet. These lengths are split down into segments and trimmed roughly to cylindical form, with a tool resembling an adze. One of these poles is placed upright on a large, flat stone and held there, while another tribesman standing on a platform or staging, constructed for the purpose, bores the hole. This usually takes the greater part of a day to accomplish, as the wood is exceptionally hard and the tools employed are primitive. The boring bar resembles a very long chisel and is usually at least a foot longer than the blowpipe.

The native chips away with this long chisel and a hammer, frequently turning the chisel as the work progresses, while his assistant pours water into the hole, to allow the chips of wood to float to the top. The upper end of the blowpipe is firmly attached to the platform and guides are provided to keep the tool absolutely vertical.

When the tube has been bored, the outside is trimmed and finished, and the bore is then polished until it is perfectly smooth and even.

These blowpipes are especially durable and are capable of extremely accurate and deadly results. The largest known animals can be killed with them, provided the dart pierces some exposed part, so that the poison is introduced into the bloodstream.

It is of great importance that all native blowpipes remain perfectly straight, or they would become useless, and it is the usual practice to store them, when not in use, by hanging them up vertically by the mouthpiece. This minimizes the risk of their warping or bending.

For sporting use, clay balls or pellets are sometimes used instead of darts, particularly when shooting at small birds, as these missiles do not damage the plumage and have sufficient weight to stun or kill such small game, depending on how much lung power is applied to the mouthpiece.

Blowpipes have a surprisingly long range and instances have been recorded where a dart has been blown as far as a hundred yards.

Naturally the range depends to a large extent on the length of the tube and to a far greater extent on the lung power of the user. When we consider that native children learn how to use the weapon almost as soon as they can walk, and go on using it all their lives, it is natural that their lung power should develop to a far greater extent than in others who do not have such stimulants. I have spoken to travellers who have seen mere children repeatedly bring down birds using these weapons with unfailing precision.

A European would not have much success with the very long blowpipes of ten to fifteen feet in length, since to achieve any degree of penetrative power calls for far greater lung capacity than the average man possesses. It is not only a case of who can blow the hardest; he who can blow the greatest volume of air through the pipe will produce the best results.

About thirty years ago it was possible to buy in England weapons known as walking-stick blowguns. These were sold by Lang of 22 Cockspur Street, Jackson of 37 Brewer Street, and several other firms, and looked exactly like ordinary walking canes. Of the several differently shaped specimens I have seen, the commonest were of ordinary bamboo and had either a plain knob or a crook-shaped stag-horn handle.

Through the centre of the stick ran a brass tube, usually about three-eighths of an inch internal diameter. In the case of the knob-handled stick, the knob was removable by pulling or unscrewing, thus giving access to the brass tube. The crook-handled variety had the blowing end of the tube permanently visible. Both types had a removable end ferrule, which was either unscrewed or pulled off.

These walking-stick blow-tubes were chiefly intended for amusement, and while the novelty lasted, they provided much good sport, especially as rats and other vermin could be quite easily killed with them if one attained the necessary proficiency. They were sold with a bullet mould for making clay bullets, together with several darts; whilst ready-made clay balls and extra darts were available at a nominal price.

The bullet mould resembled the ordinary scissors type of mould used for casting spherical lead bullets, except that there was no pouring hole, and the two halves of the mould had chamfered faces instead of the usual flat ones.

The balls were made by simply putting a piece of clay between the two halves of the mould and squeezing the handles together. The action pressed the clay into the cavity of the mould, whilst the chamfered edges cut off the surplus; and on opening the mould, the clay ball could be extracted.

These clay balls were delightful missiles to shoot with, as their impact against anything solid resulted in their smashing up in a most realistic and satisfying way. They were popular with ornithologists, who could, with practice, bring down small birds at short ranges without damage to their plumage. For longer ranges, and for shooting rats, sparrows, etc., darts were used. The dart was made of steel and resembled a large darning needle, to which was attached at the blunt end a paper cone which provided the seal between dart and tube.

A remarkable degree of accuracy could be attained with practice, and the penetrative power and range of these missiles was really astonishing. It is quite easy to blow such a dart a distance of thirty yards with such force that it will penetrate a plank of wood and will be impossible to remove except with the aid of pliers.

If there are any readers who would like to experiment for themselves and make a simple but effective blow-tube, they may easily prove this for themselves.

An ordinary piece of seamless brass tube about three feet long is ideal, provided the bore is perfectly smooth and clean and the tube absolutely straight. The bore of the tube is not of great importance, but I would suggest $\frac{5}{16}''$ to $\frac{3}{8}''$ as being quite suitable.

If the tube has been cut to length, there will be burrs on either end and these should be removed by filing or scraping. It is essential that the bore be perfectly dry, as otherwise much friction will be set up between dart and tube and the results will be disappointing.

All that is needed now are some darts. Excellent ones can be improvised from large darning needles with some kind of flight or tail attached in order to make them fit the tube.

These can be made from cork, as follows: Take a small piece of brass tube, of the same bore as the blowpipe and about six inches long. Sharpen one end with a file on the outside only, making the bevel as long and as smooth as possible. If the sharpened end is pressed against a large cork and rotated at the same time, it will bore a hole right through the cork, leaving a cork plug inside the boring tube. This cork plug should be pushed out and a darning needle inserted carefully through the centre until the eye of the needle is level with one face of the cork.

The cork, complete with needle, must now be placed on a smooth floor and carefully rolled with the foot, using a very light pressure until it will just drop through the blow-tube with its own weight.

All you have to do now is to hold the blow-tube horizontally, insert the dart, and blow. Every care should be taken when using such a blow-tube, as these darts will travel a long distance and will penetrate deeply.

The average man can blow with the mouth a pressure of under two pounds to the square inch. How much more powerful, therefore, are pneumatic weapons, using pressure of five hundred to a thousand pounds to the square inch!

CHAPTER 4

A REPEATING AIR-RIFLE OF 1792

THIS interesting sporting gun, of Austrian origin, was designed on military lines. I have chosen it as being a typical specimen of a fine quality old time sporting air-rifle of large calibre. A similar performance could be obtained by any ancient air-rifle of the same calibre provided such weapon has had the valve and mechanism overhauled and put in good working order.

The repeating air-rifle (Plate 3) was made in Austria by Joseph Lowenz in 1792. It was originally fitted in a brass-bound oak case, but woodworm had so damaged this that it was past repair. Similar arms were made by Contriner, Giradoni, Fruwirth, and other continental makers who specialized in repeating air-guns.

This weapon, a high-class sporting air-rifle, closely follows the pattern of the old Austrian Army air-rifle; the only apparent differences being that:

(a) The gun shown has a certain amount of decorative carving on the woodwork.

(b) The lock is provided with a small knob which was not fitted to the military weapon.

This knob (located on the left lock-plate) when pressed downwards disengaged the mechanism connecting the striker-pin and the hammer. The hammer was then allowed to fall, releasing the tension on the spring, without any air being emitted from the reservoir.

This was undoubtedly a very useful device since, when

hunting, the opportunity of taking a shot may pass as quickly as it occurs.

Provided the shooter presses down the small knob, the hammer may be lowered, either with the thumb or by pressing the trigger, without discharging either air or bullet, Half-cock and full-cock positions are provided. The hammer could, of course, be lowered from half-cock without using the knob, as the air-releasing mechanism is not set until the hammer has been raised to the full-cock position.

To appreciate fully the utility of this knob, it must be remembered that a peculiarity of nearly all the old multi-shot pneumatics was that once they had been fully cocked, they had to be fired. The reason for this was that (unlike spring air-rifles) the pin which depresses the valve, and thus allows the air to escape, completes its full travel irrespective of whether the hammer is allowed to fall quickly or slowly.

In actual practice, if the hammer was lowered slowly with the thumb, the pin would also travel slowly, and this would cause the valve to remain open for a considerable time and result in the loss of all the air in the reservoir. I am assuming that the hammer-spring is strong enough to depress the valve without actually delivering a blow, as usually very strong springs were employed.

The accessories shown consist of the air pump, valve key, bullet mould and tool for releasing the air from the reservoir.

An additional flask-shaped butt reservoir (not shown) completes the outfit.

The overall length of the rifle is 43½ inches of which the flask butt measures 12 inches. The circumferences at either end are 9¾ inches and 5¼ inches respectively. The air pump is 21 inches long and is constructed of hexagon section steel. The bore is $\frac{17}{32}$ inches and the working stroke 17¼ inches. The pump-rod is made of ¼-inch square steel.

The fore-end of the rifle is tipped with the buffalo horn

and the cleaning rod, carried in thimbles, is also horn-tipped.

The rifling of the barrel is of the poly-groove variety, the bullets fitting the bore fairly tightly.

The lead balls measure ·470 inches in diameter and weigh 147 grains each, 16 balls filling the tubular magazine. The hollow air-reservoir is constructed of sheet metal hammered to a conical shape and riveted and brazed along its length. The domed end of the butt is also brazed in position and the large end of the cone is hammered over it to give additional strength.

To prevent rusting, the butt or flask is coppered and was originally leather-covered. The leather covering is missing, but apart from this the weapon is in very fine condition and in perfect working order. A covering of leather or fabric was essential on a metal stock in a country where winters were very severe.

Pumping was carried out in the same manner as for walking-stick air-guns, the air-reservoir being first detached from the gun and screwed to the pump-nozzle.

The magazine was filled with bullets from the forward end of the tube which was provided with a swivelling lid that locked in the closed position by means of a spring catch.

Assuming the reservoir to be fully charged, and the magazine filled with bullets, it was necessary only to elevate the gun muzzle, press and release the sliding breech-block, and pull back the hammer to full-cock. The weapon was then ready to fire. The same actions were repeated for successive shots. The action of elevating the muzzle kept the balls (by gravity) against the breech-block.

Pushing the laterally-sliding block to the right against the pressure of the return spring allowed a ball to fall into a hole in the block. This hole was drilled right through, but was slightly tapered so that the bullets would not fall through but would remain in position approximately in the centre of the hole. On releasing the breech-block the return-spring brought it back to its normal position of rest, carrying the ball into the breech ready to be discharged.

A very high rate of fire was possible by this simple mechanism and the 16 bullets could be fired extremely rapidly, almost silently, and without recoil. And there was, of course, no smoke to give away the shooter's position.

The pump shown is the original one and is longer and thinner than those supplied with walking-stick air-guns. With it, a pressure of 600 lb. per square inch can be reached without Herculean effort.

Two bullets are shown, one unfired, and the other flattened after being shot at a steel plate. Using the pressure mentioned, 30 shots, or approximately two full magazines of bullets, could be discharged by the air contained in one air-butt without any noticeable drop in power. Using a pressure of 900 lb. per square inch the bullets are almost completely shattered.

I find that this weapon shoots high at 25 yards, but at 50 yards it is really accurate. At 100 yards, if the higher leaf of the sight is used it will still put up a very good performance, while if the rifle is elevated 33 degrees its extreme range is nearly 200 yards. This is a remarkable performance for an air-rifle when we consider its age and the very heavy bullet projected.

I well remember showing this particular weapon to a friend living in Hampshire who was very sceptical of my claims for its astonishing power.

We hadn't a target handy so my friend chalked a large white spot on the door of his outhouse, then retired a measured 60 yards and fired five shots at the chalk mark. So far so good.

We walked leisurely back to the outhouse and examined the bullet holes, all of which were grouped well within the mark. When he opened the door however, he found that the bullet had passed right through the $\frac{7}{8}''$ thick wooden door, and much to his dismay had made five neat holes through his mackintosh which was hanging up behind the door, passing through both sleeves in the process.

When the cussing had ceased, we noticed that there were also five holes through the weather boarded back of the outhouse.

The climax came as my friend suddenly remembered that he had left his bicycle leaning against the wall at the back of the shed, right in the line of fire. We quickly ran round to see if any damage had been done, and there was the bicycle with its front wheel looking like a figure 8. My friend's language was unprintable, but ever since this episode he has had a very healthy respect for antique air-rifles.

When valve-adjustment was found necessary, the tool shown was first screwed into the neck of the flask butt, the projecting pin pressing on the valve-head and allowing the air to escape. The valve could then be unscrewed with the key provided.

The inside surface of the reservoir was coated with grease so that any small particles of dust finding their way in might stick to the grease and remain there. In this way they would not pass through the valve where they might cause leakage of air.

The muzzle velocity of this weapon is approximately 500 feet per second.

CHAPTER 5

WALKING-STICK PNEUMATIC RIFLES AND GUNS

WALKING-STICK air-rifles, or 'air-canes' as they were often called, were at the height of their popularity about fifty years ago. They were first made over a hundred years ago and many specimens of the early ones exist to-day in museums and private collections. They were the most popular of all the old pneumatic weapons.

These air-canes were last made about 1914 although a few makers accepted special orders for them until about 1916. Quite a number of old gun catalogues listed and illustrated air-canes as recently as 1920, but the weapons were merely old stock that the makers or their agents wished to clear.

Since the air-cane became outmoded by the newer spring-operated air-rifles, all air weapons commercially produced in England have been of the spring-operated type.

The only exceptions were a few experimental models made by inventors, and also a few special types constructed by enthusiasts for their own enjoyment and personal use.

Many firms produced walking-stick air-rifles, including Blisset, Townsend, Reilly, Greener, Blanche, Cogswell and Harrison, and several other equally well-known makers.

Townsend and Reilly were the two most prolific makers and between them produced more air-canes than all the other firms put together.

Of these two makers, Reilly was the specialist and

manufactured a range of pneumatic walking-stick guns and rifles of various sizes ranging from three-quarters of an inch up to two inches in diameter. The smaller sizes really did look and feel like walking-sticks but the very large ones were heavy and cumbersome, and although they did not look like guns they were hardly light enough to be used as walking-sticks. Perhaps their owners were tougher than we are to-day.

The most popular diameter size was an inch and a quarter and this was the size that most of the makers adopted. This measurement was taken across the face of the valve, roughly in the middle of the weapon.

These air-canes were usually straight in shape and furnished with either a horn knob or a crook-shaped horn handle. On the better quality ones, the handle was made of ivory and often had a small silver initial plate let in level with the surface.

A bent or crank-shaped walking-stick was also fairly popular because this type could be shot from the shoulder whereas the straight ones had to be held in front of the shooter. A steadier way of holding the straight stick was by resting the knob on the right cheek just below the eye, when the sights could be clearly aligned.

In common with all other pneumatic rifles, there is no recoil from an air-cane, so this method of holding was perfectly safe.

The bent-shaped sticks were never made in anywhere near the same quantities as the straight ones, probably due to the extra cost of constructing the cranked air-chamber section.

All, irrespective of shape, size, or quality were arranged to unscrew into two sections, the upper part being an air-reservoir and containing the valve, while the lower section contained the barrel and air release mechanism.

The pump was always a separate unit, and although patents have been taken out in the past for walking-stick air-rifles with self-contained pumps, I have never actually seen such a thing, although there are many other types of antique pump-guns that do have a self-contained air-pump.

Air-cane prices varied from as little as fifty shillings to as much as two hundred and sixty-five shillings each. When we remember the purchasing power of the pound in years past, it will be appreciated that the price of the better weapons represented a very considerable sum of money.

Both breech-loading and muzzle-loading systems were employed, and usually the cheaper sticks were straight-shaped muzzle-loaders, often having only a smooth-bore barrel.

The more expensive ones were generally breech-loading, of straight or cranked shape, and furnished with a rifled barrel for firing round lead bullets and also a smooth barrel for firing scatter shot. This was arranged by having the rifled tube fitted inside the shot barrel, and it was unscrewed and withdrawn when the shooter wanted to use his walking-stick as a shotgun. The very thin sticks of three-quarters and seven-eighths of an inch diameter had rifled barrels only.

Most of the best walking-stick air-rifles were supplied in handsome oak or mahogany plush-lined fitted cases, complete with a profusion of accessories. These often included spare valves in boxwood, screw-topped containers, oil bottle, spare leaf springs and recoil spring, valve key, folding cleaning rod and sometimes an extension stock and fish harpoons, in addition to the pump, bullet mould, and cocking key.

Such air-canes were intended to be operated at air pressures of 400 lb. to 500 lb. per square inch. Calibres varied according to the make, but usually the large heavy sticks had a rifled bore of about half an inch, and the popular $1\frac{1}{4}$-inch size fired a lead ball of $\frac{5}{16}$ inch diameter and had a $\frac{7}{16}$-inch diameter shot-tube.

Using the special pump provided with the weapon, it took three to four minutes hard pumping to reach 400 lb. per square inch pressure. This necessitated about 260 strokes of the pump. A muscular man could continue pumping and obtaining maximum of 500 to 550 lb. per square inch.

The highest pressure I have personally hand pumped was 580 lb. per square inch and this was reached by using a thinner pump of ½-inch bore and 15-inch stroke and I was assisted by a friend who pumped in the first 300 lb., leaving me to complete the job.

Using an air pressure of 400 lb. per square inch these air-canes would shoot with really amazing force, and fifteen consecutive bullets could be put through an inch-thick plank of wood at fifty yards. It was then merely necessary to top up the air pressure with the pump. A total of something like twenty shots could be discharged, all of which had ample power for killing game. The last few pounds pressure were of no use for shooting but it was a good thing to leave some air in the reservoir as this helped to keep the valve seated tightly and minimized leakage. The extreme range of these weapons was about 350 yards if the muzzle was elevated 45 degrees, and the killing range was up to 120 yards. Small fixed open sights were fitted to these walking-sticks and were arranged to be correct for 30 yards range. At distances less than this it was usual to sight slightly low, while at ranges of over 30 yards, a slightly higher aim was taken to allow for the drop of the bullet.

The largest air-canes were even more powerful still but were not in such general use owing to their massive construction and weight. The largest one I have seen measured 2⅛ inches diameter at the thickest part and (believe it or not) fired a spherical lead bullet of exactly ¾ inch diameter, weighing an ounce and a half! This particular walking-stick weighed seven and a half pounds. Normally pneumatic weapons have no recoil whatever, but this monster specimen was something really outstanding and it *did* have a very considerable recoil. As a matter of fact, I once discharged it at the cast iron fireplace of my workroom.

The result was astonishing in more ways than one. There was a tremendous report, the air was filled with flying lead and, as I staggered back, feeling as if someone had given me a violent push in the chest, the room appeared to fill with a sort of white smoke.

When the fog cleared, I took stock of my surroundings and was appalled at the mess. The cast iron fireplace was smashed and the walls peppered with fragments of lead. The blast of air had stripped the wallpaper from a large area of the wall, and had also blown off the mantelshelf all my bottles and jars containing oils and chemicals, and these lay broken in the hearth. It was the plaster dust from the wall that had caused the white smoke. Several hours were spent clearing up the debris and repairing the damage. This particular air-rifle was easily the most powerful one that I have ever handled. It is now on display in the Milwaukee Museum, U.S.A.

The thinnest air-canes weighed only 1½ lb. and fired bullets of about ¼ inch diameter. These are rarely met with to-day.

The method of operating all these walking-stick pneumatic guns is as follows:

1. Assuming the reservoir to be empty, screw the pump tightly to the air-chamber and, placing your feet on the pump handle and holding the reservoir with both hands, proceed to pump with even strokes. When pumping becomes hard, bend your knees and utilize your weight in order to lessen the amount of muscular energy needed.
2. Remove the muzzle-cap and screw the two halves of the weapon together.
3. Insert the bullet either by dropping it into the loading hole or, if muzzle-loading, by pushing it down the barrel with the loading rod, which is attached to the muzzle-cap. (Bullets were a tight fit in the poly-grooved rifled barrels and were used without a greased patch or other sealing device.)
4. Cock the internal air release mechanism by inserting the cocking key in the square hole provided in the

front half of the stick and turn the key until the trigger stud flies out. This is accompanied by a click as the sear engages in its notch.

5. Take aim and press the trigger stud with the left thumb. Repeat for successive shots.

To fire scatter-shot, three methods were used. First the rifled tube was unscrewed and withdrawn and then either:

1. A small quantity of shot was screwed up in very thin paper and introduced into the breech loading hole. (The breech-loaders had a loading tap very similar to those fitted to modern air-rifles, but it was arranged to rotate in the same direction as the curvature of the surface in order to be as little noticeable as possible). Or:
2. A felt wad was first pushed down the barrel from the muzzle end by means of the wooden loading rod, the shot then being poured into the barrel and another felt wad pushed down. This sandwiched the shot between the two wads and prevented it falling out. Or:
3. Shot cartridges were sold ready-made by the various makers and these were simply pushed down the barrel. They fitted the bore closely enough to remain in place until the weapon was discharged. These shot cartridges consisted of a thin paper cylinder containing a quantity of small shot and closed at either end with a cardboard or felt disc.

It was recommended that for best results the charge of shot did not exceed the amount that could be contained in a cylinder with a diameter the same as the weapon's bore and a length one and a half times the bore.

It must be borne in mind that the smooth-bore shot barrels of air weapons were all true cylinder and not choke-bored like most of the modern cartridge shotguns, and scatter-shot could therefore only be relied upon to give a close pattern at up to about fifteen yards range.

Fish harpoons for use in walking-stick air-guns were made in various patterns, having the barbed head either flat or triangular in section and made of hardened and tempered steel. The shaft of the harpoon was usually made of cane or some similar wood and was thinned down in the middle, leaving each end a close fit in the smooth-bore barrel of the gun.

A cord was attached to the harpoon either by knotting it around a groove between steel barb and the shaft, or by passing it through a hole drilled through the shaft near the barbed head.

The harpoon was then fitted into the muzzle of the walking-stick with the head projecting, and the cord was laid up and down the river bank and the end tied to a piece of wood upon which the shooter stood. It was usual to shoot at fish which rose to the surface and if you were successful in harpooning one, all you had to do was to pull in the cord and there was your dinner! Considerable skill had to be shown in shooting fish that were below the surface as allowance had to be made for the refraction of light when passing through water. This refraction or bending of the rays of light can quite easily cause an error of several inches.

Specimens of these old fish harpoons are very rare to-day, chiefly because a miss very often resulted in the spear being shattered to pieces against a stone in the river bed.

The air-valve fitted to the air-chamber was of simple construction, being merely a spring-loaded spindle fitted with a horn disc or head and seating in a hollow cone-shaped recess. I have seen some valve-heads made of ivory or bone, but horn was the substance always used by the makers and we can conclude that valve-heads made of any other substance have been fitted instead of the horn, probably at some later date in an effort at improvement.

Air-valves of all the old-time pneumatic weapons (in spite of the makers' claims to the contrary) invariably gave trouble.

Horn was used because it was the best material available at the time, but it left much to be desired. When first fitted such valves were airtight. but the tiniest particle of grit getting into the pump usually lodged in the valve, causing leakage and rapid loss of air pressure. To assist in trapping as far as possible any grit or dust that might find its way past the valve and into the air-chamber, the inside surface of the reservoir was thickly coated with grease. By this means any dirt entering the pressure-chamber stuck to the grease and was at least prevented from doing any damage. For this reason the inside of air-gun reservoirs will generally be found covered by a layer of a sticky, dirty, evil-smelling substance, usually green with age, which is the remains of the original grease dust-trap.

Another cause of leakage was due to excessive oiling of the pump piston. Oil soaked into the horn valve and distorted its circular shape.

After experimenting with very many different substances, I have succeeded in solving the valve problem, and have found the ideal material. This is a special plastic made to my own specification. It is just soft enough to make a perfect seal, yet hard enough not to distort under high air pressures. Moreover, valves made of this material will remain airtight whether or not they are lubricated, and will give absolutely reliable and very long service. I have had several pneumatic walking-stick guns and other old-timers which I have fitted with these new valves and they have held pressures of 500 lb. per square inch for over a year without measurable loss. For these reasons I always scrap the old horn valves and replace them with the new plastic, knowing that whenever I want to use such a weapon it will not let me down. In many cases when fitting these new trouble-free valves, it is necessary to alter the angle of the valve seat to prevent the valve sticking. The plastic is more resilient than horn and therefore the valve seat angle must not be too acute or the valve may jam.

For those interested in the old-time gunsmiths' methods of lapping a horn valve, this is how it was done. The valve unit was unscrewed from the air-chamber and dismantled. The valve spindle, complete with horn valve-head, was then revolved in a lathe and skimmed up true, after which the valve and its seat were cleaned free of oil and grease and the unit put together without the spring. The valve-stem was then pressed hard against its seat and revolved until it emitted a peculiar high-pitched shriek. When this occurred, the spring was replaced and the complete assembly screwed back into the air-chamber. The end of the valve-spindle was usually squared so that it could be gripped firmly while being lapped, and pressure was applied by a specially shaped steel bar which the craftsman held against his stomach.

Lock mechanisms were of fine workmanship and cleverly designed. The action of cocking the weapon with the key compressed a strong leaf-type spring. This was held compressed by the trigger stud lever which engaged in a small notch in the movable piece to which the spring was connected. Pressing the trigger stud allowed the spring to expand and deliver a blow to the valve-head by means of the trip mechanism.

The spring opened the valve and allowed a blast of compressed air to escape down the barrel, the air pressure in the reservoir and the spring-loading of the valve immediately closing the valve again. As the air pressure decreased, the valve would remain open for an infinitesimally longer space of time, thus keeping the power of the weapon fairly even. The blow delivered to the valve-head remained, of course, at constant strength.

This was the usual arrangement in most air-canes, although one particular air-cane made use of a coil spring instead of a leaf-type flat spring. This was Cook's Patent Air-cane. Very few of these were made and they are rarely met with to-day.

A method recommended by at least one air-cane maker for equalizing every shot was as follows: When the air-chamber had been pumped up as hard as possible, the two halves of the walking-stick were not screwed completely together, but were left about a turn and a half open. After a few shots had been fired, the two halves were screwed right home. The effect of this procedure was to vary the distance between the valve-head and the striker so that when pressure was at its greatest the valve would only be lightly struck, but as the air was used up and pressure decreased, the further screwing together of the two halves of the stick resulted in the valve being depressed to a greater extent to compensate for the reduced air pressure.

A walking-stick air-rifle, shooting a $\frac{5}{16}$-inch spherical lead bullet, experimentally charged with carbon dioxide gas at a pressure of approximately 900 lb. per square inch pressure was discharged repeatedly at a thick steel plate. Thirty-seven consecutive shots were fired before the reservoir was exhausted. Some idea of the remarkable power of these weapons can be seen from the illustration which shows how the bullets were flattened.

Mention should be made of another similar type of weapon which was made principally by Blanche, Townsend and Reilly. These were known as 'stocked air-canes', and operated in exactly the same way as the walking-sticks. These 'stocked air-canes' however, had the air-chamber shaped like an orthodox gunstock, which meant they could be shot from the shoulder and therefore could be held steadier. Contrary to popular belief, these stocks, although larger than the straight air-chamber of the walking-stick gun, did not hold any more air. The actual reservoir was approximately the same size, and the stock shape was made up by a shaped piece of metal with plaster filling between. Such stocks were usually covered with sharkskin, pigskin, or calf leather.

If you should ever acquire an air-rifle or gun which has a stud trigger, you will most likely find that it shoots slightly to the right. This is a human error and not in any way due to a fault in the sighting of such a weapon. What actually happens is that when you press the trigger stud with the left thumb, you subconsciously press the whole weapon over to the right. This can be eliminated with practice, but enthusiasts who do not shoot such weapons often may find it more convenient to allow for the error by sighting slightly to the left.

A peculiarity possessed by these pneumatic weapons, and in fact by nearly all the older pump-up types, is that once the air release mechanism has been cocked, the arm can only be rendered safe again by (a) shooting the weapon, (b) unscrewing or partly unscrewing the two halves of the gun and then pressing the trigger stud. This prevents the striker pin from touching the valve-head and therefore no air is released.

Walking-stick air-rifles and any of the old-time pneumatic weapons can be operated on either air or gas, provided the air-chambers have first been properly tested at a pressure considerably in excess of that normally used. Suitable gases would be nitrogen or carbon dioxide, of which the latter is to be preferred.

Such gases can be obtained under compression in steel cylinders and, assuming the air-chamber of your weapon has first had a thorough safety test under high pressure, all you have to do is to connect the air-chamber to your steel gas cylinder by a suitable screw adaptor. Filling takes only a few seconds and saves the labour of manual pumping.

Compressed air is available in cylinders but it is usually bottled at too great a pressure to be safely used in a pneumatic weapon, unless a pressure gauge is fitted to the adaptor so that pressure can be cut off as soon as the gauge shows the desired reading.

Carbon dioxide gas is also available in steel cylinders, the pressure varying between 850 and 900 lb. per square inch, according to atmospheric temperature. In very hot weather such pressure may reach or even exceed 1,000 lb. and therefore gas cylinders should not be exposed to excessive heat. This gas is ideal for operating compressed-air rifles, as it is cheap and easy to obtain. A 7-lb. cylinder (that is, a cylinder containing 7 lb. by weight of CO_2 gas) will provide sufficient to fire many thousand shots.

Do not, under any circumstances, be tempted to fill a gun or rifle air-chamber with oxygen. Such procedure is fraught with the greatest danger, because the slightest trace of oil or grease, which is always present in such air-chambers, will combine with the oxygen to form an extremely unstable and highly explosive mixture, and the whole container is likely to explode without warning.

A walking-stick air-gun once solved a problem for me. I wanted to install a private telephone line between two houses that were next door to one another. The telephone was required to run from the back room of one three-storey house to the front room of the other. There were special circumstances that necessitated the telephone wire passing over one of the roofs and the problem was how to get it there. Various methods were tried without success until I thought of using the air-gun.

A large ball of string was obtained and a rough wooden harpoon made and attached to the end of the string. The harpoon was then inserted in the muzzle of the walking-stick air-gun and shot right over the rooftop. It was then only necessary to attach the wire to the string, and by pulling on the string draw up the wire.

In actual fact the harpoon would have easily cleared the roofs of two or three houses, had it been necessary.

CHAPTER 6

SPRING-OPERATED AIR-RIFLES

ALL the air-rifles and guns made in this country are spring-operated. This is due principally to the fact that restrictions would be imposed on any extra-powerful, commercially produced pneumatic arm. These restrictions have resulted, however, in the spring-operated air-rifle and pistol being developed to a very high degree of efficiency, and an equally high standard of quality and reliability.

It must be appreciated that the muzzle velocity and penetration obtained from a spring air-rifle is limited. In fact, it is my considered opinion that the practical limit of power has already been achieved.

By the words 'practical limit' I wish to convey that while power could undoubtedly be still further increased by means of stronger springs and larger pistons and cylinders, to do so would necessitate the whole weapon being made larger and stronger. This would, in turn, add to its weight and size and the rifle would become cumbersome and unmanageable.

The B.S.A. 'Airsporter' and the Webley and Scott 'Mk. III' are classic examples of the most powerful and finest quality British air-rifles, and these represent the highest practical limit in power and efficiency.

In other countries, notably the U.S.A., the pneumatic rifle has during the past few years gained in popularity to such an extent that there seems to have been a big swing over from spring air-rifles to pneumatic types.

Indeed, the spring air-rifles now made in the U.S.A. appear to be chiefly of the Junior variety, and, while these are of good design, in my opinion they do not compare in any way with the quality of our own weapons.

Spring air-rifles possess many advantages over the modern pump-up or pneumatic rifle and we will shortly consider these strong points in their favour.

Early air-guns were mostly of the breakdown type and all suffered from the same major faults. Briefly these were:

1. Considerable loss of air at the breech joint where the barrel was hinged or pivoted.
2. Rapid wear at the hinge causing the barrel to wobble, the air leakage to become worse, and the gun to become inaccurate.
3. The impracticability of using a really strong spring in the weapon, because the force needed to cock such a spring often resulted in barrels becoming bent.

The 'Gem' air-gun was a typical example, although there were many others made by continental firms on similar lines. These guns, although admittedly of ingenious design, were not built to stand up to continued use, and were always breaking or rapidly becoming unserviceable. They were, in fact, built more on the lines of a toy than of a practical weapon and the strain produced by cocking its very powerful spring usually resulted in the breaking or bending of various parts of the mechanism. The 'Gem' was the first commercially produced spring air-gun to sell in large quantities and although many thousands were sold, their popularity soon waned because they were always giving trouble.

Present-day breakdown air-rifles are accurate, practical weapons of precision that have none of the drawbacks of the old 'Gem' and its contemporaries. This has been achieved by the use of high-grade steels and modern methods of hardening and tempering the working parts, together with a policy of working up to a standard rather than down to a price.

Among the advantages of good-quality modern spring air-rifles are the following:

1. Reliability.

2. Simplicity.
3. Longer life.
4. Consistent power.
5. Greater efficiency.

They are reliable because they are well designed and made of fine-quality materials, and also because they have fewer working parts than a pneumatic weapon and are therefore less liable to go out of order. Because the number of moving parts has been reduced to a minimum, they are simple to use and have a long life.

The mechanical operation of these weapons is self-explanatory to anyone dismantling them and the principles involved are well known. Spare parts are inexpensive and easy to obtain and therefore repairs are cheaply and quickly executed.

Consistent power is provided by the compressing and releasing of the mainspring, and until this spring becomes weak through long usage, or wear occurs on some other easily replaceable component, the power will remain constant.

There is greater efficiency because for all practical purposes the whole of the energy stored in a compressed spring is given out again when the spring is allowed to expand.

I am often asked whether the power of a spring air-rifle can be increased by fitting a stronger mainspring than the one supplied by the manufacturers. The answer to this question is that provided there is sufficient space to accommodate a stronger spring, then power can be increased. This increase, however, is usually very slight, and is obtained at the cost of creating excessive wear on all the working parts.

It must be realized that air-rifles are not haphazardly produced. On the contrary, an enormous amount of time and money has been spent in perfecting them; and they are designed to give the maximum power compatible with reasonable dimensions and weight, and the minimum of wear. The springs fitted to new air-rifles will allow of reasonably easy cocking without undue strains being created.

Stronger springs will definitely subject the cocking levers, sear, and other working parts to excessive stresses which they are not built to withstand, and trouble will generally result. The power increase is more pronounced in the case of breakdown air-rifles to which extra strong springs have been fitted, but the rapid wear created is out of all proportion to the gain in power. It is the old story that you can't get something for nothing!

A phenomenon which often occurs with air-rifles having a high compression, especially if they have just been lightly oiled internally, is known as 'diesel action'. In effect, it is exactly what the name implies and the result is that occasionally the air rifle shoots its pellet with nearly double its normal power for no apparent reason.

What really happens, however, is that the atomized oil present in the air-chamber, together with the air also present, form an ignitible and mildly explosive mixture. The sudden compression of this mixture by the spring-driven piston causes the firing of this vapour and the pellet is projected with the power of two forces behind it, in other words, the power of the normal air compression plus the explosive force resulting from the compression-ignition of the oil vapour. If an air-rifle is discharged at night and this phenomenon occurs, a small flame or spark can be seen at the muzzle.

Such diesel action can be induced by putting one drop of light oil into the cylinder and firing the weapon first without a pellet and then firing again with a pellet in the breech. The first discharge will vaporize the drop of oil and the second one will usually cause the oil to be exploded. I do not recommend your making a practice of doing this because it is harmful to shoot a spring-operated air-rifle without using a pellet. If you try it, look on it in the nature of an experiment—do it once and then forget it.

Cocking and discharging an air-rifle repeatedly without using pellets is detrimental to the piston head and the end of the air-chamber. This is because most of the cushioning effect of compressing the air is lost when the air is not doing any work and the piston will smash down against the end of the cylinder and may result in a cracked piston or other damage.

I once designed a gadget that could be fitted to any underlever air-rifle, which would produce this diesel action continuously without any harmful effects on the rifle.

It consisted of a small cylinder and piston and a tiny reservoir which held about a thimbleful of thin oil. There were also two very fine tubes with the ends set at right angles to one another in a similar way to the nozzle of a scent spray. It was arranged in such a way that the action of cocking the rifle caused the small piston to blow air down one of these tubes and oil to rise in the other one. When this oil was met by the air jet it was atomized and injected directly into the air-cylinder of the rifle. Best results were obtained when only one drop of oil was injected for each cocking of the rifle. Various kinds of oils were tried, and maximum power was found to be nearly three times the normal performance. The device was made and fitted purely for experimental use and is never likely to be commercially made as it would produce power in excess of allowed standards.

I am often asked if I can recommend any particular make of air-rifle. This is a difficult question indeed, and frankly it is one that is best left to the purchaser to decide. Every make has its own special features which appeal to some but not to others, and I fully believe that there will never be an air-rifle made that will satisfy everyone. You must therefore weigh up the good points of each—weight, balance, trigger pull, general finish, and so on—and you will probably want them all! The muzzle velocities of every make are much the same provided the weapons compared are of the same type and calibre.

The best-known makes are probably B.S.A. and Webley, but the Diana series are also good weapons and there are in addition many excellent rifles of German manufacture on sale in England. Most of these are available in both ·177 and ·22 calibres.

The German 'Original' brand air-rifles, for instance, are obtainable here in eight different models, two of which are underlever actions, while the rest are breakdown types. There are also three Junior model air-guns which have smooth-bore barrels.

The 'Original' New Model 35B breakdown air-rifle deserves special mention. It is easily the most powerful weapon of its type and undoubtedly has a higher muzzle velocity than any other modern breakdown air-rifle. The sighting arrangements are unique. The aperture backsight is very large and robust and is fully adjustable and clearly calibrated, and moreover is easily detachable. The sight base is 33 inches.

The large eye disc can be detached from the sight unit and this brings into view an open backsight with a reversible blade that rotates to give either a V or a U opening. Provision is made for attaching the complete sight unit in the usual position roughly midway along the weapon's length, as, of course, an open sight cannot be used near the eye.

The foresight, too, is novel in the extreme. It consists of a good solid ramp with a protecting hood.

A choice of four different sights are instantly available at the touch of a finger. These are: a large bead, small bead, blade, and barleycorn, and they are cunningly arranged round the circumference of a steel disc. To change from one sight to another is very easily accomplished by pressing a small locking catch on the right of the sight-ramp and rotating a knurled knob until the desired sight appears. This is one of the cleverest ideas I have seen and it embodies everything that a foresight should be.

Other good points include an adjustable trigger with double pull, and the quality, finish, and general handling of the weapon are excellent. The dimensions are:

Overall length	.	45 inches.
Barrel length	.	20 inches.
Weight	. .	7 lb.

Messrs. Frank Dyke & Co., Ltd. of 10 Union Street, London Bridge, S.E.1, are the importers and English agents for the 'Original' series. They do not sell retail, but can supply you through your local dealer.

A fact that is not generally known is that all air-rifles sold in England under the brand name 'Original' are manufactured by the German firm who were the makers of the old (and original) Diana air-rifles before the war. The present Diana air-rifles are manufactured by Messrs. Millard Bros. of Lanarkshire who acquired the rights to the trade mark 'Diana' from the Germans some years ago.

There were, until a few years ago, a series of German air-rifles available in England, known by the brand name of 'Falke'. The German 'Falke' series consisted of eight different models of breakdown air weapons of which four were Juniors with smooth barrels and four were available with either rifled or smooth barrels.

The 'Falke' underlever air-rifles Models 80 and 90 are worthy of special mention. Both models had the same specification except that Model 80 had an elm wood stock, whereas the stock of the Model 90 was of walnut, making the weapon five ounces heavier.

These air-rifles were designed especially for club shooting and were the finest match rifles I have handled. They were very heavily constructed, on the underlever principle, and had a breech loading tap which opened automatically when the cocking-lever was operated. Other good points were an adjustable trigger with a very smooth action, a massive one-piece pistol-grip stock, and fitted sling swivels.

The sights were really first rate. There was an extremely robust aperture sight with a large eye disc, which was fully adjustable for both windage and elevation, and was of the micrometer type with calibrated knurled adjusting screws. This aperture sight was instantly detachable by means of a thumb screw, and zeroed automatically when attached.

There was also an open sight which was likewise fully adjustable for elevation and windage and the sight blade was reversible, giving either a U or a V slot. This open sight was also instantly detachable and was capable of being slid along the length of the air-cylinder and locked in any position to suit individual sight. This is a feature I have never seen before on any rifle. The foresight was interchangeable for either a blade or a barleycorn by depressing a spring locking catch, and both sights were supplied with the rifle.

Both Models 80 and 90 were available in either ·177 or ·22 calibre. The Model 90 was 44 inches long and weighed 9 lb. 7 oz.

Diana air-guns and rifles are manufactured in a range suitable for persons of all ages. The selection of weapons includes Junior air-guns with ·177 smooth bores and four breakdown air-rifles available in either ·177 or ·22 calibre.

A desirable feature incorporated in the Model 27 Diana is the patent double-pull trigger action. This entirely eliminates the rather harsh trigger pull which was often associated with air-rifles, and gives a smoothness comparable to the trigger action of a high-grade firearm. The length of the second pull can be regulated by means of a conveniently located adjusting screw.

The well-known German-made 'Diana' underlever air-rifles known as Models 26, 45, and 48E have been out of production for many years. They were extremely powerful weapons, particularly the model 48E. This was very similar in appearance to the pre-war B.S.A. underlever air-rifle, but had a bad balance and was muzzle heavy, although it was one of the most powerful spring air-rifles ever made.

Messrs. Webley & Scott manufacture two excellent air-rifles known as the 'Webley Junior' and the 'Mark III'. The Junior, as the name implies, is made specially for the younger generation and is a handsome little breakdown rifle. It is extremely accurate and is equally suitable for target practice and killing small vermin. Good points include an adjustable rear sight, light trigger pull, robust construction and a fine finish. It is available in ·177 calibre only, and is surprisingly powerful. The overall length is 37 inches and the weight 3 lb. 4 oz.

The Webley 'Mark III' is a really fine underlever air-rifle of the highest quality, and is extremely powerful and accurate. This weapon has the usual tap loading and is very well designed throughout. I particularly like the way it handles and I have never known one that has not given its owner entire satisfaction. Good points include a seasoned walnut stock and an adjustable trigger pull. The overall length is 43½ inches. Barrel length is 18½ inches and weight 6 lb. 13 oz.

The 'Mark III' is available with either ·177 or ·22 barrel and the stock can be supplied with chequering (at slight extra cost) if required. Sights fitted as standard comprise an elevating U backsight and blade foresight, but a V backsight and a bead foresight can be supplied if preferred. An additional aperture sight, designed specially to suit the rifle, can be had from the makers, but it is best to order this when purchasing the rifle as two holes have to be drilled and tapped into the metal body of the weapon in order to attach it. This aperture sight, incidentally, is a precision instrument and has both lateral and vertical click adjustments and calibrated scales, and is strong enough to withstand even rough usage.

Many shooters will remember the pre-war Webley 'Mark II' Service air-rifle. This is now no longer made, but many are still in use and are still giving excellent service.

These rifles were unique in many respects and (together with the earlier 'Mark I' rifle) were the only air-rifles ever made with instantaneously detachable barrels. This was a great advantage for travellers because the rifle could be immediately 'taken down' and would pack into a suitcase.

The weapon was cocked by using the barrel as a lever to compress the spring, but was arranged quite differently from a normal breakdown air-rifle. Loss of air at the joint between barrel and air-cylinder was entirely prevented by a bolt handle attached to a screwed nut, which was provided with a quick action thread. This bolt drew the end of the barrel tightly against a fibre washer and positively prevented any escape of air.

Another ingenious device included a patent intercepting sear which prevented discharge until the barrel had been returned to the firing position.

An aperture sight, fully adjustable for windage and elevation, was provided as an integral part of the rifle and this could be folded down into a recess when the adjustable open sight was in use. Barrels were available in ·177, ·22, and ·25 calibres and were interchangeable so that it was possible to possess all three calibres with one rifle. The piston of the 'Mark II' was fitted with a metal piston ring instead of the usual leather cup washer.

All air-rifle manufacturers now appear to have discarded the piston ring in favour of the leather air-seal because this reduces production costs and gives a more nearly airtight fit between piston and cylinder with less wear and less maintenance. Leather absorbs and retains a certain amount of oil and this is sufficient to give a good seal without frequent lubrication over quite a long period. The metal ring, on the other hand, needs constant oiling and even then it is doubtful whether it is so efficient in operation, whilst if it is allowed to become dry it rapidly wears and becomes unserviceable and the rifle loses power.

Two fine underlever air-rifles are manufactured by B.S.A. Guns of Birmingham. These are known as the 'Club' and the 'Airsporter'.

Both are identical in general design except that the 'Club' has a ·177 calibre barrel whereas the 'Airsporter' has a slightly larger power unit and the calibre is ·22. Both are very robustly constructed and will virtually last a lifetime provided they are treated with reasonable care.

The 'Club' model is, as the name implies, eminently

suitable for the air-rifle clubman and is accurate at ranges up to 50 yards, and even at this distance has ample power to kill rats and other vermin. Dimensions are: barrel length, 20 inches; overall length, 44 inches; weight 7½ lb.

The 'Airsporter' is designed chiefly for sporting purposes but can be used equally well for general target practice. The accurate range is 60 yards. This is a remarkable performance for a spring-operated air-rifle, and I have actually seen rabbits killed instantly at this distance with one of these rifles. When using such a weapon against rabbits, it is absolutely essential to hit them in the head to be certain of a kill. Body-shots will only wound them and they will crawl away and die miserably in their holes. This is bad sportsmanship, and is to be condemned, both because it causes unnecessary suffering to the rabbit and the loss of a dinner to the shooter. These remarks apply equally to the use of any small-bore arm for sporting use.

Good points common to both the 'Club' and the 'Airsporter' are the absence of muzzle heaviness, the ease of cocking, and the self-opening breech-tap.

The underlever folds neatly into the forepart of the stock and this keeps the weight well to the rear. Easier cocking is obtained by so arranging the cocking-arm that the distance between its fulcrum and the second lever pivot is as short as possible. This lever actually pulls the piston into the cocked position, whereas in other air-rifles there is a pushing action.

The 'Airsporter' weighs 8 lb. and has the same length of barrel as the 'Club', but the overall length is ⅝ of an inch more to allow for the longer air-chamber. Both rifles have open backsights which are graduated and adjustable for elevation only, and both have a sight-base (distance between sights) of 16⅝ inches.

B.S.A. also manufacture two very good breakdown air-rifles known as the 'Cadet' and the 'Cadet Major'. These are not so powerful as the larger and heavier underlever models, but are nevertheless really excellent weapons which have been specially designed for the use of the younger shooters. They are equally suitable for target work or sporting purposes and will kill rats, grey squirrels, and other vermin at up to 30 yards' range. Both are sturdily made and are easy to cock and load, combining high quality with really fine finish.

The 'Cadet' is 37¾ inches in length and has a ·177 rifled barrel of 15 inches, a fixed open backsight and a sight-base of 12½ inches. The weight is 4¾ lb.

The 'Cadet Major' is the more powerful of the two models and has a ·177 rifled barrel 18½ inches long, with an overall length of 42 inches. The backsight is an open V-type and is adjustable for elevation, while the sight-base is 16 inches. This rifle is fitted with a screw for the purpose of adjusting the trigger-pull to meet individual needs. The weight is 5¼ lb.

Both 'Cadet' models have a one-piece stock and fore-end and are as pleasing to the eye as they are pleasant to shoot with. A special feature is the patent filter disc which is permanently fitted between the barrel and the cylinder. This allows a perfectly free flow of air but effectively prevents the entry of any dirt or other foreign matter into the cylinder where it could cause damage.

About thirty years ago there were many repeating spring air-rifles and pistols on the market. These weapons had various types of pellet magazines into which the pellets or slugs were inserted, and the mechanisms were so arranged that the action of cocking the rifle or pistol automatically inserted a pellet into the breech.

Probably the most successful were the German Haenel repeating air-rifles which were on sale in England in 1927. Two models were made, the ·177 calibre Model V and the heavier and more powerful Model IV.E of ·22 calibre.

Both weapons were fitted with a revolving drum magazine holding 18 pellets, which was positioned immediately over the breech cap, just behind the backsight. The drum was provided with a cover through which holes were drilled to correspond with the 18 holes in the drum itself, these being arranged in a circle having a radius of approximately $1\frac{1}{2}$ inches. The cover was capable of being manually rotated a fraction of a turn so that the two sets of holes did not quite correspond and this prevented the pellets from falling out if the rifle were inverted.

The drum magazine and the breech loading tap were both inter-connected to the lower arm of the cocking lever, on the left side of the rifle, and this ingenious arrangement left the shooter free to discharge the 18 shots just as quickly as he could operate the cocking lever, take aim, and shoot.

To operate the weapon, the magazine was first filled with pellets through the holes in the cover plate, care being taken to use only well formed slugs inserted head downwards. The cover plate could now be rotated $\frac{1}{36}$th part of a turn, when it would be held in this position by a spring loaded plunger, but it was not essential to do this manually if the weapon were about to be cocked and used.

The underlever was now operated to cock the spring, and the first part of the movement of this lever caused the cover plate to close the holes in the drum, if this had not already been done by hand. As the lever continued its travel, the breech tap was opened and the drum revolved $\frac{1}{18}$th part of a turn depositing the pellet in the already open breech tap. When the cocking lever was returned to its normal position the breech tap closed again and the rifle was then cocked and loaded and ready to fire.

I have never been able to understand why such an excellent idea did not last more than a year or two. The mechanism worked beautifully and it saved groping about in one's pocket for pellets every time one wanted to shoot the rifle. I can only assume that the automatic pellet-feed devices were discontinued on safety grounds as it was only by a very close inspection that one could say with certainty whether or not there were pellets in the magazine.

A very ingeniously constructed and beautifully made air-rifle was the 'Britannia' which was made by Bonehill of

Birmingham about forty years ago. This was a breakdown rifle but the mechanism was differently arranged from the usual weapons of this type.

The air-cylinder, complete with spring and piston, was located on the underside of the stock and in this way the rifle was able to accommodate a much longer air-cylinder than is usual in breakdown rifles, and the weapon was extremely compact. Another difference resulting from the layout was that although the barrel was 21 inches long, the total length of the weapon was only 35½ inches. There was also a removable screw which could be put in one of two positions, and this was located towards the rear end of the spring-chamber. This screw controlled the degree of compression to which the spring was subjected and gave two separate cocking positions and therefore two separate powers. I have never quite understood the real reason for this device, but it was certainly useful to be able to vary the velocity according to whether one was shooting indoors or outdoors. These weapons were made in ·177 calibre. A very few were made in ·22 and ·25 calibre, but I have never personally seen any with these bores. The 'Britannia' was one of the most powerful ·177 calibre breakdown air-rifles ever made and if in good order would literally blow a ·177 pellet to fragments.

Another breakdown rifle, made at a later date than the 'Britannia', was the Greener air-rifle. This was a superbly made weapon and was very powerful indeed. It was last produced about fourteen years ago.

It had a rifled barrel of 19⅞ inches and the overall length was 44½ inches. Sights fitted were a good solid blade foresight set on a ramp, while the backsight was an open V which was fully adjustable both laterally and vertically. The sight-base was 18 inches. Both ·177 and ·22 calibres were made. Trigger pressure was adjustable by means of a setscrew which passed through the trigger-guard. The best and most original feature of the Greener rifle was the provision of a special lever attached to the pivot pin. This lever operated a cam which locked the breech by drawing the barrel backwards against the breech-washer. The cam was adjustable, and there was no doubt that this device gave a positive and absolutely hermetic seal. The rifle was very solidly made and weighed approximately 6⅜ lb.

I understand from the makers that in spite of the fact that these air-rifles have not been recently manufactured, they are by no means obsolete. Production ceased solely on account of the difficulty of obtaining sufficient skilled labour.

For many years Messrs. W. W. Greener Ltd. of Birmingham have put all their available craftsmen on the production of the high-class shotguns for which they are so well known. It is to be hoped, however, that one day the Greener air-rifle will be on sale again, as it was a very fine weapon, and was accurate, powerful, and easy to operate.

There are, of course, very many old spring air-rifles in use to-day, most of which have given good and faithful service and are still performing satisfactorily, while others which are not actually in use could be made serviceable again by the replacement of the spring, piston head, or some other small component.

When using any spring-operated air weapon, it is important that it should not be cocked until needed for shooting and also that it should be discharged as soon as possible after cocking. It should not in any circumstances be kept cocked for any length of time, as this will weaken the mainspring and cause rapid loss of power.

If, therefore, you have cocked your air-rifle and the opportunity of firing a shot passes, you should either discharge the weapon into the ground or else uncock it.

Most breakdown air-rifles may be uncocked by holding the barrel down hard with your left hand, pressing the trigger, and at the same time *slowly* allowing the barrel to resume its normal position. Underlever air-rifles can be uncocked by the same procedure, but in this case it is the lever that must be held firmly, instead of the barrel.

Another method of releasing the spring is to turn the breech-tap into the 'load' position and press the trigger, thereby allowing the spring to expand without shooting out the pellet. If you do this, do not forget to shoot out the pellet before putting away your rifle or pistol, as neglect of this precaution is one of the commonest causes of all air-gun accidents.

CHAPTER 7

SPRING-OPERATED AIR-PISTOLS

AIR-PISTOLS are particularly fascinating weapons because they are so much more portable than air-rifles and because to use them requires a much greater degree of skill.

Their power, however, is generally much less than the power of a rifle on account of the considerably smaller air-chamber with its limited space for the spring. It is this space restriction that enables only a small and comparatively weak spring to be employed, and in view of this it is surprising that air-pistols are as powerful as they are.

Pistol shooting is more difficult than rifle shooting mainly because the pistol must be held, aimed, and discharged with one hand, and also because of its very short sight-base. In the hands of an expert a good air-pistol can give a very good account of itself, but the tyro will need much regular and constant practice before he can put up a good score. It must be appreciated that a modern spring pistol is a weapon of precision and is capable of grouping its shots far better than the average man can hold.

A factor common to both air-rifle and air-pistol shooting is that you get an awful lot of it for your money. Pellets are cheap and so are targets, and at the moment the air is still free! These reasons alone should be sufficient to interest potential 'air-gunners' in such a healthy sport.

I am often asked the range of an air-pistol and whether such a pistol will kill at a hundred yards! It may interest readers to know that the standard ranges for any type of pistol shooting are 10 yards and 20 yards and pistols are not normally used at ranges over 20 yards. This is not intended to imply that air-operated (or cartridge) pistols are incapable of longer ranges, but that the difficulties of holding the weapon steady enough for long-distance shooting are enormous. It takes a really expert shot to make a good score at 20 yards and most readers will do well to content themselves with shooting at 10 yards until they have become proficient enough to attempt the greater distance.

There are several air-pistols manufactured in Britain, among which are the Webley series, the Acvoke, Diana, Gat, Thunderbolt, and others. Of these the Webley pistols are perhaps the best known and are made in a range of three models. These are known as the 'Junior', the 'Mark I' and the 'Senior'. The 'Junior' is, as the name implies, suitable for use by young people, and is a robustly made weapon which should delight the heart of any boy. It has a 6⅛-inch, ·177 smooth-bore barrel, so that darts as well as pellets can be fired. The overall length is 7¾ inches and the weight 24 ounces.

The Webley 'Mark I' pistol is larger, heavier, and more powerful. It has an adjustable trigger and a rifled barrel, and as barrels are interchangeable, it is possible to have both ·177 and ·22 calibres in one pistol. The overall length is 8½ inches and the weight 30 ounces. It is a very accurate pistol and ideal for the older lad who wants something better than the 'Junior' model.

The Webley 'Senior' is the best of the three models and is largely used, by adults as well as adolescents, for target practice. It has sufficient power to kill small birds and vermin at normal pistol ranges and is an ideal weapon for keeping in practice with. It is constructed on the same general lines as the 'Mark I', but has several additional good points. The backsight is adjustable both laterally and vertically. Cocking is easier on account of the provision of a patent double joint in the cocking-arm. The trigger-pull is lighter and the weapon has a higher muzzle velocity. The barrel length and overall length are the same as the 'Mark I' but it is more heavily built, bringing the weight up to 33 ounces. Accuracy, general handling, and ease of operation are first class. Barrels are interchangeable, as in the 'Mark I', and are available in both ·177 and ·22 calibres. I have a very high opinion of the Webley 'Senior'. Spare parts are obtainable from the makers or through any good sports shop or gunsmiths.

A German-made pistol that has recently become available in England is the Walther Model 53. This pistol also makes use of the barrel as a cocking-lever, but whereas in the Webley series the barrel is superimposed on the top of the air-cylinder, the Walther pistol has the cylinder built into the butt. Cocking is very similar to that of a breakdown rifle, but the trigger guard is pivoted to the underside of the barrel and acts as the cocking-arm.

There are several other unusual features about this pistol that are worthy of comment. The mainspring consists not of one spring, as is the usual practice, but two. These are arranged one inside the other, presumably to give the strongest compression compatible with the short cylinder. The foresight has interchangeable bead, blade, and taper-blade sight elements, which can be quickly changed by the removal of a set screw. The rear is of the micrometer type and is fully adjustable for both elevation and windage. It is arranged for positive click adjustments, each click denoting $\frac{1}{8}$-inch variation at 7 yards range. The rearsight, moreover, has interchangeable V and U blades which can be snapped into position, using the fingers only, and these zero automatically when in position.

The pistol has a very strong snap action at the breech and has an excellent compression. The moulded grip plates give a comfortable hold and the left plate has a thumb rest. Balance is excellent and the general lines and handling of the weapon compare favourably with those of a target automatic pistol.

Dimensions are: Overall length, 12·2 inches. Height, 5·9 inches. Weight, 40·6 ounces.

The pistol is extremely accurate, but power is disappointing. This is probably because its appearance leads one to suppose that it should be outstandingly powerful—which it isn't. It is available with a rifled barrel of ·177 calibre only.

The Diana, Gat, and Thunderbolt pistols are suitable for the very young shooter. They are all good in their way but they are built on the lines of toys and are not intended for more serious work.

The Acvoke pistol is a weapon of precision and is very well designed. It is manufactured in ·177 calibre only and has a nicely rifled barrel that is arranged concentrically with the piston and outer barrel casing. That is to say, the barrel actually runs through the centre of the air piston. Such an arrangement is not entirely new, and there are at least two other air-pistols which employ the same system. The Acvoke pistol, however, appears to have overcome successfully the disadvantages previously associated with the central barrel design and the makers assure me that nearly twenty thousand are in use and giving complete satisfaction.

Special features include: Easy cocking by simple opening lever action. Fully adjustable backsight, positive breech seal, all working parts correctly hardened and tempered and complete elimination of all leather washers.

I particularly like the clean lines of the pistol and its robust construction and fine finish. Power is quite up to the standard expected of such a weapon. As regards accuracy, each pistol is individually tested on final inspection and must produce, from a fixed rest, a consecutive 'five shot' group to cut an inch diameter circle at thirty feet.

From above it will be seen that although specifically designed and built so as to come in the lower price range, this Acvoke pistol has in fact both the power and the accuracy of products costing a good deal more. It is in every way a man's size weapon.

Spring-operated air-pistols date back to the days of the

old smooth-bore breakdown air-guns and there have been dozens of different kinds produced over the years. At no time, however, has there ever been a spring air-pistol of outstanding power. This may be disappointing news to the pistol enthusiasts who are always seeking such an imaginary weapon. The fact remains, however, that a super-powerful spring air-pistol of reasonable proportions is an impossibility. The only way that such a weapon could be constructed would be by sacrificing lightness and portability and making the pistol considerably longer, and therefore heavier. Such procedure would transform the pistol, as we know it, into a cumbersome affair resembling a rifle without its stock and would be far too heavy and awkward to be used with one hand.

An interesting old air-pistol was the Westley Richards 'Highest Possible' (Plate 9, bottom). It was manufactured about 1910 and at the time was one of the finest pistols on the market.

Dimensions are: Barrel length, 9¾ inches. Overall length, 12 inches. Weight, 44 ounces.

It was made in ·177 calibre only, had a rifled barrel and an adjustable trigger. It was an accurate weapon and had just about the same power as our modern air-pistols, but it was far too heavy and the balance was bad. Pistols such as this are desirable specimens for the collector.

Plate 10 includes two illustrations of a pre-war German repeating air-pistol. The lower picture shows the method of cocking, and the upper, the weapon ready to fire. This pistol is no longer in production. It was the EM-GE 'Zenit' Model M. and was available in ·177 calibre. The magazine held ten pellets and these were fed into the breech one at a time at each cocking of the pistol.

Another German repeating air-pistol is illustrated in Plate 10. This, too, has long been obsolete, and will probably never be made again.

There is an American-made repeating target air-pistol called the 'Hy-Score' which is being produced at the present time. The pistol has a breech magazine of six shots capacity and resembles a Luger automatic. The barrel is 10¼ inches long but does not appear out of proportion because it passes through the piston and spring in a similar manner to the Acvoke pistol and much of it is therefore hidden in the casing or body of the weapon. Cocking is accomplished by using the butt as a lever. The general finish is very good and the pistol handles nicely. Its muzzle velocity is stated to be higher than any other American-made spring air-pistol. It is also made as a single-shot weapon with a choice of blued or chrome finish with either ·177 or ·22 calibres. Similar models can also be supplied with 7¾-inch barrels. The 'Hy-Score' is the only repeating spring-operated air-pistol being manufactured at the present time.

The other pistol using the centrally arranged barrel design was the 'Abas Major'. This was made by a Birmingham firm and was in production until about three years ago. Manufacture ceased only because materials were in short supply, and not on account of any fault with the pistol or its performance.

This weapon was unique in many respects and among its many good points were ratchet action cocking and breech loading by means of a tap arrangement similar to that employed in underlever air-rifles.

The 'Abas Major' was a powerful pistol and was not only extremely well made and finished, but was very robust, compact and well balanced. It was made only in ·177 calibre with a rifled barrel, and was the only air-pistol to be provided with a loading-tap. This tap was very neatly designed and provided a positive seal at the breech, giving, at the same time, convenient and quick loading. Cocking was extremely easy and was accomplished by means of a lever that was pivoted at the muzzle. This lever also formed the trigger guard and ended at the heel of the butt. The portion that followed the line of the butt was not visible when the lever was closed as it fitted into a recess and formed the front part of the grip. A ratchet device ensured perfect safety in cocking as the weapon could not be fired until the lever was closed. Moreover, this ratchet prevented the lever flying back from any position during cocking.

The backsight was fully adjustable, both vertically and laterally.

The overall length was $7\frac{3}{4}$ inches, the barrel was 7 inches long and the weight approximately 2 lb. Muzzle velocity was 400 feet per second.

I sincerely hope that we shall one day see this pistol back in production again, as it was an excellent weapon in every respect.

CHAPTER 8

MODERN PNEUMATIC RIFLES

It is disappointing to have to begin this chapter by saying that pneumatic rifles are not available in England. There are, however, a few such rifles in use that have been privately imported and it is possible that the reader may be able to acquire a second-hand one that is in good order. Such weapons are manufactured in several countries, but notably in the United States of America.

Pneumatic or pump-up rifles have several definite advantages over spring-operated weapons. They are usually lighter in weight, shorter, and generally more compact. They have a very pleasant smoothness in shooting, with complete absence of 'spring kick', and power is variable according to the number of pump strokes.

However, no pneumatic weapon requiring multiple pumping can ever be quite so mechanically efficient as a spring-operated air weapon, although it can easily be much more powerful.

Pumping creates heat. You have of course noticed that when you pump up a car or cycle tyre the pump becomes warm. The same thing happens when you pump up a pneumatic rifle or pistol; both the pump and the air-chamber become warm. This heat represents a loss of energy and therefore a lowering of mechanical efficiency, because the energy expended in pumping is wasted in creating heat and not pressure.

All gases (including air, which is a mixture of gases) expand $\frac{1}{273}$ of their volume for each degree centigrade rise in temperature. If, for instance, after pumping up a pneumatic weapon the temperature rise is 10 degrees centigrade and the gun is left for a while until this extra heat is dissipated, it will be found that the air under compression has decreased by $\frac{10}{273}$ (or approximately $\frac{1}{27}$th) of its former value with a consequent lowering of pressure. In practice, however, the shooting force is not noticeably affected, although theoretically a loss of efficiency must take place.

Typical American pneumatic rifles are the Sheridan, Crosman, and Kessler but there are also several others. They are all single-shot rifles; that is to say, whatever pressure of air is pumped into the air-chamber, all the air is released on firing one shot.

There is also an air-operated small-bore shotgun called the 'Plainsman' manufactured in the U.S.A. This is an ingenious little gun and is quite successful for shooting small birds and vermin. It is a bolt-action breech-loading gun with a bore of ·280 and choked at the muzzle. The wooden fore-end forms the pump handle and is pivoted near the muzzle, and by a system of levers operates the air pump.

The cartridges are merely small cardboard tubes closed at either end by felt discs or wads and the space between them filled with shot. To load the gun, a cartridge is placed in the breech just in front of the bolt and the bolt is pushed home. The front of the bolt passes through the cardboard tube of the cartridge, carrying the wads and shot with it and pushing them just ahead of the air inlet holes, and sealing the breech. The air pump is then operated until sufficient pressure is created. This takes from five to ten strokes, according to the power needed.

After shooting, the bolt is drawn back, allowing the empty cartridge case to drop off. Each cartridge contains about half a thimbleful of small shot and, using maximum power, all the shot will penetrate below the surface of a pine plank at 10 yards range and give quite a small group.

As far as I am aware this is the only modern version of a pneumatic shotgun. A few years ago an American firm marketed a double-barrelled pneumatic rifle which was called the 'Apache'. This was pumped in the same way as the 'Plainsman' gun, but the two barrels were mounted side by side on top of the weapon. Both barrels were rifled, one being ·177 calibre and the other ·25. A small lever operated a two-way tap which directed the air to whichever barrel one wanted to fire. I have often thought that such a weapon would have possibilities apart from its novelty, but I have not heard any more of the 'Apache' rifle so must conclude it was not a commercial success.

The Sheridan rifle was originally made in two grades, known as the 'Super' and the 'Sporter'. Both were outstandingly accurate and extremely powerful weapons, the 'Super' being easily the finest modern small-calibre pneumatic rifle ever produced. The demand, however (in a country where the use of firearms is not so restricted as it is in England), was limited, and these two models have been discontinued.

In their place, are two models known as the 'Silver Streak' and the 'Blue Streak' which are both identical except for the external finish being silver and 'gun blue' respectively. Both are excellent weapons, having nearly the same performance as the more expensive 'Super' and 'Sporter' but they do not have aperture sights, cheekpieces, or the same superior finish. All give wonderful accuracy and penetration. Much thought and care has been embodied in the design of Sheridan rifles and they are robustly constructed with good quality materials. All working parts, for instance, are machined from steel which is afterwards hardened and tempered, and most of the other troubles usually associated with pneumatic rifles have been eliminated.

Penetration is outstandingly good, and five or six smart strokes of the pump will provide power great enough to shoot through a deal plank one inch in thickness.

The overall length is a very compact 37 inches, of which the barrel measures 20 inches. The calibre is 5 mm. (or ·20) not ·22 as is standard practice. Rifling is 2½ thousandths of an inch deep and the calibre of ·20 is the measurement at the bottom of the grooves. The diameter at the top of the grooves is ·195 and the twist is one complete turn in 12 inches. The 'Super' weighs 5 lb. 14 oz., the 'Blue' and 'Silver Streak' models being approximately 5 lb.

Stocks are of walnut with a pistol grip, the forepart being pivoted and serving also as the pump handle. The pump mechanism is cleverly concealed and cannot be seen when the pump handle is closed against the rifle at the end of the pump stroke. The head of the pump piston is not made of leather, but of a special wear-resistant plastic which has been proved to be extremely efficient and trouble free. In actual manufacturing tests, no measurable wear was recorded after nearly half a million strokes of the pump.

The barrel is made of toughened bronze which, of course, is rustless; and the rifling is broached into the metal. This appears to give the rifling an unusually smooth surface or skin which results in the absolute minimum of friction between bullet and barrel and materially contributes to the weapon's amazing performance.

The present Sheridan rifles have adjustable open back-sights and blade foresight, but the 'Sporter' and 'Super' had adjustable aperture sights and ramp-type blade foresights with a sight-base of 22 inches.

The compression chamber is designed as a separate unit from the rest of the weapon, the advantage being that should any valve trouble develop, the owner can easily remove this unit and return it to the makers, instead of having to return the whole rifle.

Every provision is made to guard against valve trouble and a fine mesh gauze filter is fitted outside the air-chamber to eliminate the possibility of small particles of grit or dust finding their way, by means of the pump, into the valves.

The valves themselves are chrome steel balls which bed down into plastic seats, whereas most other pneumatic rifles use a metal seat and a resilient valve-head. The

Sheridan valve-seats provide a positive hermetic seal and are practically unaffected by climatic conditions.

Cocking and loading is by means of a bolt, plenty of space being left for the fingers when inserting the pellet. The bolt handle needs only very light pressure to ensure an airtight seal at the breech, and on the 'Super' and the 'Sporter' adjustment was provided so that the knob could be set in a high or low position. The original Sheridans also had a trigger that could be adjusted to individual needs.

All the Sheridan models are operated as follows:

1. Lift up the bolt handle and open the bolt. Now hook the first finger round the bolt handle and pull back hard until a click is heard and the sear engages.
2. Insert slug in breech and close bolt.
3. Apply safety catch.
4. Operate the pump with quick, smart strokes. This looks easy and *is* easy for the first few strokes but quickly becomes harder as the pressure rises in the air-chamber. It is, however, largely a question of knack and once this has been mastered pumping presents no difficulty.
5. Release safety catch, aim, and shoot.

The muzzle velocity of these weapons naturally varies according to the number of strokes of the pump, the approximate muzzle velocities being as follows.

2	pump	strokes	..	400	feet	per	second
4	”	”	..	510	”	”	”
6	”	”	..	620	”	”	”
8	”	”	..	707	”	”	”
10	”	”	..	750	”	”	”
12	”	”	..	770	”	”	”

By comparison, the approximate muzzle velocities of the finest modern spring-operated air-rifles are:

·177 calibre,	8 grains pellet weight.	600 feet per second
·22 ” ,	15 ” ” ”	540 ” ” ”

Sheridan rifles fire special conical, hollow-based bullets which weigh 15·3 grains and are ·195 inches in diameter, and have a narrow driving band (to grip the rifling) at the base, which is ·200 inches in diameter.

Tests carried out on prototypes using various pellets and calibres proved that this shape and size of bullet was best suited to the rifle and gave the best all-round performance.

There are quite a number of experimenters and others who stoutly maintain that ·200 is the ideal calibre for all air-rifles irrespective of type. I am open to conviction on this matter, but even if such is the case I do not think a rifle of this calibre would have much success in England as a commercial proposition. To market any type of rifle whose calibre did not conform to present accepted standard would be difficult, to say the least.

Another American pump-up rifle is the Benjamin.

This is made in ·177 and ·22 calibre with rifled barrel and also in ·22 with a smooth barrel for use with darts or round BB shot.

In addition there is also a 25-shot Benjamin smooth-bore air-gun which has a tubular magazine alongside the barrel and is designed to fire round shot only.

This is operated by filling the magazine with BB shot and pumping-up the air reservoir. Every time the bolt is operated a shot advances into the breech, and while the air-chamber holds enough air to fire several shots, the air pump must be given a few strokes occasionally to maintain a good pressure. It is a quite well designed job but will not give the accuracy of a rifled bore weapon. The makers claim that it will give a 2-inch group at 15 to 20 yards; and this is also claimed for the single-shot smooth-bore Benjamin.

The Benjamin single-shot models with rifled bores are claimed to group one inch from a machine rest at 20 yards range, and power is very good. Normal shooting needs only four to five strokes, while maximum power is sufficient to shoot through an inch of soft pine wood.

The overall length is approximately 36 inches and the weight 4 lb. Good points include a very smooth, light, trigger pull, real walnut stock and pump handle, and adjustable backsight.

The Crosman pneumatic rifle is yet another example of American pump-up weapons.

Formerly, Crosman rifles were available in many different models both single-shot and with magazine feeds, and in both ·177 and ·22 calibres. Now only the popular ·22 calibre single-shot model is available; but the makers also produce three models of gas-operated rifles which seem to be finding greater favour. The improved Model 140 Crosman pneumatic rifle replaces the Model 120 which is now discontinued.

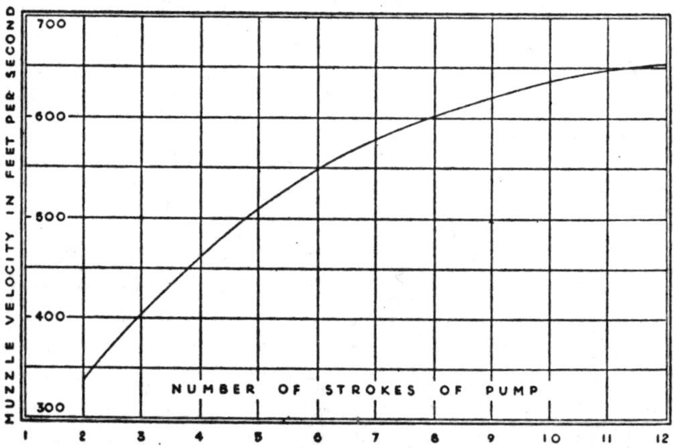

Graph showing muzzle velocity of Crosman 140 pneumatic rifle

It follows the same general lines as other American pump-up air-rifles but has, of course, its own special characteristics. These include a 19½-inch barrel containing six rifled grooves with a twist of one complete turn in 16 inches. The back sight is an open V and is adjustable and the foresight is a fixed blade.

Cocking and loading are by means of a bolt, but this bolt is quite different to the usual type of loading bolt with which the Model 120 was equipped. The new bolt incorporates a sleeve which slides externally over the breech and completely encloses the loading-chamber. This gives the breech of the rifle a very neat appearance and also assists in excluding dirt and other foreign matter.

The exhaust valve mechanism has been redesigned to make an air lock impossible, and at the same time give an absolutely instantaneous air release. (An airlock is a condition which can exist in pneumatic weapons when the internal air pressure is too great for the spring of the air-release mechanism to overcome. It is caused by over-pumping and renders the weapon temporarily unusable.)

The outlet valve is closed by pushing forward a small button located on the left side of the rifle. This closes the valve which is held closed by the trigger mechanism. Pressing the trigger when the weapon is charged with air results in the valve being blown open by the air pressure. This arrangement supersedes the spring and plunger air-release system employed in the Model 120 rifle and literally gives fingertip cocking. Overall length is 35½ inches and weight 4 lb. 10 oz. Power is about the same as in the Benjamin rifle.

Provision is made for detaching the stock by the removal of a single screw with a convenient coin slot. This is very useful for people who travel and want to take their air-rifle with them, as the weapon can be taken down and re-assembled in a matter of seconds.

An earlier Crosman rifle was fitted with a tubular pellet magazine and was the only modern pneumatic rifle that would feed ordinary ·22 waisted slugs from the magazine to the breech, simply and effectively. The magazine tube was located on the left side of the rifle parallel to the barrel and held twenty slugs. Loading was carried out by holding the rifle vertically and filling the tube with pellets, afterwards sliding a cover over the filling hole.

The weapon was pumped up in the ordinary way but had to be held muzzle upwards when operating the bolt, to feed the slugs to the breech. The pellets were thus kept in contact by gravity with a laterally moving breech-block. Opening the bolt caused the block to move towards the left and a slug then dropped into it. Closing the bolt caused the block first to move to the right carrying the slug with it until it was opposite the breech end of the barrel, while complete closure of the bolt pushed the slug up the barrel, just in front of the air inlet hole, and sealed the breech by contact against a shoulder on the bolt.

The Kessler pneumatic rifle is similar to the other rifles already described. It is 36½ inches overall length, weighs 6½ lb., and is a single-shot breech-loader. Both calibres ·177 and ·22 are available and it is fitted with both open and aperture sights. The finish is gun blue and the stock is oil finished. It is a very well made weapon and is extremely accurate and very powerful. General design, balance, and handling are well up to expectations and its maximum muzzle velocity is over 600 feet per second.

Modern pneumatic rifles have the reputation of going wrong quickly. Whilst it is fact they are more complicated and contain a greater number of working parts than spring-operated rifles and for these reasons there are more potential sources of trouble, I maintain that most breakdowns are due to abuse by their owners. Instead of being content to use such weapons in a normal manner, the average shooter seems determined to use a pneumatic weapon in the manner of a 'Try-your-strength machine'. This continual over-pumping creates stresses far in excess of what the weapon is intended to bear and results in rapid wear on the pivots, bent levers, and scorched valves. If you treat a pneumatic rifle with reasonable care there is no reason whatever why it should not give you many years of excellent service without ever letting you down.

It is important to remember that all pump-up weapons mentioned in this chapter and also those in Chapter 9 should be given the same number of strokes of the pump for every given range.

If you usually shoot at 20 yards and use say six strokes of the pump, don't pump up six strokes one time and seven or eight another. Your shooting will not be consistent if you do. It is best to find by experiment the number of strokes needed at different distances to give sufficient normal power, and to keep rigidly to these numbers. Pumping should be rhythmical. Do not pump quickly one time and slowly another. All these factors will affect your shots.

Pneumatic weapons are of course far more suitable for sporting purposes than for target work, as they take longer to prepare for shooting and much pumping is likely to render the user unsteady in his aiming.

CHAPTER 9

PNEUMATIC PISTOLS

WITH these magic words we can let our imagination run riot and conjure up mental pictures of silent and fearful weapons made especially for criminals, spies, and assassins.

We should, however, be a long way from the truth. Although it is quite possible that in the olden days murders may have been committed with such weapons there is no evidence in support of this.

There is no doubt, however, that the old-time large calibre pneumatic pistol, rare as it was, had ample power to kill, and was intended to be used as a personal protection weapon. As stated in Chapter 2, very few such pistols were made. I have handled and shot with many of these vintage pneumatic pistols by such famous old makers as Fruwirth, Colnot, Giradoni, Hansen, and others, and can testify to their almost unbelievable power.

One of the most powerful that I have examined was an unnamed pistol of English origin. It was constructed on the 'outside lock' principle and was almost entirely made of brass except for the working parts, which were of steel. It was complete except for the striker pin, and, as expected, the valve also needed attention. When I had put it in order, I took it to a friend's garage to try it out and charged the air-chamber at a pressure of 600 pounds per square inch.

Not only did it give a one inch group at 10 yards range, but the hitting power of the ⅜-inch diameter bullet was so terrific that it literally knocked large pieces off the brick walls. My colleague was as astonished as I was, and we concluded that much firing at the same spot would pretty well wreck the wall.

An illustration of this particular pistol is shown facing page 99. The butt of the weapon acted as the air-reservoir and contained the valve mechanism. It was far from silent although the noise would be less noticeable out of doors. This weapon is a typical example of a real old-timer, the butt being detachable for charging by means of a separate air pump.

By comparison, modern pneumatic pistols seem like mere toys. The only pneumatic pistols made at the present time are all of American manufacture.

Two typical weapons are the Benjamin and the Crosman, but there are others built on similar lines and having similar characteristics.

The Benjamin Company of America manufacture pump-up air-pistols in quite a large range, in both ·177 and ·22 calibres and with smooth and rifled barrels.

The first pistols made by this company had plunger-type pumps set underneath the barrels with the end of the pump rod terminating in a flattish knob or flange under the muzzle. This arrangement had the advantage that the piston of the pump had a full and long stroke and therefore only a few such strokes were needed to charge the air-chamber. It had the serious drawback, however, that it required great force to push the piston home and this could not be done with the hand alone. The result was that unless you had a hard surface on which you could rest the knob, at the same time pushing the pistol hard against it with both hands, you could not obtain maximum compression.

Benjamin pneumatic pistols now have a lever action air pump which is far easier to operate and can be worked with the hands alone without the aid of a convenient tree, wall, or other solid object and, due to the double lever design, a higher air pressure can be reached. The only disadvantage is that the pump tube has to accommodate these levers and therefore the working stroke of the piston is considerably shorter. In other words, although the pumping action requires far less effort, more strokes have to be made.

These pistols are really accurate and have a very light, smooth trigger pull. Power is adjustable according to the amount of pumping; and the maximum power is greatly in excess of that of any spring-operated pistol. In fairness to spring pistols, however, it must be borne in mind that a pneumatic pistol requires about seven or eight strokes of the pump to equal the power of the spring pistol and this is a slower process than the instantaneous cocking of a spring. For this reason all such pneumatic pistols are far more suitable for sporting use than for target work. Anything in excess of seven or eight strokes of the pump builds up power sufficient to outshoot any spring pistol.

All the air pumped into these pistols is released at one shot. Dimensions are: overall length, 11 inches; weight, approximately 1½ lb.

A repeating air-pistol is also available but this is made only with a smooth-bore barrel, and operates on round shot. It has a magazine capacity of eight shots and is loaded by first filling the tube magazine, the shots being fed one at a time into the breech by the action of opening and closing the bolt.

Crosman pneumatic pistols were originally made in two models, one having a ·177 rifled barrel and the other a ·22 barrel. They followed the same general design as the Benjamin range, but had shaped grips with a thumb rest, a rather longer barrel and greater overall length. The pump lever had an oval-shaped space for the fingers and other small differences. Power and penetration were about the same as in the Benjamin pistols, but if anything, they were a shade more powerful if the same number of pump strokes were used for each. Of the two makes I preferred the Benjamin. They seemed to handle better, and pump pivots and levers appeared to be tighter and freer from side play.

The Crosman Arms Company have now substituted in place of their two models, a lower priced pneumatic pistol with a very modern streamlined appearance. This weapon is claimed to have many excellent features and to be an improvement on the two previous models. I obtained one of these recently. It handles well and has a nice light trigger pull, but its power is much less than that of the former Crosman pistols.

Pump-up pistols are nearly always fitted with a safety catch, whereas spring-pistols are not. Safety catches are a useful and very necessary refinement on such weapons.

A pneumatic pistol, like a pneumatic rifle, can be pumped up fully and carried around on a sporting expedition without the slightest harm being done to the weapon. As a matter-of-fact, this is the standard practice, because if carried empty of air many shots would be missed. If pumped up and the safety-catch applied, the pistol can be carried without fear of accidental discharge, it being only necessary to insert a pellet in the breech to make it ready to shoot.

A spring-pistol on the other hand, must not be carried with the spring compressed, or the spring will rapidly become weak. As spring-pistols are intended to be cocked only when required, there is no real necessity to fit safety-catches.

The most powerful ·22 pneumatic pistol ever made was designed by O. H. Brown of Davenport, Iowa, U.S.A. It was of abnormal proportions and had a very long barrel. Its outstanding power was derived from a two-stage air pump located at the breech of the weapon. By this means, the air entering the pump tube was first compressed by the outward or pulling stroke of the pump while the second and higher stage of compression was produced by the inward or pushing stroke. The pump was highly efficient, and this factor, together with the extremely long barrel, gave this pistol about the same power as a ·22 calibre pneumatic rifle.

The weapon does not appear to have been a commercial success and only a very few were made. Presumably the ungainly size did not appeal to shooters generally. It was a beautifully made weapon, however, and sold at a high price on account of its complicated mechanism and high-class workmanship.

American manufacturers now appear to be concentrating on the production of gas-operated pistols and rifles, and in my opinion these are the weapons of the future as far as air-gunners are concerned.

It is therefore to be hoped that the 'powers that be' will relax our stringent regulations sufficiently to allow our own manufacturers to compete in this market. Given this necessary encouragement, I feel sure that we could design and produce first-class, practical, 'compressed-gas-operated' weapons which would delight the hearts of all our enthusiasts and would also produce considerable revenue from export markets.

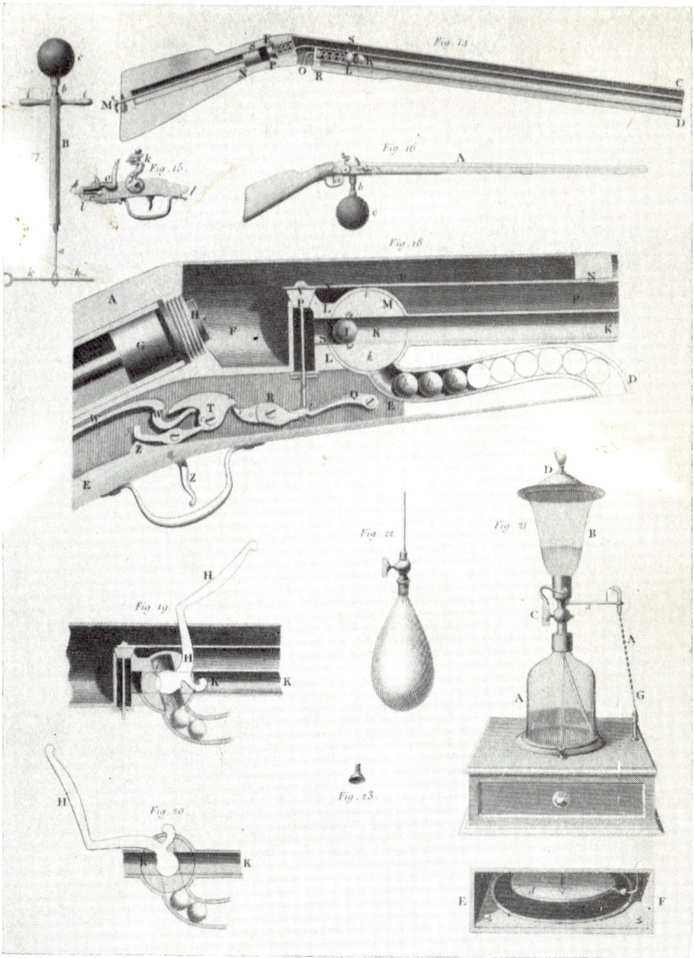

Page of pneumatics from an old scientific encyclopaedia

Detail of Kolbe flintlock air-rifle

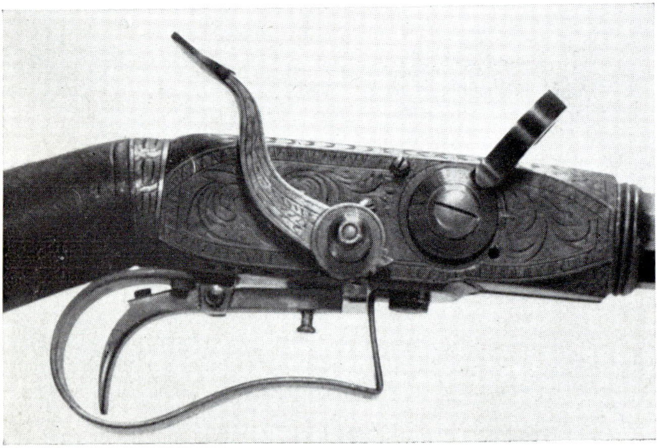

Antique pneumatic rifle by Hansen of Huddersfield

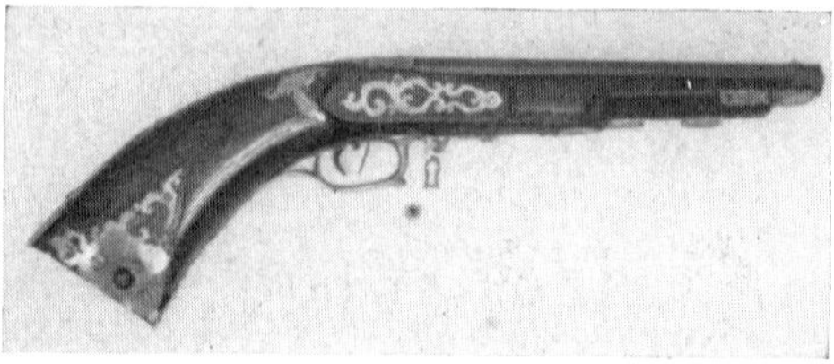

Antique bellows air-pistol

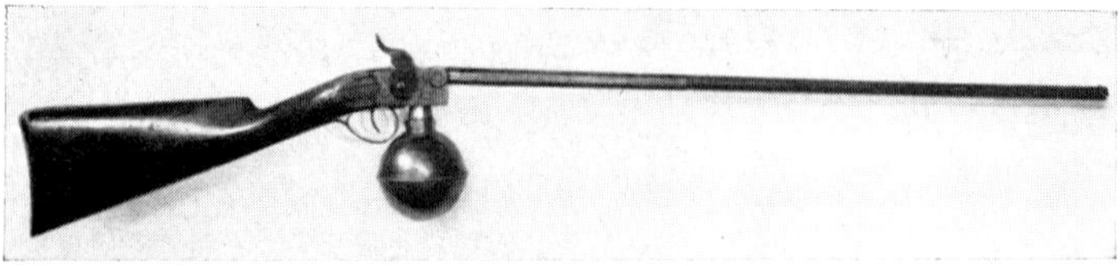

Antique pneumatic rifle with ball reservoir

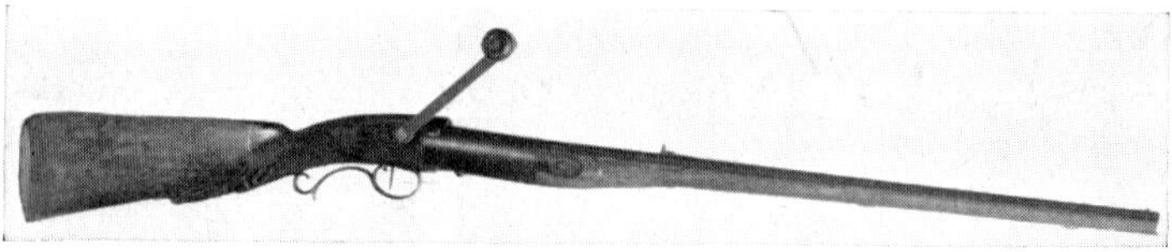

Antique crank-wound air-gun

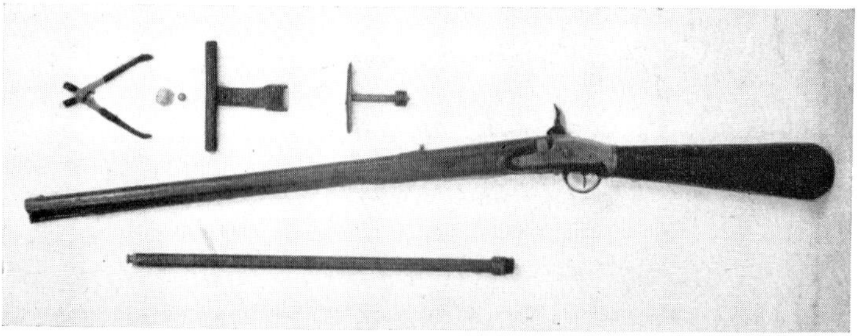

Repeating air-rifle of 1792

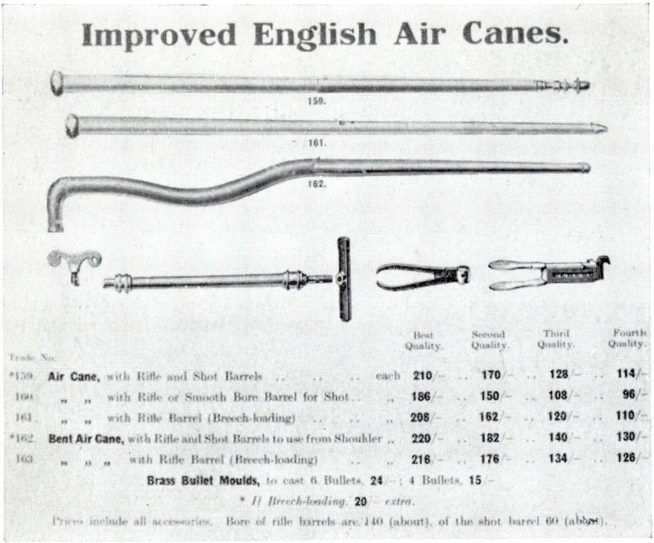

Improved English Air Canes.

Trade No.			Best Quality.	Second Quality.	Third Quality.	Fourth Quality.
*159.	**Air Cane,** with Rifle and Shot Barrels	each	**210**/-	**170**/-	**128**/-	**114**/-
160.	„ „ with Rifle or Smooth Bore Barrel for Shot ..	„	**186**/-	**150**/-	**108**/-	**96**/-
161.	„ „ with Rifle Barrel (Breech-loading)	„	**208**/-	**162**/-	**120**/-	**110**/-
*162.	**Bent Air Cane,** with Rifle and Shot Barrels to use from Shoulder	„	**220**/-	**182**/-	**140**/-	**130**/-
163.	„ „ „ with Rifle Barrel (Breech-loading) ..	„	**216**/-	**176**/-	**134**/-	**126**/-

Brass Bullet Moulds, to cast 6 Bullets, **24**/-; 4 Bullets, **15**/-

* *If Breech-loading,* **20**/- *extra.*

Prices include all accessories. Bore of rifle barrels are 140 (about), of the shot barrel 60 (about).

Page from an old gun catalogue

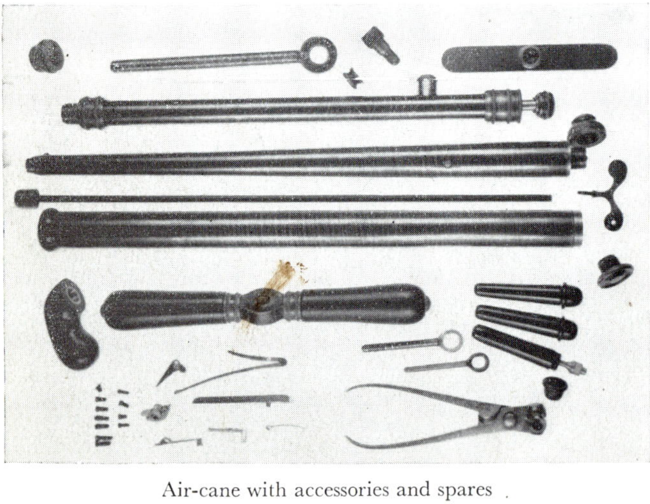

Air-cane with accessories and spares

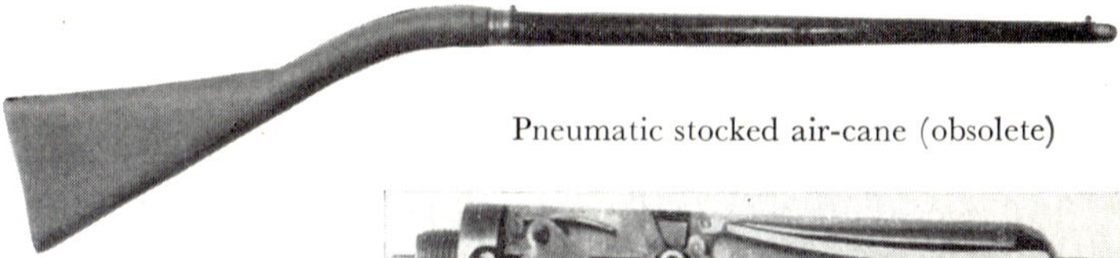

Pneumatic stocked air-cane (obsolete)

Walking-stick air-rifle lock. Cover plate removed

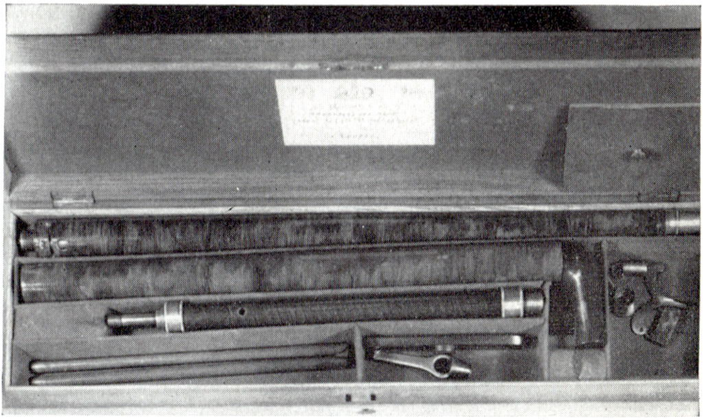

Cased walking-stick pneumatic rifle (obsolete)

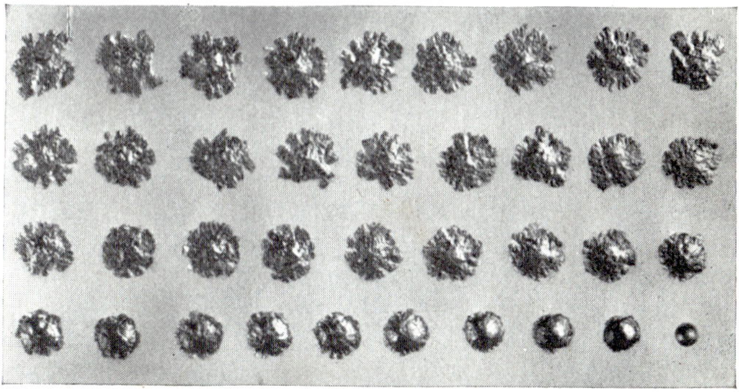

Consecutive shots from a walking-stick pneumatic rifle

German Original air-rifle. Model 50

German Original air-rifle. Model 35B

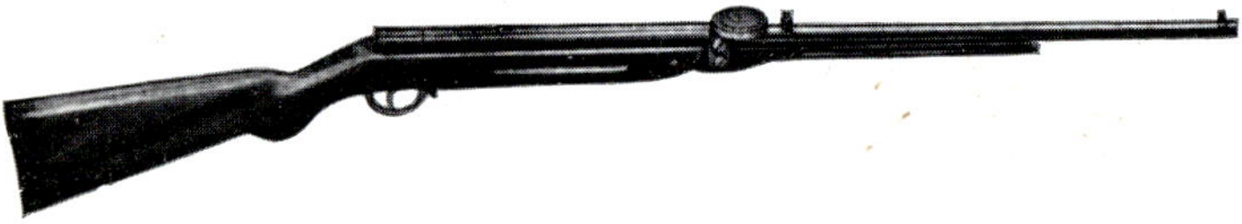

Haenel repeating air-rifle. Model V (obsolete)

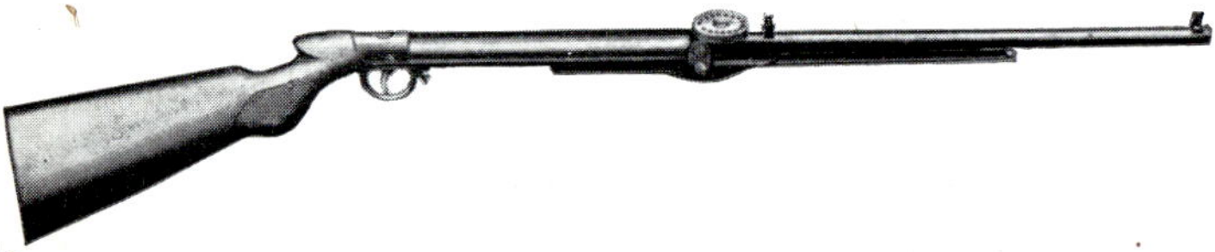

Haenel repeating air-rifle. Model IV E (obsolete)

Faulke air-rifle. Model 90D

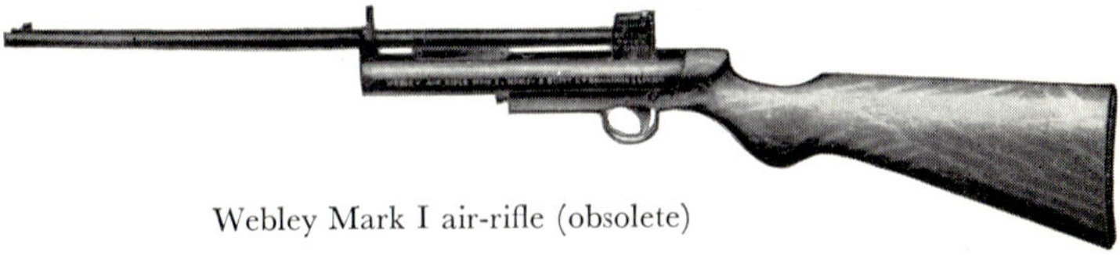

Webley Mark I air-rifle (obsolete)

Webley Mark II air-rifle (obsolete)

Webley Mark III air-rifle

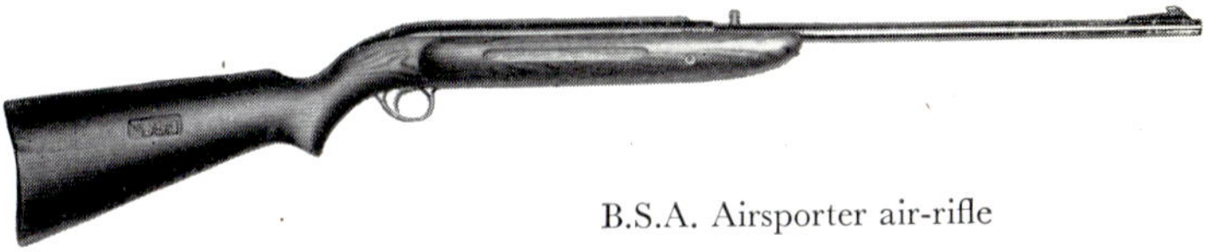

B.S.A. Airsporter air-rifle

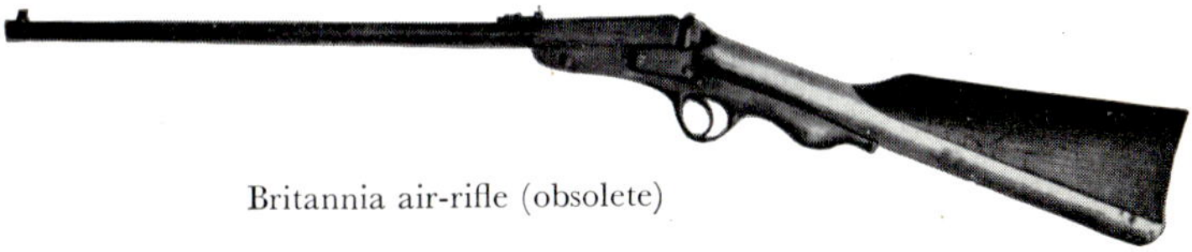

Britannia air-rifle (obsolete)

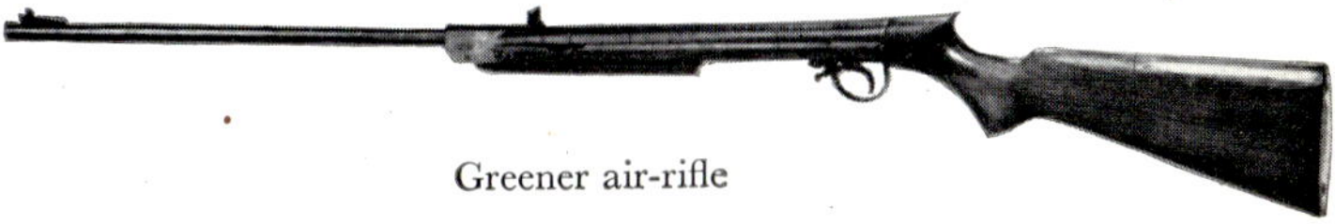

Greener air-rifle

Plate 8

Webley Junior
air-pistol

Webley Mark I
air-pistol

Webley Senior
air-pistol

Walther air-pistol.
Model 53

Acvoke
air-pistol

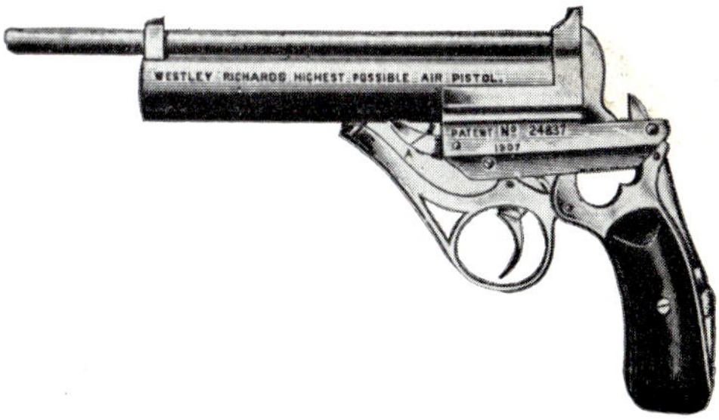

Westley Richards
'Highest Possible'
air-pistol
(obsolete)

Plate 10

Zenit repeating air-pistol (obsolete)
Below: Method of cocking

Haenel repeating air-pistol (obsolete)

Abas Major tap-loading air-pistol (obsolete)

Sheridan Blue Streak pneumatic rifle

Sheridan Sporter pneumatic rifle

Crosman repeating pneumatic rifle. Old model

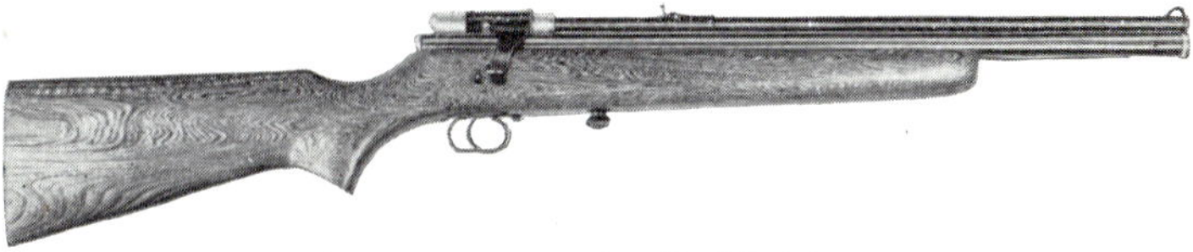

Crosman pneumatic rifle. Model 140

Giffard gas-rifle with external hammer (obsolete)

Plate 12

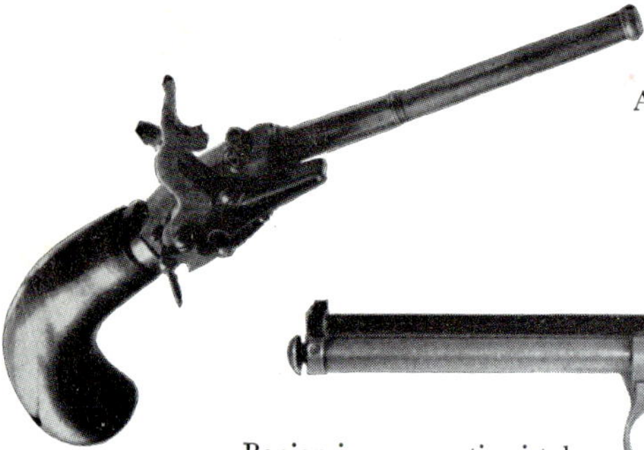

Antique English pneumatic pistol

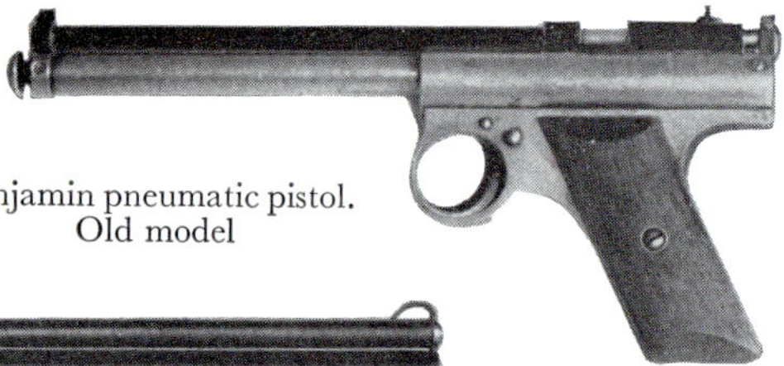

Benjamin pneumatic pistol. Old model

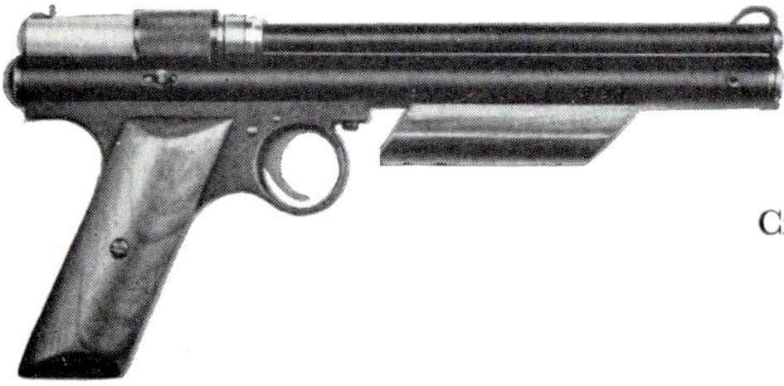

Crosman pneumatic pistol. Model 130

Brown pneumatic pistol

Giffard pneumatic pistol (obsolete)

Giffard gas-pistol (obsolete)

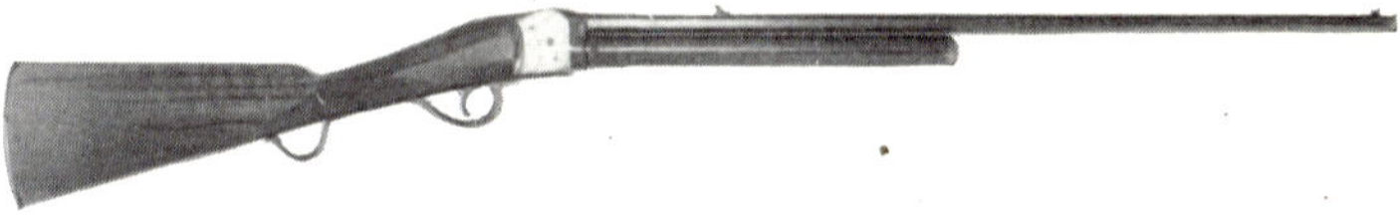

Giffard hammerless gas-rifle (obsolete)

Crosman single-shot gas-rifle, Model 113, with gas refill cylinder (old model)

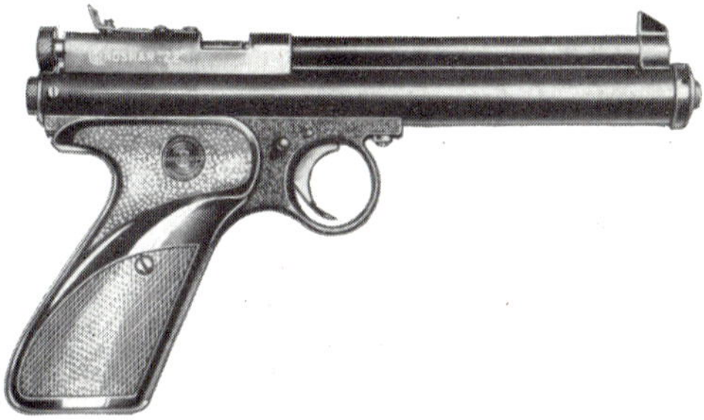

Crosman gas-pistol,
Model 110
(old model)

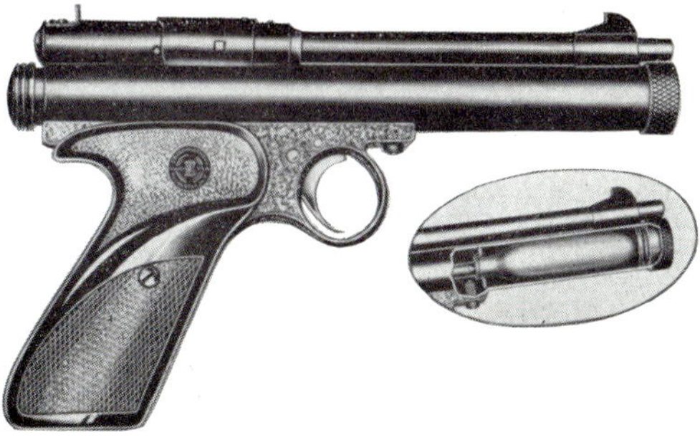

Crosman pellgun
gas-pistol,
Model 150

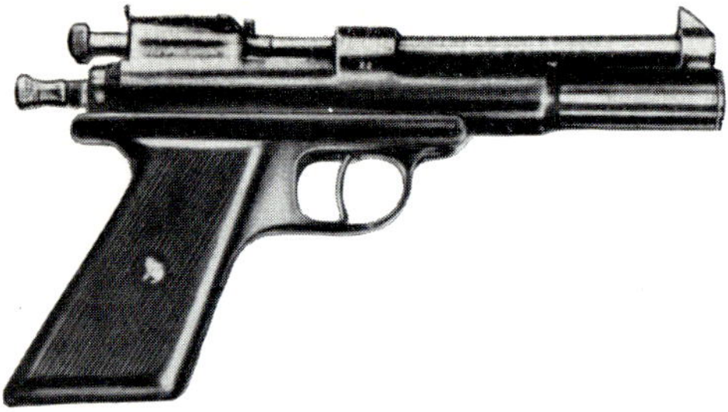

American Plainsman gas-pistol (obsolete)

American Schimel gas-pistol (obsolete)

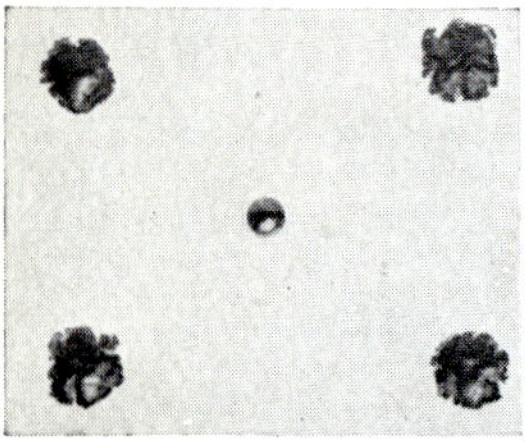

McGlashan air machine-gun. *Inset*, Fired BB pellets

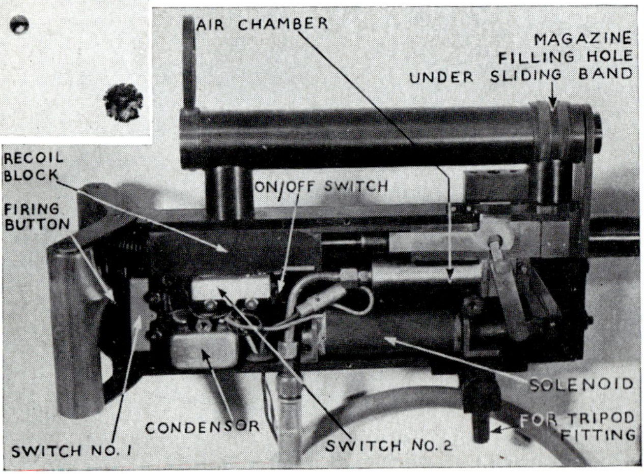

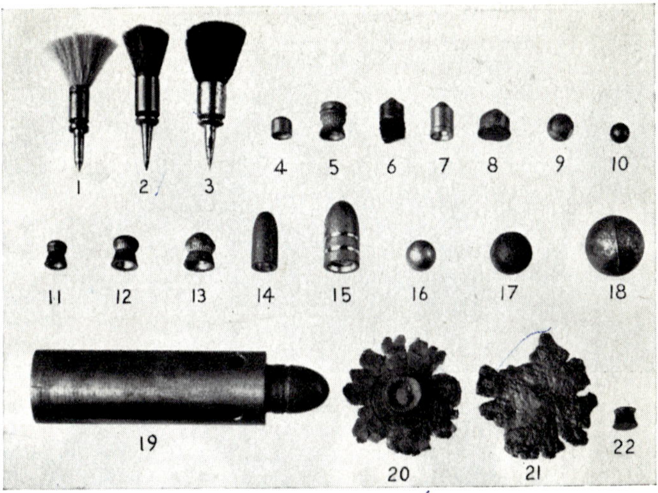

SOME AIR-RIFLE PROJECTILES OLD AND NEW
(*Those marked* are now obsolete*)

1. No. 1-bore air-gun dart (·177)
2. No. 2-bore air-gun dart (·22)
3.*No. 3-bore air-gun dart (·25)
4. Ordinary No. 1-bore hollow 'cat' slug
5.*No. 2-bore Triumph air-rifle pellet with additional circular fin (·22)
6.*·200 felted slug for use with Quackenbush, Excelsior and Hurricane air-guns, and Pope, Champion and Eureka air-pistols
7. ·200 air-rifle slug for use in Sheridan pneumatic rifles
8.*Bank's No. 3-bore solid air-gun/rifle slug
9.*·22 round lead shot
10. ·177 round lead shot for use in Daisy and other repeating air-guns
11. Modern No. 1-bore waisted slug
12. Modern No. 2-bore waisted slug (·22)
13.*No. 3-bore waisted slug (·25)
14.*·22 solid conical bullet for high-power pneumatic rifles
15.*·295 Giffard bullet for hammerless Giffard gas-rifle
16.*6-mm. round lead shot for Giffard hammer gas-rifle
17.*8-mm. round lead ball for Giffard hammer gas-rifle
18.*·44 round lead ball as used in the Austrian army air-rifle
19.*Giffard cartridge containing compressed CO_2 gas
20. Bullet fired at a steel plate, showing power of gas cartridge
21. Bullet fired from Austrian army air-rifle at steel plate
22. ·177 plastic air-rifle pellet

Explosive air-rifle pellet detonating on impact with a brick wall

Air-rifle target, 1909

Page from an old gun catalogue of about 1909

Hahn BB single action 18 shot gas-revolver ·177 calibre only

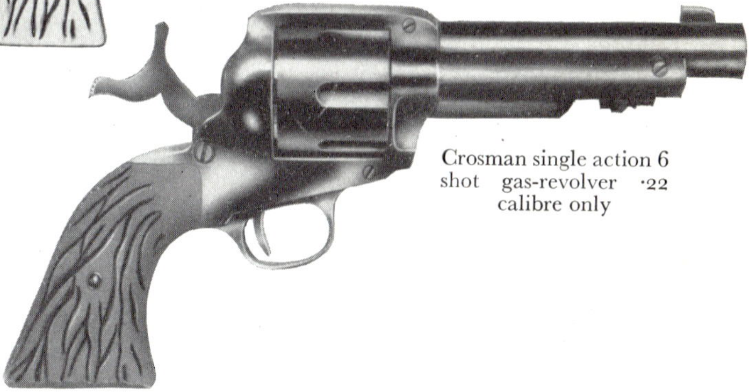

Crosman single action 6 shot gas-revolver ·22 calibre only

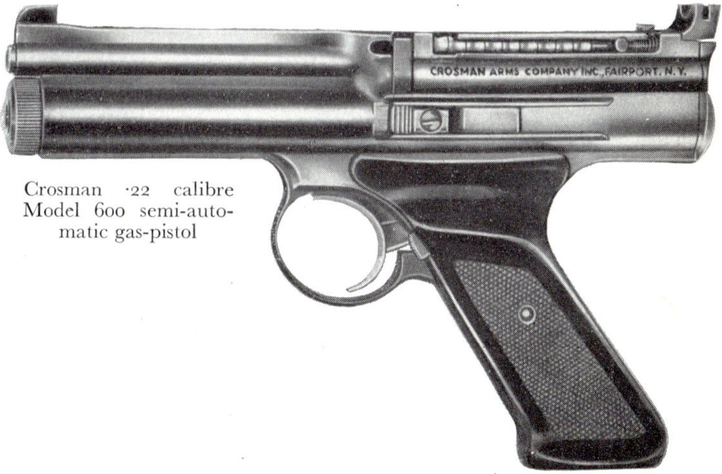

Crosman ·22 calibre Model 600 semi-automatic gas-pistol

Crosman Model 160 ·22 calibre single shot gas-rifle

Model 167 ·177 calibre single shot gas-rifle. Identical except for calibre

Hahn BB lever action repeater gas gun

Crosman Model 180 ·22 calibre gas-rifle

Crosman Model 187 ·177 calibre gas-rifle. Identical except for calibre

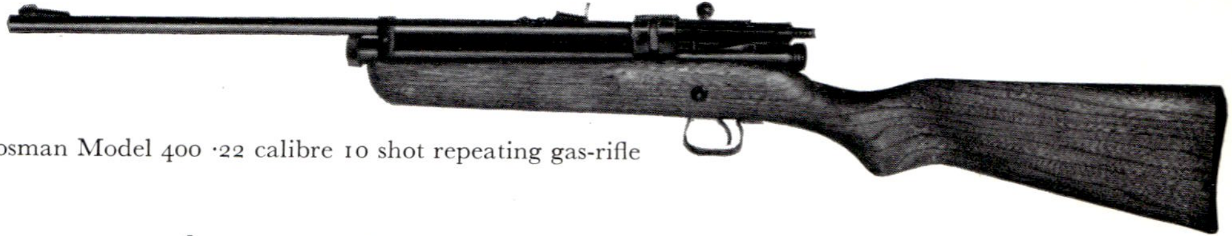

Crosman Model 400 ·22 calibre 10 shot repeating gas-rifle

Models 310-CS, 312-CS, 317-CS Benjamin super single shot air-rifle with custom stock. Calibre BB or ·177 or ·22

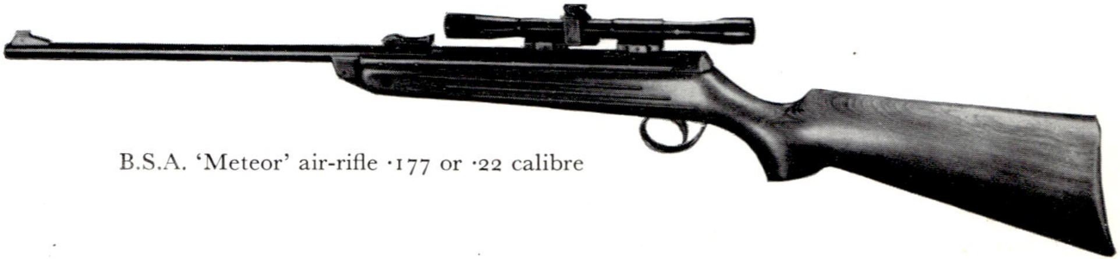

B.S.A. 'Meteor' air-rifle ·177 or ·22 calibre

Models 360, 362, 367 Benjamin super single shot CO_2 carbine gas-rifle with regular stock. Calibre BB or ·177 or ·22

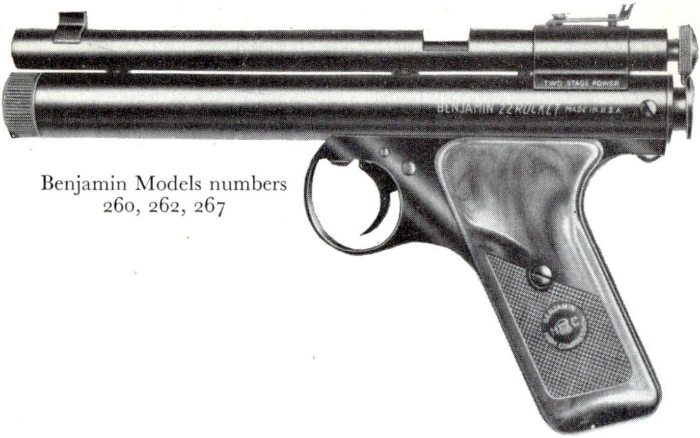

Benjamin Models numbers
260, 262, 267

Benjamin Models numbers
132, 137

Hammerli ·177 Model R.D. target gas-pistol

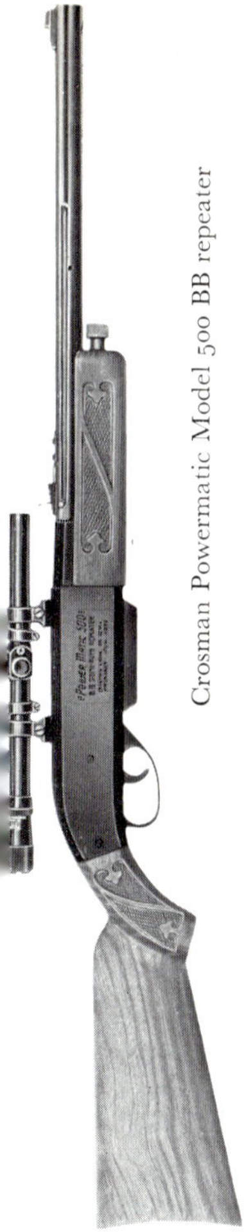

Crosman Powermatic Model 500 BB repeater

Crosman Model 1400 pneumatic rifle

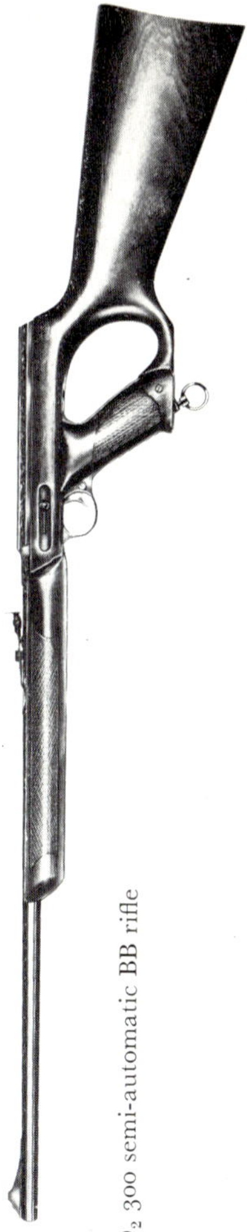

Daisy Model CO_2 300 semi-automatic BB rifle

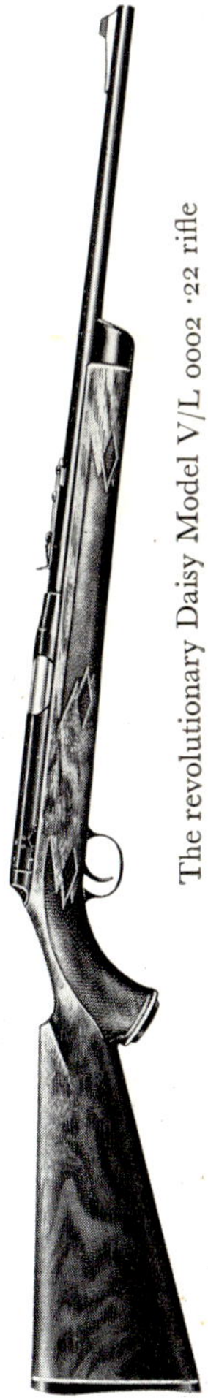

The revolutionary Daisy Model V/L 0002 ·22 rifle

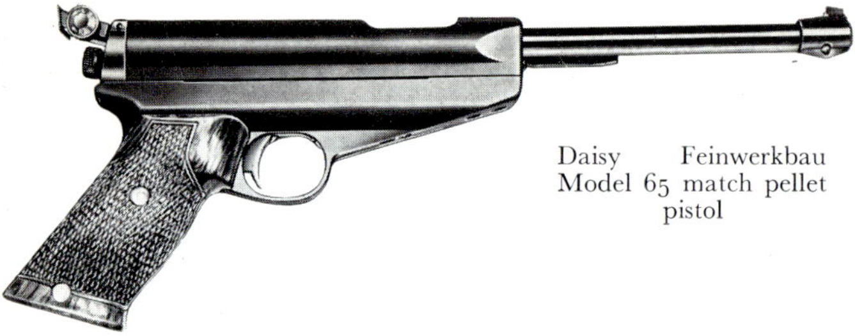

Daisy Feinwerkbau Model 65 match pellet pistol

Crosman Model 1300 pneumatic pistol

Daisy Model CO_2 200 gas-operated semi-automatic BB pistol

Daisy Model 179
pneumatic revolver

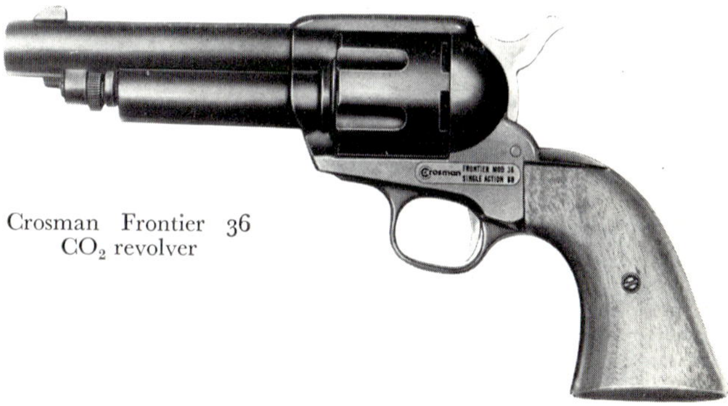

Crosman Frontier 36
CO_2 revolver

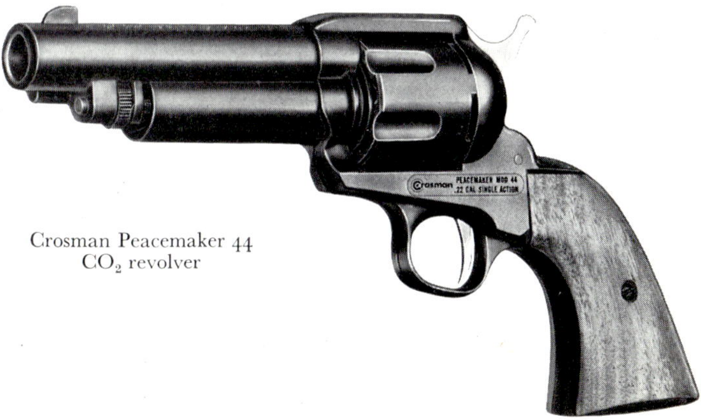

Crosman Peacemaker 44
CO_2 revolver

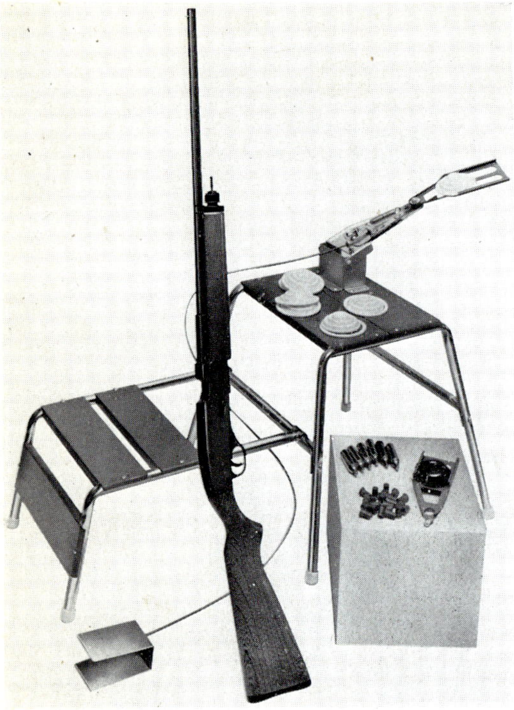

Crosman Trapmaster CO_2 skeet gun with plastic clays, clay-trap, CO_2 powerlets and shotshells

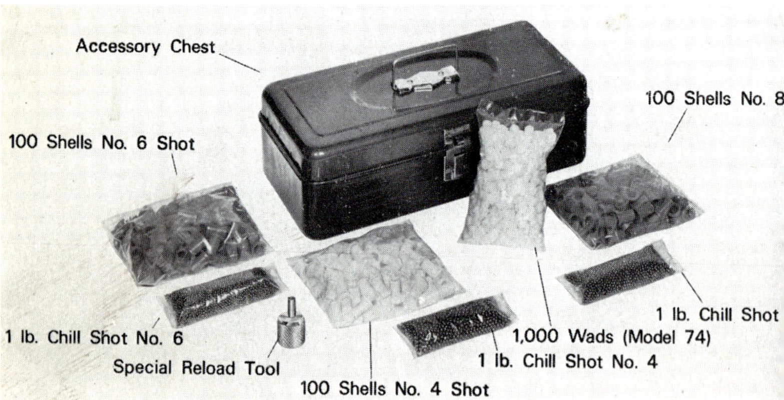

Reloading equipment for the Trapmaster

CHAPTER 10

GAS-RIFLES

THE idea of using compressed gas as a propellent in guns and rifles, instead of a charge of explosive, is not new. It would be correct to say that gas-rifles and pistols appear to this generation to be quite a new and novel invention, but if one has the time and the inclination to make a thorough search of the Patents Office files, it will be seen that the modern gas-operated weapon is merely a variation of previous patents.

Paul Giffard of Paris applied for a provisional English patent for his gas-rifle on 9th July 1889, and lodged the complete specification on 29th July. The patent was granted on 21st September of the same year, and shortly afterwards these gas-rifles were in production in London.

An earlier patent by Giffard in 1872 related to 'Improvements in Compressed or Liquefied Air or Gas cartridges and firearms and in apparatus employed therein'.

A further patent, also by Giffard, which was granted in 1890, referred to 'Improvements in apparatus for charging metallic cartridge cases with Liquefied Carbonic Acid Gas and in the construction of such cartridge cases'.

It would be a lengthy and costly procedure to attempt a complete search of the Patent Records, not only in England but of the world, to discover who first thought of using gas for this purpose. I am quite content, however, to regard Paul Giffard as the father of the modern gas-rifle.

The Giffard 'guns' produced by the Giffard Gun Company of London were actually *rifles* and fired a conical bullet of ·295 calibre.

These weapons were most beautifully made and resembled a modern hammerless rifle. The gas cylinder was located underneath and parallel to the barrel and the rifle was cocked by pulling down on a lever which also formed the trigger-guard. The operation of this lever performed several functions simultaneously. Not only did it open and close the breech and cock the internal hammer (which struck the air-valve) but it automatically applied the safety-catch and worked a counting device which showed how many shots had been fired.

The end of the trigger-guard lever was connected to a rotating breech-plug so that when the lever was down the bullet could be inserted. The safety-catch was located on top of the rifle behind the loading hole and had to be pushed forward before the rifle could be discharged.

A disc numbered 0.10.20.30.40.50.60.70.80.90 was positioned behind one of the lock-plates and by a ratchet (operated by the cocking lever) was caused to revolve $\frac{1}{10}$ of a turn for every tenth cocking of the rifle. The numbers were visible through a small hole in the lock-plate. It was possible, therefore, to see at a glance how many shots had been fired and, more important still, to tell how many more shots could be fired before the cylinder was empty.

These gas cylinders were available in two lengths, the standard size which would fire eighty shots and the long ones which would fire a hundred times.

The cylinders were filled with liquefied carbonic acid gas (carbon dioxide) and when empty could be exchanged for full ones at a modest price. Extra cylinders could also be purchased if required.

The power and accuracy of the Giffard rifle were really remarkable, and shooting costs were low, but the weapon was not a commercial success. The reason for this was the difficulty, or more correctly the impossibility, of keeping the valve airtight.

A peculiarity of these hammerless Giffard rifles was that the air release was constructed on the rebounding lock principle, and owing to this a hard valve had to be used. These suffered from the same troubles as the old walking-stick or air-cane valves, and were always leaking. It must be appreciated that the tiniest leak will very soon empty a gas cylinder and therefore an absolutely airtight seal is essential.

Unlike the walking-stick, whose valve was opened a definite amount each time the weapon was discharged, the Giffard Rebound System did not work this way. If, therefore, a soft valve was used, its resilience absorbed most of the hammer blow, the valve barely opened, and practically no gas was released.

These Giffard rifles are the only weapons with which my special plastic valves are unsuccessful. The choice is, therefore, a hard valve that will leak but give maximum power while the cylinder is full, or a soft valve that will definitely remain airtight, but gives very little power.

The earlier Giffard rifles which were made in France were available in 6 and 8 mm. bore with rifled barrels. These rifles had a visible but low-set hammer and a screw with a large milled head which could be set to regulate the fall of the hammer and so vary the power. The gas container was arranged as before, but loading was by a manually operated semi-rotary bolt and only round bullets could be used. The weapon had no underlever, and cocking was by means of the hammer. These rifles can be fitted with plastic valves and will operate successfully with them.

There is no doubt that the Giffard rifle created quite a sensation in France, and nearly all the newspapers of the time printed long articles about 'the new Liquid Gas Shooting System'. In England, the rifles also caused much comment, but Englishmen are conservative creatures and no one became particularly excited. I have always felt that the Giffard was ahead of its time and had it been produced at a later date with an improved gas release system, it would have been a great success.

The following are extracts from an old catalogue of the Manufacture Française d'Armes de Saint Etienne (Loire) of about 1895, describing the rifle:

'No powder, no heating, fouling, recoil, wear and tear, smoke, harmful gas, or expensive upkeep. Absolute safety, perfect accuracy, ammunition costs reduced to the cost of the bullets only.

'According to the bore and range (the gas release adjusted accordingly) one charge of gas will be sufficient for fifty to three hundred shots.'

The Giffard rifle was described in this catalogue as 'Giffard Rifle cal. 6 mm, steel barrel of first quality, rifled and longitudinally polished, moulded rubber butt plate, Swiss army backsight with moving indicator, bead foresight, trigger with screw adjustment, American type trigger guard, checkered hand, all parts engraved, rustless brown finish. Perfectly made and accuracy guaranteed . . . . 100 francs.'

Similar weapons were available with 8-mm. rifled barrels or smooth-bore shot barrels and also Giffard pistols with either 6-mm. or 8-mm. rifled barrels, and all were priced at 100 francs.

Exchanging empty rifle cylinders for full ones cost 1.25 francs for rifle size and 75 centimes for pistol size and spare cylinders for either size cost 10 francs. Round bullets were quoted at 2 francs per 1,000 for 6 mm. and 4 francs per 1,000 for the 8 mm. size.

As a matter of interest only—as it has really nothing to do with this chapter—a man named Cornelius Borda once invented an Oxy-hydrogen gun. This was constructed with two reservoirs, one containing oxygen and the other hydrogen. The gun was so designed that a small quantity of each of these two gases was admitted into a combustion chamber behind the barrel, where they were allowed to mix together and were then electrically ignited. It was said that the gun 'propelled a bullet as far as gunpowder would have done', and I can quite well believe it, but knowing the highly explosive nature of such a mixture, I should imagine the weapon was far more dangerous to the user than to anyone else.

A steam-gun was also invented by a man named Perkins and could be seen working at the National Gallery of Practical Science in the Strand in 1833. This was an elaborate affair and projected a continuous stream of bullets; but as the gun depended on a large boiler to generate the enormous volume of steam needed to operate it, the idea was rightly considered impractical.

A more recent invention, of only a few years ago, was the Dry Ice Gun, made by Monner of Colorado. In this weapon, solidified carbon dioxide was substituted for the liquid form. This gun was never produced commercially, and never got past the experimental stage.

Modern American gas-operated rifles are made in standard air-rifle calibres only, and give about the same maximum power and penetration as the average pump-up air-rifle of the same calibre.

These gas-rifles, however, have three great advantages.

1. They need no pumping.
2. A great number of shots can be fired on each filling of gas.
3. Power is variable by merely turning a screw.

The Crosman gas-rifle is manufactured in three models. These are Model 113 which is a single-shot rifle with ·177 calibre rifled barrel, and Model 1.14 which is identical except that the calibre is ·22. Both these rifles have a gas capacity sufficient to fire about seventy shots at full power, but the pellets have to be loaded singly for each shot.

The overall length is 38¾ inches and the weight 5 lb. 10 oz. Loading and cocking are by means of the breech-bolt and both weapons are fitted with safety-catches. Sights are blade foresight and adjustable aperture backsight. The rifling has 6 grooves and the twist is one turn in 16 inches.

The third model, No. 118, is made in ·22 calibre only and has a similar specification to the single-shot models, except for the following differences.

The bolt handle is adjustable and is capable of being set to suit individual needs. The action is cocked by lifting the bolt handle instead of pulling back the bolt, as in the single-shot models, and the rifle is fitted with a detachable tube magazine holding ten ·22 waisted pellets. These pellets are fed into the breech automatically by the action of operating the bolt while an automatic 'double-loading eliminator' automatically prevents the loading bolt being operated if a pellet is already in the breech.

The Crosman repeating gas-rifle has a higher rate of fire than any other air- or gas-rifle. This is because, once the weapon has been charged with gas and the pellet-magazine loaded, the ten shots can be fired as quickly as one can operate the bolt and press the trigger. The automatic pellet-feed, however, will work only if Crosman pellets are used, and no standard English-made pellets will operate without continual jamming. Crosman pellets—although conforming approximately to the waisted shape in general use—have a particularly flat head and a rather thin tail to enable them to slide smoothly from the spring-loaded tubular magazine from which they are cross-fed to the breech. I have found that the English-made 'Marksman' brand pellets have the correct shaped head, and if these pellets are first pressed by hand through a simple die to reduce their tail diameter by ·005" they will function perfectly in the rifle.

All three models are supplied with a small cylinder of liquefied carbon-dioxide gas holding ten ounces by weight.

The gas reservoirs on the rifles are positioned underneath the barrels, and are filled from the end just under the muzzle. The method of filling is very simple and takes only a few seconds. The rifle is held muzzle uppermost and the screw plug removed from the reservoir. This plug is fitted merely to protect the threads, the inlet valve being inside the end cap. The gas cylinder is now screwed to the rifle and the hand-wheel valve on the cylinder opened. After five seconds the wheel valve is closed, the gas cylinder unscrewed, and the screw plug replaced. The rifle now only requires to be loaded with a pellet and cocked and it is ready to shoot.

The small ten-ounce gas cylinders hold sufficient gas to charge the rifle reservoir seven times, and as each filling provides seventy shots, it means that nearly five hundred shots can be fired with ten ounces of gas.

In America a widespread cylinder exchange service is available, the cost of a refill being only one dollar, thus good sport is provided at a very reasonable price.

Such weapons are very hard hitters and are quiet in operation, and very accurate. The muzzle velocity of the Crosman gas-rifle is 700 feet per second at full power.

CHAPTER II

MODERN GAS-PISTOLS

GAS-PISTOLS using liquefied carbon dioxide gas as a propellent appear to be exclusively an American manufacture at the present time.

Several different makes are in production and two separate systems are employed. In one type the filling is carried out by connecting the pistol to a gas supply cylinder which is removed as soon as the pistol reservoir has been filled. The other method, which seems to be the more popular of the two, makes use of the small steel gas bulbs filled with CO_2 which are commonly used for the home production of aerated (soda) water. These are inserted into the pistols and the gas is released and drawn off by shooting the weapon.

The Crosman gas-pistol is filled from a 10-oz. capacity gas cylinder in exactly the same way as the Crosman gas-rifle is charged. Two models are available, Model 110 (·22 calibre) and Model 115 (·177). Both can be had with either 6-inch or 8-inch barrels. Their weight is approximately 1 lb. 10 oz.

One filling of gas provides 30 shots at full power and the supply cylinder contains sufficient gas to fire a total of 800 shots at full power, or up to 2,000 at half-power. Power can be regulated by means of a knurled screw located at the breech of the pistol. This screw varies the tension on a small coil spring which actuates the gas-release valve and thereby regulates the strength of the blow transmitted to the valve by the internal hammer.

Overall length of the 8-inch barrel model is 10 inches and muzzle velocity at full power is 600 feet per second. A moulded plastic grip with thumb rest is fitted to the butt, and a fixed blade foresight and an adjustable open backsight are provided. A positive push-type, cross-lock safety-catch is located just behind the trigger. Cocking and loading are by means of a neat bolt with a knurled head. Rifling is the same as in the Crosman rifle; 6 grooves with one turn in 16 inches. This pistol is the most powerful of any up-to-date ·22 pneumatic or gas-pistol that I have recently tested.

Some gas-pistols using a gas bulb instead of filling from a cylinder are the 'Plainsman', Schimel, Benjamin and Crosman.

The 'Plainsman' gas-pistol is built on the lines of an army automatic and is big and rugged. It is charged by unscrewing the plug at the muzzle end of the pistol, inserting the gas bulb (small end first) and screwing the plug back into position. The knob at the breech, just below the bolt-head, is now pulled back to cock the pistol and the trigger is pressed. This pierces the seal at the small end of the bulb and releases the gas into the pressure chamber where it is held by a valve. The pistol is again cocked and is now ready to fire as soon as a pellet has been inserted in the breech. This is done by partly rotating the bolt-head, drawing back the bolt, and closing it after the pellet has been inserted.

Power can be adjusted by turning the cocking knob, and 25 to 30 shots can be obtained using full power, or up to 60 with half power. The pistol is made in ·22 calibre only.

The muzzle velocity is not stated, but the makers claim that maximum power will penetrate three-quarters of an inch of soft pine. As is usual with gas-pistols and rifles, shooting is extrtemely smooth and there is a complete absence of recoil. There is no safety-catch fitted to the 'Plainsman' pistol.

The Benjamin gas-pistol is operated in much the same way as the 'Plainsman' except that cocking is done by means of the bolt instead of having a separate cocking knob. The gas bulb is inserted at the muzzle end of the pistol as before. The Benjamin pistol is, however, a smaller and neater weapon, being only 7⅞ inches overall, is less powerful, and has no power adjustment. The muzzle velocity is not stated, but the makers claim that it will penetrate up to ⅜ inch of soft pine and will fire 40 shots from one gas bulb. Both ·177 and ·22 calibre pistols with rifled barrels are made, and also a similar model with a smooth-bore barrel for shooting round shot and darts.

The trigger pull is very light and smooth and a safety-catch is provided. Sights are the usual blade foresight and open adjustable backsight. The pistol is well finished; and accuracy is such that a one-inch group can be obtained when the pistol is shot from a rest.

The third gas-pistol to use the gas bulb method of charging is the Schimel.

This weapon is a very lethal looking job and so strongly resembles a Luger automatic that at a first glance it could easily be mistaken for one. It is quite different from both the 'Plainsman' and the Benjamin pistols although it is charged by means of a gas bulb.

The Schimel is made in one model only and has a ·22 calibre rifled barrel. Dimensions are: barrel length, 6 inches; overall length, 9¼ inches; maximum width, 1¼ inches; height, 5⅜ inches.

Sights are a fixed blade foresight and an adjustable open backsight and the length of the sight-base is 8 inches. The weight is 40 ounces, and the weapon has a muzzle velocity of approximately 580 feet per second.

Operation is as follows (see Plate 14):

To charge with gas, the breech lever (shown marked with vertical lines) is pulled backwards. This causes the gas-chamber to slide slightly downwards through the pistol butt and the screw plug to become exposed. The screw plug is now removed, the gas bulb inserted, small end first, and the plug replaced and tightened with a coin. Now the small button on the right-hand side of the pistol near the breech opening is pushed forward. This closes the outlet valve. The breech lever is now pushed home, this action piercing the seal on the gas bulb. The breech lever is now opened and closed again, allowing a charge of gas to pass into the expansion chamber where it is retained until the pistol is fired.

To load a pellet into the breech, the knuckle bar (shown with circular end) is raised and a pellet dropped into the breech end of the barrel. The knuckle is now pressed down again into position and this causes the pellet to be pushed past the gas inlet hole and at the same time hermetically seals the breech. The pistol is now ready to fire.

For successive shots it is only necessary to insert another pellet, push forward the valve button; and open and close the breech lever and so on until all the gas has been used up.

It is absolutely essential that the valve button must be pushed forward *before* operating the breech lever. If this is not done the whole content of the gas bulb will be lost when the lever is pulled back. It might have been better if the makers had interconnected the breech lever and valve button, as by doing so one operating movement would have been eliminated, and the pistol would have been made foolproof at the same time.

When shooting this pistol for the first time nearly everyone forgets about this button after a few shots and loses all the gas. However, after this has happened a few times one acquires the habit of automatically pushing the button forwards after every shot. Apart from this criticism, the pistol shoots very well and is really powerful and accurate.

No provision is made for varying the power, but a safety-catch is fitted just in front of the trigger. 25 to 30 shots can be fired from one charge of gas.

The Crosman Arms Company of U.S.A. have recently introduced a gas-pistol using a gas bulb which is inserted into the body of the weapon. These pistols are made in both ·177 and ·22 calibres and are known as Models 157 and 150 respectively.

The gas bulb is inserted in the muzzle end of the pistol body and the cap screwed up by hand pressure only. The pistol is cocked by pulling back the cocking knob at the breech. The first time the trigger is pressed the seal on the gas bulb is pierced, allowing the gas to pass into the compression chamber. It is only then necessary alternately to cock and shoot the pistol until all the gas is used up. The cocking knob also acts as a power regulator. The knob is twisted to the right for maximum power and to the left for low power, while several intermediate settings are also available. Using maximum power, 50 shots can be fired from one gas bulb, while the lowest power setting will give up to 200 shots. Dimensions are: barrel length, 6 inches; overall length, 10 inches; weight, 1 lb. 10 oz.; maximum muzzle velocity, 600 feet per second.

In common with other similarly operated pistols, the trigger pull is crisp and light, and the weapon handles nicely and shoots with very little noise and no recoil. The pistol is provided with a safety-catch, and has a sliding cover to the loading chamber similar to the Model 130 pump-up pistol.

Although these weapons cannot be purchased in England, gas bulbs are available at every chemist and large stores throughout Great Britain which will operate in these pistols. These gas bulbs are marketed under the name of 'Sparklets' and are made for use with the 'Sparklets' syphon for producing soda water at home. The bulbs contain liquid carbon dioxide gas at a pressure varying between 850 and 900 pounds per square inch according to atmosphere temperature, this being equivalent to ·15 cubic feet of expanded gas at normal temperature and pressure.

A peculiarity of gas-operated pistols and rifles is that they are noticeably more powerful in summer than in winter. The reason for this is that the rise in temperature in summer causes the gas pressure to rise, and this gives a greater muzzle velocity.

Gas-operated and pneumatic weapons of all types can be

discharged without having a pellet or bullet in the breech, and no harm whatever can be caused by this 'dry snapping' provided the weapon is charged with air or gas.

As we have already seen in a previous chapter this should not be done with spring-operated weapons, or serious damage may result.

Many pneumatic and gas weapons are made with a brass or bronze rifled barrel instead of a steel barrel. The reason for this is not, as one would suppose, for cheapness or ease of manufacture, but because the sudden release of air or gas under pressure creates coldness. This cooling of the barrel is likely to cause condensation and rusting of a steel barrel, and the use of a non-ferrous barrel eliminates this possibility.

CHAPTER 12

AN AIR-OPERATED MACHINE-GUN

REPEATING air-guns of various types have been made for well over two hundred years.

The Swiss gunmakers were making 10- and 12-shot large-calibre repeating air-guns even before 1700 and these have been developed and improved on throughout the years.

These weapons were all of the semi-automatic type, because the bullet feed mechanism and also the cocking had to be operated manually. Not until modern times was there such a thing as a fully automatic air-gun, and because this is a weapon that very few people have seen or even heard of, a description of it should be of interest to all air-gun enthusiasts.

These fully automatic air-guns were made by the McGlashan Air Machine-Gun Corporation of Long Beach, California, U.S.A., and closely resemble aerial machine-guns. I believe, however, that very few were made and I doubt whether there are many in existence at the present time.

The gun is fitted with two handles, with the firing button set centrally between them so that it can be pressed with either or both thumbs.

The McGlashan gun was manufactured for training air crews in aerial gunnery, and on account of the extremely low cost of operating must have effected a very considerable saving in ammunition costs.

The gun is designed to operate from a steel supply cylinder or tank filled with compressed air, carbon dioxide, or other suitable gas and a 12-volt D.C. supply of electricity. The air is conveyed from the supply cylinder to the gun, through a length of flexible, high-pressure, laminated rubber hose. The gun barrel has a smooth bore of ·177 inch diameter and the weapon is designed to use round steel shot. This steel shot was usually copper coated to prevent corrosion by rust when stored in bulk.

The object of using steel, instead of lead, shot was twofold:

1. To reduce to a minimum any possibility of the feed mechanism jamming, lead shot being softer and far more liable to distortion while passing through the automatic feed.
2. To effect economy. After firing practice, a powerful magnet could be drawn over the ground and practically all the shot recovered and used many times over.

In point of fact, the gun will operate quite successfully using BB lead shot similar to that used in No. 1 bore repeating air-guns of the Daisy type.

A comparatively low air pressure of only 150 pounds to the square inch is quite sufficient to operate the gun, but using such a low pressure very little power is developed.

The weapon is capable of a rate of fire of 300 to 500 shots a minute (varying with the air pressure used) if the firing button is kept depressed. Single shots can be fired, if the button is pressed and instantly released. This, however, needs practice, since unless the pressing and releasing is very quickly done a short burst will be fired. Sighting is by means of a bead foresight set on a high post and a ring-type backsight fitted with fine central crosswires.

The magazine consists of two concentric tubes of different diameters, the space between them being exactly the diameter of the shot. The outer tube is provided with a sliding band which forms a cover for the filling hole, into which the shots are poured. The magazine has a capacity of about two thousand shots.

The cylindrical space enclosed by the inner tube allows an electric torch to be fitted; the light, at night, illuminating the stream of bullets and giving a very realistic tracer effect.

Using a pressure of 400 pounds per square inch, a 12-volt 30-amp. accumulator will provide ample power to operate both the electro-magnetic air-release valve and also the automatic feed mechanism. At higher air pressures a more powerful battery is needed because the electro-magnet has to overcome the increased pressure against the valve-head. Also, of course, a much heavier flexible air hose must be used.

In operation, the gun makes a typical chattering sound very similar to a real machine-gun, although, of course, less noisy.

In the illustration (Plate 14, bottom), the right cover-plate is removed, exposing the mechanism which consists essentially of two switches, a condenser, an electro-magnet (solenoid), and an air pressure chamber provided with a valve.

The operative cycle is as follows:

When the firing button is pressed, switch No. 1 (immediately behind the back plate) is closed.

Assuming switch No. 2 to be also closed, the current flows from the battery to the solenoid. (This is the coil positioned on the bottom plate.)

When energized, the solenoid pulls the air-valve lever which opens the valve and allows air to flow into the breech. The air thus released drives the shot out of the barrel, and pushes back the recoil rod.

Simultaneously the solenoid actuates another lever which operates a slider which it pushes forward.

Attached to the slider is a spring arm which engages the ratchet of the automatic feed mechanism, moving it forward one notch. The ratchet teeth are cut on the periphery of a steel disc which has ten equally spaced holes drilled in it, and arranged in a circle, one hole behind each tooth. The shot is gravity fed into the holes in this revolving disc, which allows them to drop one at a time into the breech.

When the air-valve is open and the shot is fired, the pressure blows back the spring-loaded recoil block and a small stud is allowed to slip into the block. This opens switch No. 2 and cuts off the current from the solenoid, allowing the air-valve to close, while a spring causes the feed slider to move back, the slider spring arm engaging the ratchet ready to advance the next shot.

As soon as the recoil block has completed its recoil, it moves forward under spring pressure, allowing the stud to pop out again. This stud, pressing against a light, flat spring, closes switch No. 2 and the whole cycle commences again.

The condenser is connected across the terminals of switch No. 1, to minimize sparking.

The inset at the bottom of Plate 14 shows one unfired shot (centre) and several others which have been fired against a steel plate. For this test the gun was supplied with air at 300 pounds per square inch pressure and was using ordinary No. 1 bore round lead shot.

CHAPTER 13

BULLETS, PELLETS, CALIBRES, AND SIGHTS

In the early days of air-guns and rifles, there was no standardization of calibres, and every gunmaker constructed his weapons according to his own particular ideas. As a result there were literally dozens of different calibres, some only varying by a few thousandths of an inch from one another. This was not of great concern in bygone times, because each weapon was sold complete with its own special bullet mould, with which the exact size of bullet could be cast to fit the bore. Although in later years the conical bullet began to be used in air-rifles, most of these early weapons fired a round lead bullet. The advantages of the spherical ball were as follows:

1. It was easier to load into the muzzle of the old air-guns and rifles.
2. Friction between the ball and the barrel was infinitely less than in the case of the conical shape. The ball touched the rifling only around the line of its circumference, whereas the old conical bullet engaged the rifling for the whole of its 'parallel' length.
3. The spherical bullet is less affected by wind than conical or other shapes.
4. Round balls were the only sort that would function in any of the early breech-loading mechanisms as all these repeating systems depended on gravity for successful working.

It was a simple matter to cast bullets, and several hundred an hour could be made using a single cavity mould. Bullet moulds were available with one, two, or up to six cavities, and if a multiple cavity mould was used, enough bullets could be cast in an hour to provide a week's shooting.

The method employed was first to melt the lead in an iron pot, then heat the bullet mould; and, using a small spoon-shaped ladle, pour the lead carefully into the mould, while holding the mould over the pot of melted lead.

It was important to heat the mould before starting, or otherwise the first few bullets would be spoiled by the rapid cooling of the molten metal when it entered the cold mould. This resulted in the lead solidifying before the cavity was full and only partly formed balls being produced.

If the mould was of the pliers type with a single cavity it was necessary to open the mould and give it a tap to release the ball, and when the bullets had cooled down, they could have the 'sprue' or 'pour' removed by trimming with the cutters provided on the mould.

If a multiple cavity mould was used, these usually had a sprue cutter attached to the face of the mould. This cutter consisted of a flat steel plate with deeply counter-sunk holes through which the lead was poured into the mould. Directly the pouring was done, a projection on the steel plate was struck and this caused the plate to pivot sideways, cutting off the surplus lead from every bullet. The mould was then opened and the bullets tipped out, when they were ready to use without any further preparation.

If, therefore, the reader desires to shoot with an old-time air-rifle, he will have to cast his own bullets, unless by a remote chance the weapon's calibre is such that it will use a standard size of moulded shot that can be purchased ready-made from a gunsmith.

Early spring air-rifles were made in three standard calibres. These were No. 1 bore, No. 2 bore, and No. 3 bore and corresponded to ·177 inch, ·22 inch, and ·25 inch respectively.

Round shot was frequently used in spring-operated guns, and was made in all three sizes, but to-day is available only in No. 1 size for use in single-shot and repeating air-guns of the Daisy and Junior types.

Round shot was succeeded by the conical slug and later by the modern, waisted pellet.

Air-rifle calibres are now standardized and only ·177 and ·22 barrels are made, but at least two firms still produce the old ·25 waisted pellet for the convenience of owners of old No. 3 bore rifles.

No air-rifles of ·25 calibre are in production to-day nor have they been made for many years, the reason being that they were generally unsatisfactory. The muzzle velocity of a ·25 air-rifle was much lower than that of a ·22 weapon and the extra weight of the ·25 pellet with its theoretically greater killing power was more than neutralized by the lower velocity and therefore greater bullet drop.

I have never handled a ·25 calibre spring-operated rifle that was really powerful, although I did once have a Gem-type breakdown air-*gun* of No. 3 bore that would shatter a pellet, but it was hopelessly inaccurate and, therefore, useless.

Some early American spring air-guns and pistols may be met with, which are neither ·177 nor ·22. Examples of these are the Pope and Eureka air-pistols and one model of the Quackenbush breakdown gun. These were ·200 calibre and were intended to shoot a special felted slug.

Felted slugs were of the plain, solid, non-waisted type and had a small disc or circle of black felt glued to their base. This provided a really good air-seal between pellet and bore with the minimum of friction. These slugs were on the whole quite successful, but were rather expensive and this was probably the reason why they were discontinued.

Another type of pellet available in bygone days was the Bank's Patent Pellet. These, I remember particularly, were obtainable in No. 1, 2, and 3 bore and were solid, conical tipped bullets with a slightly larger flange at the base to grip the rifling. They were too heavy to be useful except at short ranges.

Darts were also made for No. 1, 2 and 3 bore air-guns, and were at one time very popular indeed, but these seem to have almost died out nowadays and perhaps it is just as well. They cannot be used in underlever air-rifles, as the breech tap will not accommodate their length; but can be used in breakdown air-rifles and guns and spring air-pistols. Their use, however, is not recommended in any rifled weapon as the steel part of the dart is liable to damage the rifling.

It is not generally realized why the modern waisted air-rifle pellet is so shaped. The real reason is to reduce friction between pellet and rifling to the absolute minimum and so increase power and penetration. The front portion of such a pellet slides easily into the bore of an air-rifle without gripping, and the base flange, being made a few thousandths of an inch larger in diameter, grips the rifling and causes the pellet to spin on its axis as it travels up the barrel, and continue to spin for a long time after it leaves the muzzle. It is this spin imparted to the pellet that causes its gyroscopic stability in flight, and results in the super accuracy of modern air-rifles.

Modern pellets of the waisted shape are made to close limits and only a few thousandths of an inch tolerance is allowed. For example, No. 1 bore ·177 pellets should have a head diameter of between ·176 and ·178 of an inch, and a skirt or tail diameter of ·183 to ·185.

The larger No. 2 bore or ·22 pellets usually have a head diameter of ·215 to ·217 and a skirt diameter of between ·226 and ·229.

It is popularly supposed that the reason for the hollow base is to allow the skirt of the pellet to expand as soon as the compressed air strikes it.

Such expansión does take place in high-power air-rifles, but only to a very small extent. The real reasons for having the pellet hollow at the base are:

1. To concentrate the weight in the head of the pellet, thus giving stability in flight and
2. To leave the skirt or driving part of the pellet as thin

as possible so that it will 'take' the rifling of the barrel with the minimum of friction. If the skirt were made any thinner than is usual, the pellets would be very liable to become damaged before use, and also the absence of a sufficient body of metal would cause 'stripping'.

'Stripping' is a term used to denote the passing of a projectile straight through a rifled barrel without a turning motion being imparted to it. In the old days, 'stripping' was caused by having too many turns in the rifling of barrels. Modern air-rifles have a comparatively slow twist to the rifling in order to facilitate the high speed at which pellets travel through their barrels.

There is another shape of waisted pellet which was patented many years ago and is still in production to-day, although very few dealers appear to stock it. This pellet is nearly double the weight of the ordinary waisted pellet and is slightly longer. It has the usual flange as the base, and an additional flange immediately behind the head.

They were made originally for use in smooth-bore guns but I find they work very well in high-powered spring rifles and pneumatic and gas-operated weapons. They are useful for game or vermin shooting, as the extra weight makes them especially deadly. These pellets are made by Lanes Ltd. of Bermondsey and are known as 'Triumph' Brand. They used to be available in both No. 1 and No. 2 bore but are now procurable in ·22 calibre only.

Another kind of ammunition which was popular many years ago was 'Air-Gun Spread Shot'. This was originally of continental manufacture, but was afterwards made in England. Such ammunition was last produced about 1930, although by a strange coincidence I was able to purchase some quite recently at a Guildford tool and cycle dealer's shop.

These spread shot pellets looked exactly like tiny sticks of chalk and in fact that is just what they were. Embedded in the compressed chalk were several (usually six) very tiny shots. When the chalk stick was fired through the air-rifle barrel, the compression of the air caused the chalk to disintegrate and the tiny shots were projected from the muzzle. The chalk dust, of course, was blown out at the same time. These were useful pellets if one was not a particularly good shot and wanted to appear a crack shot. Small birds could be brought down by using these spread shot pellets, much to the amazement of the onlookers.

Other pellets even more novel, and comparatively unknown, are explosive air-gun pellets. These were obtainable many years ago on the Continent and were also manufactured in London in 1906 and sold under the name of 'Bango' air-gun bullets in ·177, ·22, and ·25 calibres, the ·177 size retailing at sixpence a hundred. This was quite a high price in those days, as ordinary air-gun slugs could be purchased in a great variety of different brands and shapes at sixpence a thousand. Happy days!

'Bango' air-gun bullets were guaranteed to 'go bang' when fired at a hard surface but it is extremely doubtful if such pellets could be marketed to-day, as no doubt many irksome restrictions would be placed on their sale.

I have, however, made two different types of explosive slug for use in air-rifles, but these were made purely for experimental purposes.

One type was made by filling the hollow back of an ordinary ·22 waisted slug with an explosive substance which would detonate only on impact. Such a pellet would be projected only by the normal power of the air-rifle, but would fly to pieces with a loud report when it reached its billet.

The second and more interesting type had the hollow loosely filled with a non-sensitive, slow-burning explosive, with an admixture of a minute portion of a highly sensitive composition.

If these pellets were used in air-rifles having a high compression ratio, the rapid compression detonated the explosives and the air-rifle performed very much in the same way as a ·22 cartridge rifle. The characteristic flash and kick were present, and the power of the air-rifle was increased enormously.

From pellets we pass to sights.

A fact that is not generally appreciated is that every air-gun, rifle, and pistol projectile has what is known as a 'trajectory'.

This means that every pellet, dart, slug, arrow, or other missile fired from any weapon whatsoever, does *not* travel in a straight line, but follows a curved path. The pellet, slug, or dart fired from any air weapon must follow the laws of gravity, and any such projectile is acted on by gravity directly it leaves the muzzle. This causes the bullet to drop. This bullet drop is not very noticeable at short ranges as the amount of drop depends on the length of time the bullet is in flight. The initial velocity or speed at which the pellet is travelling is greatest near the muzzle of the weapon, and the time taken by the pellet to travel a short distance is extremely small. For this reason the pellet drop is negligible. The longer the distance, however, the slower the pellet will be travelling, due to the continued resistance of the air through which it passes, and therefore the longer it will take to complete its journey to the target. During the whole of this time the forces of gravity are at work, pulling the bullet towards the ground, and therefore the bullet drop is quite considerable and must be allowed for if the pellet is to strike the target.

This is why elevating backsights are fitted to most good air-rifles. Elevating sights are also fitted to many air-pistols, but as pistols are never used at long ranges, it would be as well to consider such pistol sights in the nature of 'good selling points' rather than aids for practical use. I do not think the average pistol shooter ever has need to elevate his sight unless he intends carrying out experiments in long-range shooting.

I wish to make it quite clear that the amount of drop of any projectile does *not* depend on the distance it has travelled, but upon the *length of time it has been travelling*. This means that an air-rifle having a high muzzle velocity will have a flatter trajectory than another air-rifle whose muzzle velocity is lower.

It must be clearly understood that if you look along the sights of your rifle, keeping them correctly aligned on your target, this imaginary straight line is the 'Line of Sight' and is *not* the path that the pellet follows.

The 'line of sight' can be considered as a straight line passing through the sights of your rifle to the bull's-eye of the target. We have already seen that the path taken by the pellet is a curved one and, of course, the longer the pellet is in flight the more pronounced the curve will become.

The sights on all air-rifles are so arranged that when the weapon is correctly aligned on the target, the barrel is actually pointing in a slightly upwards direction.

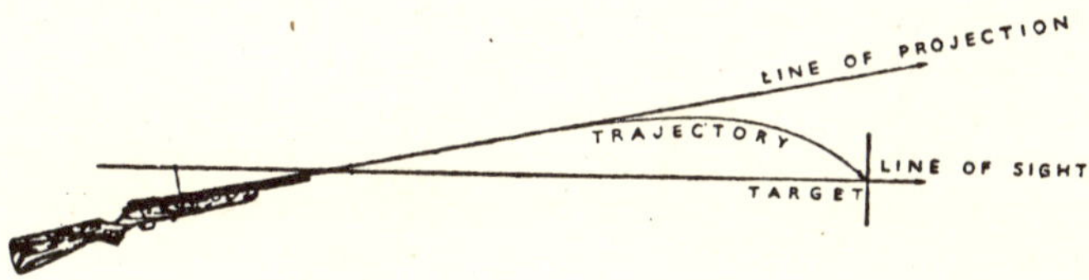

(In this drawing the elevation is exaggerated for the sake of clarity)

If we consider the tip of the foresight as being approximately ¾ inch above the centre of the bore, it means that the pellet commences its journey ¾ inch below the 'line of sight'. As the barrel of the rifle is pointing slightly upwards the pellet will cross the 'line of sight' and continue to rise above it for the first part of its flight but will soon commence falling and (if your elevation is correctly set for distance at which you are shooting) the pellet will strike the target at the point where the line of sight crosses the curved path of the bullet.

If the bullet were not projected in an upwards direction, it would hit the ground long before it reached the target if the range were long, or would strike low on the target at short distances.

Some air-rifles are also provided with a lateral adjustment on the backsight. This is sometimes useful if a strong wind is blowing across the direction in which one is shooting. This feature, however, is of no real consequence as it is very easy to shoot slightly right or left of the target according to which way the cross wind is blowing and a little practice will enable anyone to dispense with the need for using such an adjustment.

Open sights are usually fitted as standard to most modern air-rifles and are generally quite suitable for both target practice and sporting use. For match shooting the aperture sight is much to be preferred, however, and finer shooting can, as a rule, be done with it.

Aperture sights can be used for sporting purposes also, but are only advantageous if the aperture is fairly large and the light is good. An aperture sight with a fine hole is worse than useless in poor light and whatever advantage could be gained is more than counteracted by the difficulty in peering through a hole too small to let enough light through.

I am often asked if a telescopic sight can be fitted and used successfully on an air-rifle. The answer is, yes—but there are several things to be borne in mind if you are thinking of having this done.

Firstly, the cost of a good telescopic sight is considerable, and may easily be as much as the air-rifle itself—or more. The cheapest 'scope sight on the English market costs just over £3 and you can pay as much as £30 or even more for specially good ones.

There are many factors governing the cost of telescopic sights, among which are: (a) size of the field of view; (b) magnification; (c) light-gathering properties; (d) provision of adjustments and (e) cost of mounting on the instrument.

For general sporting use, the magnification should be somewhere between 2 and 4 diameters. 'Scopes are often available in 2x, 2½x, 3x, or 4x, the x denoting the number of times the object is enlarged or magnified.

If powers greater than 4x are used it is almost essential that shooting is done only from the prone position.

It must be made clear that the fitting of a 'scope sight does not increase the weapon's power, and such sight should be fitted with the sole object of seeing more clearly at distances within the weapon's normal range.

It must also be remembered that as well as magnifying the object at which aim is taken, the telescopic sight also magnifies the slightest movement of the rifle. This can be most disconcerting to anyone using a 'scope-sighted rifle for the first time and may cause him to wonder whether he will get anywhere near his target. Much to the shooter's amazement he then usually proceeds to put his shots exactly where he wants them to go.

As a rule, the better the telescope, the better its light-gathering powers, and conversely it is a fact that while the cheaper 'scopes are quite satisfactory in a good light, they are not of great use on a dull day or in the failing light of evening.

A large field of view is very desirable, but not essential. It is obviously more convenient to be able to see a large area when looking through your telescopic sight than to have a restricted view of only a small area. However, it is far better to sacrifice a large viewing area if extra clarity can be obtained with a smaller field of view.

The provision or absence of external adjustments also affect the price of the 'scope. Some 'scopes are non-adjustable and, once zeroed to the air-rifle, cannot easily be altered. These are more difficult to mount on the rifle in the first place, but once this is done, they should give every satisfaction. The absence of adjustments is of no real importance, and in fact is considered by some to be an advantage as there is no possibility of anyone fiddling with the knobs and altering the sight setting.

Telescopic sights with external adjustments for elevation,

windage, and focusing, are usually expensive, and these adjustments are rarely used. As a rule, air-gunners will have no need for such trimmings, which are only intended for long-range shooting with a high-powered cartridge rifle, and only in certain circumstances can be well worth their cost.

Graticules can be of several different sorts but a 'post' or fine crosswires are the commonest, of which the latter is the best for the air-gunner.

'Scopes are best zeroed or set for 25 yards range, and elevation for distant shots obtained by placing the crosswires slightly higher on the object aimed at. For instance, if your 'scope is zeroed for 25 yards, so that the crosswires exactly quarter a pigeon at this distance, you will probably find that you may have to get the crosswires on the pigeon's head to drop him at 35 yards. This, naturally, depends on the trajectory of the rifle you are using.

There is another point that is not generally appreciated when talking of telescopic sights and air-rifles.

The fitting of a 'scope sight does not, and cannot, make a rifle more accurate than it was previously. It only provides the shooter with a magnified, and therefore clearer, view of his target and enables him for this reason only to improve his score. Therefore, do not be tempted to fit such a sight to any air-rifle that is not both powerful and accurate.

Only first-class air-rifles that are in perfect order are worthy of that 'greatest of all shooting aids'—the telescopic sight.

CHAPTER 14

AIR-RIFLES AND THE LAW

THERE is much confusion between the terms *gun licence* and *firearm certificate*, so it may be as well to state here the legal aspect of the purchase and use of air weapons.

A *firearm certificate* is issued by the Chief of Police of the area in which the applicant resides. It enables its holder to acquire and legally possess one or more breech-loading firearms, or weapons classed as firearms, and/or bulleted cartridges. *Firearm* usually denotes a single-shot or repeating pistol or rifle operated by the insertion of cartridges containing explosive, or any type of breech-loading shotgun or shot pistol if the barrel length is less than 24 inches.

Firearm certificates are granted to suitable applicants who have a good reason for wanting a firearm and have access to a place where it can safely be used. Members of rifle and pistol clubs should have no difficulty in obtaining a certificate for target rifles or pistols, but applicants who wish to use rifles for pest control or for general sporting purposes must have permission to shoot in places where they will not endanger public safety. Whether the land over which you propose to shoot is your own or whether you have permission to shoot over someone else's land is not important. What *is* important is that the safety of the land will be checked and shooting permission verified. For example, rifle shooting on a small farm located in a hollow could well be classed safe, whereas permission to use firearms on a very large farm could be refused if there were public footpaths or rights of way across it, or a public road near by.

Firearm certificates now cost £7·00 and remain in force for three years from the date of grant, although they may be revoked by the police at any time if there are any good grounds for doing so. A certificate covers the purchase or acquisition of the weapons for which it is granted, and must be obtained before the purchases can be made. Any subsequent variation of a certificate which increases the number of weapons owned costs £5·00, and renewal for a further three years costs £4·50.

A *gun licence* is an entirely different thing from a firearm certificate. A gun licence used to be needed to *carry* any type of gun including air-guns, air-pistols, shotguns, *and* firearms too, and was obtainable up to 1967 from any general post office on payment of a 50p fee. This no longer applies.

Shotgun licences are now issued by the police only. The new Shotgun Act came into force on 1 May 1968, and all shotgun owners were required to obtain a licence for any guns in their possession; as from 1 May 1968 anyone requiring a shotgun must first apply to the police for the necessary licence before he can make his purchase.

The fee payable for a shotgun licence is now £2·00; the licence remains in force for three years from the date of its grant, and covers the purchase or acquisition of any number of shotguns. Applicants must be prepared to complete a form and to prove their identity by having this form signed by a person of repute (doctor, bank manager, etc.) who knows them personally. No difficulty should be encountered in obtaining a shotgun licence unless the applicant is a lunatic, drunkard, or criminal.

It should be noted that the new shotgun licence relates solely to shotguns, and is no longer needed by firearm certificate holders wishing to carry their firearms from place to place.

Other points worth noting are that every shotgun owner must hold a licence, whereas prior to the 1968 Act anyone could own a shotgun without holding a licence, *provided he used it for vermin destruction or bird scaring in or on his own house or grounds.* Using or carrying a shotgun elsewhere without a licence was a civil offence carrying a maximum fine of £10. The offence is now classed as a criminal one and carries a maximum penalty of £200 plus six months' imprisonment! A shotgun may not be sold by one private individual to another unless both hold valid shotgun certificates, but it is permissible, without holding a shotgun licence, to carry and use a shotgun on farm or other land on behalf of the farmer or landowner provided he is a licence holder.

All dealers in shotguns must now be registered with the police, and anyone wanting to buy or sell a shotgun or have any gun repairs carried out must produce his licence. Dealers must keep a register of all transactions, recording customers' names, addresses and licence numbers and the descriptions and serial numbers of all weapons passing through their hands.

A new Act of Parliament was passed in 1962—the 'Air-guns and Shotguns, etc., Act'—restricting the sale, possession and use of air-guns, air-pistols, and shotguns by young persons. This Act prohibits the possession of any air-gun or pistol, or any air-gun ammunition by anyone under the age of fourteen; and no person under the age of seventeen may have any air weapon in his possession in any public place unless it is covered and the cover securely fastened so that the weapon cannot be fired. (A public place means any place to which the public have access, whether or not any charge is made for admittance.)

A young person of fourteen or under is permitted to carry and use an air weapon when he is accompanied by, and under the supervision of, someone over twenty-one years of age.

No person under the age of fifteen may have an assembled shotgun in his possession unless under the supervision of a person of twenty-one or over; or unless the shotgun is covered and the cover securely fastened so that the gun cannot be fired. A penalty of three months' imprisonment, or a fine of £20, or both, is prescribed for transgressors, and the courts have the power to confiscate the weapons involved. It is now a punishable offence to give, transfer, sell or part with any air weapon to a person under fourteen years of age. The minimum age for obtaining a shotgun certificate is now fifteen.

The Home Secretary has always been empowered to declare any unusually powerful type of air weapon 'specially dangerous' and restrict its sale if he considered it necessary; and prior to 1 May 1969 no air weapon had been so classed. The Home Secretary thought fit, however, to introduce his 'dangerous air weapons rules', which came into operation on 1 May 1969. Prior to this no air weapons needed any kind of licence or permit (except the 50p gun-carrying licence if they were to be carried or used away from the owner's own premises).

From 1 May 1969, any air-gun or air-rifle producing a muzzle energy of 12 foot pounds or over, and any air-pistol producing a muzzle energy of 6 foot pounds or over, is automatically classed as a 'dangerous air weapon' and can only be owned or purchased by the holder of a valid firearm certificate; such certificate being usually granted more readily than it would be for an actual firearm.

From the results of tests carried out on a representative selection of air weapons available in England it appears that all *spring-operated* air-guns, rifles and pistols are *not* classified as 'dangerous air weapons' under the new Act, and at the present time need no licence or permit of any kind whatsoever. I have heard, however, that it is eventually planned to have some sort of licence for spring air weapons; but it is to be hoped that this will not come to pass, as it would be a severe blow to the millions of air gunners throughout the country, and to the gun trade.

Sad to relate, all pneumatic rifles and pistols (except for the ·177 Walther pistols Models LP2 and LP3, and Crosman pistols Models 130 and 137) produce muzzle energies in excess of the limits laid down, and firearm certificates are now *definitely needed for them.*

To shoot animals or birds classed as game you need a *game licence*. The air gunner need hardly consider the purchase of such a licence (unless he owns a powerful pneumatic weapon and has some very good shooting rights), as opportunities for shooting small game do not often occur. The possessor of a current game licence still needs a gun licence. Yearly game licences expire on 31 July no matter when they are bought, and cost £6. They can also be bought on a three-month basis, expiring also on 31 July, and these cost £4; a short-term game licence covering a period of any fourteen consecutive days costs £1. All are obtainable from any general post office. It is illegal to shoot game on Sundays, Christmas Day, or during the close season.

The following information may be of interest to those who wish to use air-rifles and pistols in their gardens or back yards. It is perfectly legal to use an air rifle, gun, or pistol in your own house, or in your back yard or garden, provided that various conditions are complied with.

First, the weapon must not be discharged in any place (even though it be on your own property) if such place is within 50 feet of the centre of a public highway. Some districts have local bye-laws which in some instances increase the distance up to 100 yards. Such bye-laws are equally binding, and if in any doubt it is as well to consult your local Authority on this matter.

Secondly, no pellet, bullet, dart, or other missile may go outside the boundary of your own property.

Thirdly, you must not make a noise sufficient to annoy your neighbours, or you may render yourself liable to be summonsed for causing a nuisance.

Finally, you must provide a really effective backstop for your shooting range, in the interests of public safety.

I have recently been asked whether an *antique pneumatic rifle* is classed as a firearm, as obviously such weapons give muzzle energies greatly in excess of 12 foot pounds, yet being antiques they should be free of permit.

I have made numerous inquiries from the Home Office,

the Metropolitan Police, and various legal authorities, but all are unable or unwilling to give a ruling. From the replies received I have come to the conclusion that if an antique air-rifle or pistol is in working order and is going to be actually used then it appears that a firearms certificate is needed. If on the other hand it is not in working order, and is held as part of a collection for display purposes only, and there is no intention to put it in order and use it, then no certificate should be required.

There is one particular type of *spring-operated* air rifle that does need a firearm certificate, although this type has been obsolete for over fifty years and few are in existence today. This was known as a 'combination air-rifle', first patented, and manufactured by Quackenbush of U.S.A., and followed later by other similarly designed German-made weapons. All were of the breakdown type, and were so constructed that either a ·22 air-gun slug or a No. 1 Bore (6 mm) BB cap could be fired through the barrel. Such weapons need a firearm certificate, not because they are extra powerful air-rifles, but because they were designed to fire a cartridge and therefore come into the same category as ordinary firearms.

A peculiar situation now exists regarding the possession and sale of all gas-operated weapons in England. In 1961 such weapons were available on open sale to anyone over seventeen years of age, but due to the enormous increase in accidents, restrictions have been applied to their sale, and importers have either ceased to import them or reduced them to the barest minimum.

In recent years the Home Office has instructed police chiefs to 'discourage the sale of gas-operated weapons', and this has been done by most Chief Constables by insisting that anyone who wants to buy such a weapon must first apply for a firearm certificate. Such certificates were at first rarely granted, but recently a more reasonable view has been taken, and there should be no special difficulty in any responsible adult person's obtaining a firearm certificate for a CO_2

rifle or pistol, provided he has a safe place to use it.

It appears to be left to the discretion of the police in each area to decide whether or not a firearm certificate should be demanded, and I understand that in some parts of the British Isles the local police hold the view that gas weapons are only a different kind of air weapon and no special restrictions are imposed on their sale. In these areas such weapons can be bought or sold freely without hindrance provided the purchaser is over seventeen and is a responsible person.

A CO_2 gas-operated rifle or pistol cannot possibly be called a firearm, neither can it be compared with a firearm in terms of range, muzzle energy, or capacity for danger, yet dealers and private individuals have been summonsed, convicted and fined for possessing, selling, exposing for sale or attempting to sell gas weapons without a firearm certificate being in force.

I have been unable to trace any Act of Parliament, law, or any printed legislation whatsoever which claims that gas-operated weapons are firearms and can therefore only be sold to persons holding firearm certificates. In fact CO_2 gas weapons are not mentioned at all in any Act; even in the 1969 Dangerous Air Weapons Act.

The situation is irregular, to say the least, when the public can be prosecuted for breaking laws when no one can produce any evidence to show that such laws exist. It becomes particularly unjust when owners of CO_2 weapons—bought openly some years ago—apply for firearm certificates and are informed either that such weapons must be surrendered to the police, or alternatively that a temporary certificate for one month only will be issued.

This usually means that the weapon has to be sold quickly to a dealer for a nominal sum; if it is surrendered to the police, of course, the owner gets nothing at all! Most dealers will no longer buy CO_2 weapons, as such weapons are very difficult to dispose of legally.

CHAPTER 15

GARDEN RANGES AND TARGETS

When building your own range it is of first importance to make sure that your targets are arranged in such a way that a really thick, strong, efficient stop can be provided behind them.

This stop can consist of thick planks, a bank of earth or sand, or even a brick wall. A really first-class backstop can be made from old railway sleepers, which can often be procured easily and cheaply, or an alternative stop of a similar nature can be built of old wooden road-blocks. Whatever type of stop you use, it is essential that it is of ample height and width, because at some time it is certain that shots will fly well clear of the target. This may not necessarily be due to bad marksmanship. A sight may become loose causing a bullet to stray, or you may want to try out a recent purchase whose shooting capabilities are a closed book.

It is also very necessary to make sure that whatever bullet stopper you use is amply thick enough to stop pellets from the most powerful air-rifles. Regular inspection is essential. It is astonishing how the continual impact of pellets fired from powerful air-rifles will splinter even very heavy timber.

There are other points to bear in mind when making a garden range. The targets must be set up where the light is good and away from overhanging trees and other objects that will cast shadows just where they are not wanted. Also, the targets should be able to be placed at varying

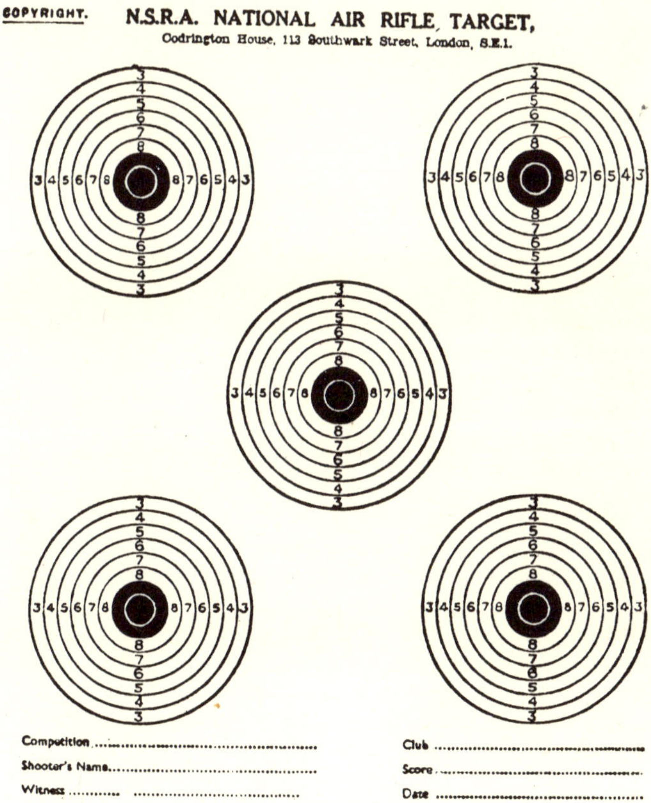

The standard type of target used by the National Air-Rifle League
(about two-thirds actual size)

heights so that they are equally suitable for shooting when standing, kneeling or lying prone.

Probably the simplest way of fixing the targets is to have two wooden posts about 3 feet apart driven into the ground in front of the backstop, and these two uprights connected by two laths about 6 inches apart and parallel to the ground. The targets can be fixed, top and bottom, to these laths by ordinary drawing pins. Never be mean with targets. They are cheap, and even if practising quietly on your own it is far more satisfactory in every way to have a fresh target for every ten shots or so. If you do not do this you will be unable to state with certainty where your pellets are striking unless you make a pencil ring round each shot hole.

If you want a more elaborate target holder there are various sorts available, ranging from the square box-type, which can be mounted directly on a wooden plank partly driven into the ground, to the patent roller target holders that can be screwed to your wooden laths.

The box-types have the advantage of being very tidy, since all pellets passing through the target are collected in the body of the holder. A further advantage is that when sufficient lead has been collected it can be sold! At first sight this may not appear to be worth while, but if you consider the weight of a box of 500 air-rifle pellets you will appreciate that if your range is in constant use by yourself and your friends it will not be very long before you have several pounds by weight of lead. Most air-rifle clubs find the sale of lead quite an asset.

Another type of box target holder which, moreover, brings an element of novelty into your sport, has the target backed by a strong steel plate in which a hole is bored corresponding with the bull's-eye. Behind this hole and inside the body of the box is a metal bell. It will be seen that any pellet striking the bull's-eye will pass through the hole and ring the bell. This type of target holder only collects the pellets that actually pass through the bull. The bell is generally spring-loaded to lessen the impact of the pellet, and spare bells are obtainable.

A tin swinging from a string is often recommended as being a good target, but I have found such things to be both annoying and dangerous. Annoying, because by the time you have started the tin swinging and taken up your position at the firing point the swinging has nearly stopped. Dangerous, because shots glancing off the side of the tin may not hit the backstop but may be deflected in any direction.

A better idea is to make a pendulum, using a long wooden lath terminating in a thick, square piece of wood carrying the target, and heavily weighted by attaching a lump of lead to the back. If the other end of the lath is pivoted so that the pendulum can swing freely it will go on swinging for a very considerable time and provide an excellent target.

About thirty years ago there used to be other types of novelty targets usually in the shape of a grotesque figure made of iron and having the head pivoted and sprung. These retailed at five or six shillings each. There was a simple catch and lever arrangement at the back of the figure and a small round button about half an inch in diameter arranged in front. To make the figure realistic this button often formed the centre of a flower or small target which the figure was holding while the movable head was crowned with a conical hat terminating in a half-inch diameter disc. The idea was to shoot the disc on the figure's hat, causing the head to pivot backwards where it was held by the catch. A further shot on the centre button released the catch causing the head to fly up again, when it was once more ready to receive its baptism of fire. These targets were really great fun and considerable skill was needed to hit the exact spot on the head and on the belly to cause the gadget to work. Any shots that did not strike the hat exactly on the disc would not result in the head staying down, and likewise, once the head had been shot down, no amount of hits on the figure would cause it to reappear until the release disc had been struck. These two bull's-eyes were painted white so that they would show up in contrast to the black finish of the figure, and the instantaneous disappearance of the head when struck gave one the impression that it had been literally shot off. It is a pity that these targets are no longer manufactured, but they can occasionally be bought in junk shops for a shilling or two, and if you are fortunate enough to acquire one you will have many happy hours potting away at it.

Moving targets add greatly to the interest of shooters using a garden range, and can be made by anyone with a little ingenuity. Naturally, if one is mechanically minded quite elaborate moving targets can be designed. An enthusiast of my acquaintance once showed me a snap-shooting target that he had constructed from odds and ends. This consisted of a wooden box covered at the front with sheet iron, and containing the works of an ancient clock. Parts of the clock mechanism had been removed and an ingenious arrangement of levers caused a white disc to appear on top of the box, and disappear again continuously every five seconds. This was an excellent contrivance for the shooting range, and incidentally this young man became a really first-rate snap-shot with his air-rifle.

Similar snap-shooting targets were also obtainable many years ago, one of which was known as the 'Dodo'. Other types of clockwork targets were available, some of which had figures of animals and birds which would keep moving for several hours on one winding of the spring. Others had rising and falling discs, or disappearing targets, which used to remain visible for only a few seconds at a time, but were capable of adjustment in order to vary the time that the targets were in sight. Thus one could start with a visibility period of, say, ten seconds and as one's marksmanship improved, reduce the time until almost lightning shots were needed. There are no English firms producing clockwork snap-shooting targets to-day, but in America a 'Dodo' target is available. This works in a very similar way to the figure target already described, except that it consists of a metal frame in which are situated two steel cut-outs of animals. When these have both been shot down, a centre button must be struck and this brings both the animals into view again.

If you can make up such an outfit for yourself you will find it will be more than worth the effort, and for those who are not handy with tools I would suggest that they try to persuade a mechanically-minded friend to help them.

A simple and very effective moving target of a different sort can be made by anyone who can use a hammer and screwdriver. In this case, the target travels bodily across the range, and will provide very good practice for the air-gunner, especially if he fancies his luck at becoming a good shot at moving game.

Firstly obtain two thick, strong posts and set them in the ground about 12-14 feet apart.

These posts will need to be 7 feet high, leaving about 5 feet above ground when erected. As they will have to stand a goodish strain it is advisable to ram pieces of brick and rubble into the hole around the ends when making them firm in the ground. Clothes posts are ideal for the purpose, especially if they are the type that have special ground sockets, as then the posts can be removed when not in use.

When you have set the posts firmly in the ground you must obtain a length of thick, strong galvanized wire and stretch this between the two posts, having one end of the wire a few inches higher than the other. It is best to fasten the wire to one post by passing it round the post and twisting the end round the wire itself.

The other end of the wire can be fixed to the second post in the same way, but a better idea is to incorporate a wire strainer or tightener between this end and the post so that the wire can be tightened when in use and slackened off to relieve the strain on the posts when it is not needed.

You now need a target that will run along the wire, and this can be arranged in any one of several ways. Probably the easiest is to get a light shallow wooden box similar to a horticultural seed tray and nail a plywood sheet over the open top. Now you want two pulleys with deep grooved wheels, having one side of the pulley bracket open. These can be bought at any ironmongers' shop. If open-sided pulleys are not available you can cut one side through with a hacksaw or ask the shopman to do this for you. These pulley brackets are screwed to one of the narrow sides of the box and the target pinned to the front with drawing pins. All you have to do now is to arrange a simple catch with a string attached. The box, complete with target, is hooked on to the higher end of the wire. The catch is released by pulling on the string. The speed can be altered by varying the height of one end of the wire.

There are two methods of shooting at such a target. One is by judging the right elevation and waiting until the target comes in line with your sights and then pressing the trigger. The alternative and preferable method is to follow the target with your rifle increasing the speed of your movement until you have slightly overtaken the moving target and at that instant loosing off the shot. If you wish to develop this style of shooting it is absolutely essential that when swinging your rifle you *must* fire while the weapon is still moving. The only successful way to accomplish this is by continuing the swinging movement *after* the shot has been fired. If you do not do this you will find that although you may think you have a correct aim you will subconsciously stop the swing of your rifle at the critical moment when you press the trigger. This will, of course, result in the pellet missing its mark, because during this momentary pause the target will have passed the line of sight. This is the technique adopted in shotgun shooting and is recommended for developing a nice easy style.

Points to remember are that when aiming at such a moving target you *must* shoot in front of and never directly at it. The amount of forward allowance naturally depends on the range and the speed of travel and this can best be ascertained by trial and error. When you can 'pot the

Black' fairly frequently you can increase the speed of the target and the distance from the firing point to make it more difficult to do so. If you are shooting at some distance and there is a strong cross wind blowing, this must be allowed for by shooting slightly towards the direction from which the wind is blowing. Also your sight must be elevated to compensate for the drop of the pellet at different distances. Do not forget that for all air-rifle shooting of this nature your backstop must be absolutely safe.

Probably one of the most difficult targets to hit—or at least I have found it so—is the dancing celluloid ball kept aloft on a jet of water. This is usually found in fairground shooting booths and can always be relied upon to arouse interest. There is no reason why anyone should not rig up such a target for themselves provided one has a garden hose and a convenient water supply. If the hose is fitted with a fine nozzle and the end fixed in such a way that this nozzle points straight upwards, it only remains to adjust the tap so that the jet is the desired height and place your ball on the jet then off you go.

I once evolved a completely self-contained water jet apparatus from an old Primus stove and it worked beautifully. In case anyone wants to try it I will describe how it was made. The first requirement is an ancient Primus stove. If this is the type with a silent burner all one has to to is to remove the cap and flame spreader from the top of the burner and throw them away. If they are missing already it saves you trouble! If the stove contains any paraffin it must be tipped out and filled up with water instead. Now the jet or nipple must be unscrewed and the jet hole enlarged with a small drill. The nipple is now replaced and on pumping the stove a jet of water will shoot into the air, the height of which will depend on the amount of pumping you give the stove.

It is best to use a small drill first and enlarge the hole if necessary, testing frequently, until the water jet will support the ping-pong ball. It is also necessary for the hole through the nipple to be quite vertical, as the slightest canting of the drill will cause the water to squirt out at an angle and it will not then support the ball.

A stove with a roarer burner is not so suitable, as it would have to be modified by removing the complete burner and refitting the nipple by means of some sort of adaptor. In either case, a further refinement can be installed by fitting a tap between the body of the stove and the nipple, as by this means the water jet can be stopped and started at will if pressure is left in the container. If the whole arrangement is stood in a bowl the ground is kept dry and the water can be funnelled back into the stove and used again. Such an apparatus will keep the ball aloft for quite a long time, the height of the jet becoming less as the water is used up.

It is advisable for financial reasons to use only low-power air-rifles for 'ball on jet' shooting, as these will, as a rule, merely knock the ball off the jet, and it can be used again and again. If powerful rifles are used the pellets will smash through the balls and constant replacements will be needed.

Such financial strain could be mitigated by a very cunning dodge I saw once demonstrated. A ten-shilling note was tied to a length of ordinary white cotton which was suspended from the ceiling of an indoor rifle range and at a distance of ten yards from the firing point. The secretary challenged any member to shoot through the cotton and thus cause the note to fall to the ground. Two pence per shot was the entrance fee and the marksman who was successful in cutting the thread was promised the ten shillings. Naturally there was a rush of would be prize-winners and the resultant expenditure of many hundreds of slugs was punctuated by the continual clink of coins, all enriching the club funds.

Several members succeeded in hitting the thread but the only result was to cause the note to dance about, and the thread remained unbroken. After some time had elapsed, business slackened off; several members voicing the opinion that it couldn't be done, and maintaining that the thread acted as a shock absorber which robbed the pellet of all its power. The secretary promptly borrowed an air-rifle that one of the shooters had been using and after two or three shots cut the thread, causing the note to fall to the ground. The note was again tied up and business resumed as before. Eventually the club closed for the night with the thread still intact, the secretary's face wreathed in smiles, and the club funds in a very satisfactory condition. It later transpired that a direct hit would not break the thread, and that the secretary had used some specially prepared pellets to do the trick. These were nicked round their circumference and shot so that they passed the side of the thread, the saw-like edges of the pellet instantly severing the cotton. I have never tried this before or since; and although I am open to correction, I believe that the thread cannot be severed except by this method.

In all forms of air-gunning it is essential to use a weapon with a rifled barrel as it is only by using such weapons that accurate shooting can be done. With a smooth-bore air-gun the accuracy just isn't there. Nothing is more disconcerting and calculated to dampen the enthusiasm of the most ardent marksman than the realization that the weapon he is using cannot be relied on to group its shots consistently

I remember when I was a schoolboy I possessed a break-down 'Gem' air-gun, with which I once potted a starling at a distance of approximately thirty yards. The bird was perched on the edge of the chimney-pot and it toppled neatly down the chimney. I was so surprised that I promptly fell off the roof of the garden shed on which I was standing. The shot was a pure fluke as the gun was absolutely unreliable and quite incapable of repeating such a performance. If, however, I had been using a good air-rifle instead of an air-gun I could easily have equalled or bettered my marksmanship and the absence of surprise would have saved the bruises. The sequel to this little story, by the way, was the violent opening of a window and the appearance of two nearly black faces uttering fearful imprecations. It appears that the couple were enjoying a leisurely Sunday morning breakfast when a dead starling came hurtling down the chimney scattering soot and blood everywhere. So if you must shoot starlings don't shoot those on other people's chimneys.

CHAPTER 16

AIR-RIFLE CLUBS

WHETHER or not the enthusiastic air-gunner has the facilities for constructing his own rifle range, it is always an excellent idea to belong to an air-rifle club.

No doubt the reader will be surprised to hear that there are such things as air-rifle clubs. I can assure you that there are in existence quite a large number of them. If there is a club in your vicinity you cannot do better than join it. You will be swelling the ranks of the most enthusiastic air-gunners you will ever meet and you will be able to take part in organized competitions and be encouraged to talk and think air-guns until you almost look like one. The competitions are great sport and are treated as seriously as our colleagues treat their small-bore shooting. An extremely high standard of shooting is regularly to be seen on these air-rifle ranges quite comparable to the standard achieved on an ordinary rifle range.

The air-rifles used at these clubs are always of ·177 calibre because these give a higher muzzle velocity and flatter trajectory, and also because the pellets are cheaper.

Shooting distances are usually six yards for indoor ranges and sometimes six, ten or fifteen yards for outdoors. Do not imagine that these distances represent the maximum ranges of an air-rifle. The short ranges are usually purely for convenience, and as most air-rifle clubs do their shooting indoors an accepted standard must be adopted. The six-yard range was the accepted standard of the National Air-Rifle League, because it is often difficult to find sufficient room indoors for longer ranges. If no standard were adopted we should find that some teams would be handicapped. If, for example, a visiting team who had only a six-yard range found themselves expected to compete on a much longer range against competitors who were quite used to the greater distance, it would go hard with the visitors. It would be comparable to a small-bore club member only able to take part in competitions at twenty-five yards, being suddenly expected to put up as good a performance at, say, a hundred yards.

I have seen air-rifle marksmen consistently putting their shots into a bull's-eye only a quarter of an inch in diameter, which, when you consider it, is about equal to scoring 'sevens' consecutively on a standard hundred-yard small-bore rifle range.

Spring-operated rifles are always used in club shooting, although some clubs also shoot air-pistols. Both the air-pistol and the air-rifle are, in my opinion, more difficult to shoot accurately than their big brothers the cartridge rifle and pistol.

For example, an air-rifle will shoot differently if used by different persons. This is because such weapons are particularly susceptible to the way they are held. If one shooter grips the rifle tightly or holds it so that the butt is positioned high on the shoulder it will group differently from one held lightly and low on the shoulder.

I do not profess to be a crack shot, and I make no apologies for not attempting to write a chapter on how to shoot. So much has already been written on this subject that to do so would merely be duplicating what has been thoroughly dealt with elsewhere. If one read all the shooting books available and tried to emulate the crack-shots one would still find eventually that a style of one's own produced the best scoring. Some men are natural shots and virtually need no teaching and others must be taught the rudiments and the accepted methods of muscle control, breathing, correct position, etc.

I will, therefore, content myself with setting down only a few words of advice for the guidance of the would-be marksman.

Do not attempt to hold the weapon rock steady as if it were clamped in a vice. There was never a man born who could do so. It just cannot be done. We will assume you have a correct hold, and have your lungs empty with your breathing temporarily stopped, and have your weapon aligned on the bull's-eye. Your rifle will still be moving and you will see your sights wandering around the point of aim. You now start gently squeezing or pressing your trigger and as you do so your weapon will wander one way or another. Stop squeezing every time the sights wander away from the bull and recommence squeezing again as soon as the sight is once again correct, but *maintain the trigger pressure you have gained* by this squeezing. One of these light squeezes will discharge the arm and you should score a bull. Remember, too, that it is almost impossible to be too gentle with your trigger pressing.

Shooting an air-rifle, however, is quite different in every way from shooting any other sort of rifle. We all know that it is necessary to get used to any particular weapon if you want to get a good score, but it is doubly necessary to get to know your air-rifle before you can hope to be a crack shot.

For this reason the shooter is strongly advised to acquire his own weapon or weapons and stick to them, rather than to rely on the casual hire or loan of a rifle which he will probably never have long enough to learn its peculiarities.

Speaking generally, however, I find that a spring-operated air-rifle must be held lightly with as much bodily relaxation as is possible. The reason for this is that the natural jump of the rifle when the spring is released *must* be allowed to take place freely. Any attempts made to prevent this jump or kick will undoubtedly have an adverse effect on one's scoring. Unlike a cartridge rifle, whose jump comes *after* the shot is fired, the air-rifle jumps *before* the pellet leaves the muzzle. This is because directly the trigger is pressed the spring expands and produces the kick or jump; and not until the air in front of the piston has been compressed does the pellet even start to move down the barrel. An air-rifle pellet is a fairly tight fit in the rifling of the barrel and it takes quite a considerable pressure of air behind it to start it on its way. It is an actual fact that the spring-driven piston practically reaches the limit of its travel before the pellet has left the muzzle and therefore if this spring kick is restrained by tight holding then the shooting suffers as a consequence.

These remarks do not apply to gas-operated or pneumatic weapons, which, having no mainspring, are absolutely devoid of jump and have a smoothness in shooting peculiar to themselves and quite incomparable to any other type of weapon.

There are many other factors which will affect the pellet grouping of your spring air-rifle. For example, the use of a thin oil on the piston head will produce a different muzzle velocity from that produced by a thicker oil, and for this reason the oil recommended by the makers should always be used.

Another point which should be remembered by the club shooter is that different makes of pellets will also cause variation in shooting. Some brands of pellets will shoot high and others will shoot low. This is mainly due to different tolerances in maximum and minimum diameters, some makes being a few thousandths of an inch larger or smaller than others. It should be safe to assume that one particular make of pellet will be fairly consistent in size, but this does not seem to be so with some of the cheaper makes. With these there is much variation, and often a good percentage of misshapen slugs that cannot be used. It is therefore advisable to buy the best pellets available as these will give the most accurate shooting. The use of cheap slugs for sporting use may be tolerated, but if used in match shooting they may be responsible for your losing those much needed points.

A simple yet very effective gadget can easily be made,

which will automatically size every pellet as it is used and also slightly increase muzzle velocity and accuracy.

This consists of a short length of stiff wire set into a small piece of wood to form a handle. A convenient wooden handle could be made from a piece of hardwood dowel rod about three inches long and $\frac{3}{8}$ inch thick.

I call this instrument a 'pellet seater' and it is used to push the pellets a uniform distance into the breech of your weapon. In the case of a breakdown air-rifle or pistol the wire needs to project about half an inch from the handle, while for underlever or other tap-loading rifles it should be long enough to push the pellet to the bottom of the tap.

This simple little device ensures that the pellets start their journey having a uniform diameter. It is of particular value when used with pistols and breakdown rifles as it forces the pellet into the rifling of the barrel and the rifling becomes imprinted on the tail of the pellet. This in turn causes the pellet to start moving more easily, and therefore faster, by lessening the friction between pellet and rifling. It really means that you are doing manually some of the work normally done by the compression of the air, and therefore causing *more* of the air to be used in projecting the pellet and *less* to be used in overcoming the initial resistance in starting it moving.

A new type of pellet which has recently been introduced especially for use on indoor ranges may be of interest to readers. These are shaped somewhat like miniature cotton reels and are made of a softish red plastic material. They are solid, not hollow like ordinary pellets, and are available in ·177 calibre only. These shoot quite accurately, but they have much less penetration than lead pellets and are only suitable for short-range shooting on account of their lightness. They have the peculiar quality of remaining undamaged after shooting them and can be used again and again. They are manufactured by Messrs. Millard Bros. Ltd., and are obtainable through your local sports dealer or gun shop.

I understand from the National Small Bore Rifle Association (usually referred to as the N.S.R.A.) that the National Air-Rifle Section which was so active in the past, was suspended during the war and has not yet started to function again. The matter is under discussion at the present time and I hope that we shall soon once again have our air-rifle clubs affiliated to the N.S.R.A.

At the moment, the existing clubs are privately owned and maintained by local bands of enthusiasts, but there are various drawbacks to such an arrangement. The chief disadvantage lies in the fact that there is at present no parent society from whom one can seek information of the whereabouts of such organizations, and thus membership suffers. The layman anxious to join a club may have difficulty in finding out whether or not there is one in his locality, even though some of the clubs have been in existence for nearly forty years.

Air-rifle shooting under League rules was always at six yards and always in the standing position. Open foresights were essential, but any type of backsight could be used, except a telescopic sight. Regulations were strict and targets had to conform to a standard type. The calibre used was ·177 only.

The air-rifle targets shown on page 119 were the standard types used by the Air-Rifle League and have been reproduced with the kind permission of the N.S.R.A.

Some idea of the enormous popularity of air-rifle shooting in days gone by may be gathered from the fact that in 1904 Birmingham alone had sixteen hundred air-rifle clubs catering for about twenty thousand enthusiasts. The sport was considered of such importance that the Saturday sports edition of the local paper devoted a whole column to the doings of the air-gunners.

Birmingham, being the centre of the English gun trade, naturally headed the list but many other towns in the Midlands and elsewhere were also well represented. Manchester, for instance, had two hundred air-rifle clubs, and by 1906 the movement had spread to such an extent that practically every town in England had its own clubs, and the National Air-Rifle Association claimed to have formed a grand total of four thousand of them. (Most of these clubs' headquarters were on licenced premises, and as each club usually took the same name as the hostelry some curious combinations were seen in the List of Fixtures—Hen and Chickens v. Bird in Hand, John Bright v. Shakespeare, Spotted Dog v. British Lion, and many others equally amusing.)

As we have been discussing targets and shooting, this is an ideal opportunity for stressing a few simple but essential safety precautions.

1. Never leave your weapon loaded with a pellet or bullet in the breech or in the barrel.
2. Never lend your gun, rifle or pistol to irresponsible persons or to children, and never leave it where any such persons can have access to it.
3. Never rest your gun against anything that is liable to be moved and thus cause the gun to fall, when accidental discharge may occur, or, at best, the gun may be damaged. Treat your air-rifle with the same care and respect you would accord to a firearm.
4. *Never* point any weapon at anyone, even in fun, and if you see anyone doing this, stop them at once.
5. Never have to say, 'I didn't know it was loaded.' Consider any and every gun as loaded until you have made certain it is not. Ninety per cent of all shooting accidents are caused by 'unloaded' weapons.

CHAPTER 17

BUYING OR SELLING AN AIR-RIFLE OR PISTOL. SOME NOTES FOR THE COLLECTOR

I AM often asked questions such as 'What is the best air-rifle or air-pistol?' or 'What is the most powerful air-rifle?' Such questions are difficult to answer because they are far too vague. If the inquirer states for what purpose he wants the air-rifle, and asks me to recommend the best weapon *for his purpose*, that is a different matter entirely.

The fact is, that an air-rifle that is ideally suited for one particular purpose may be quite unsuitable for another, and if you wish to purchase a rifle or pistol you should consider most carefully what you chiefly intend to use it for, and allow this to guide your choice.

For instance, we will assume that you are either already a member of an air-rifle club, or are about to become one, and your rifle therefore will be used only for club shooting and garden target practice. Your choice should be a No. 1 bore ·177 calibre, preferably of the underlever type and as heavy as possible. Suitable new weapons of this type would be the Webley and Scott 'Mark III' or the B.S.A. 'Club'. If for any reason such as economy you prefer a lighter-weight weapon, then I would suggest the B.S.A. 'Cadet Major', the 'Webley Junior', the Model 27 Diana, or the German 'Original' Models 23, 25, or 27. All these are available in ·177 calibre.

Air-pistol shooters are catered for with the 'Webley Senior', the 'Mark I', the 'Webley Junior', the Acvoke, and the German Walther Model 53. All these weapons are available in this country, although the German weapons are not so freely obtainable as the British ones, due to restrictions on their import. In addition to the above there are also several makes of toy air-pistols suitable for young boys but not intended for adult use.

If you have no interest in club shooting and want an air-rifle for sporting purposes, for instance rook, rabbit, pigeon, or vermin shooting, then you will definitely need a No. 2 bore ·22 underlever air-rifle, a really powerful ·22 break-down air-rifle or alternatively a pneumatic weapon.

The reason for this is that the tiny ·177 pellet is too light to have sufficient shocking power to be certain of kills, and the ·22 rifle has a longer range. It is advisable also to avoid buying a very heavy rifle for sporting use, as much carrying of it will be found tiring.

New underlever air-rifles of ·22 calibre suitable for sport are the B.S.A. 'Airsporter', the Webley 'Mark III', the German 'Original' Model 50 and other similar weapons. A ·22 calibre breakdown rifle that is outstandingly powerful and is ideal for sporting use is the 'Original' Model 35B described in Chapter 9.

There are of course many thousands of excellent and serviceable air weapons available on the second-hand market which will give absolutely reliable and accurate shooting. These may be of the types and makes already mentioned or they may be models that are out of production. Most of these weapons are still in excellent shooting order, while many more need only slight attention.

Typical examples are the Webley 'Mark I' and the 'Mark II' Service air-rifle, the B.S.A. Model 1 and Model 4, the Greener, the Britannia, and many others of British manufacture. Foreign weapons would include the Diana Models 26, 45, and 48E, the Haenel range, the Falke series, and many others too numerous to mention individually. The only British air-pistols made in ·22 calibre are the 'Webley Senior' and the 'Mark I'. Both have interchangeable ·177 or ·22 calibre barrels.

If you require something different from the standard makes and types usually available, then the pneumatic or pump-up weapon is the answer. It is unfortunate that these pneumatics are not available in English shops, but there are quite a number in daily use in various parts of the country and a judiciously worded advertisement in your local newspaper may produce what you want. Suitable American pneumatic rifles are the Benjamin, Crosman, 'Apache', Kessler, Sheridan, etc., of which several are made in different models. All (except the Sheridan, whose calibre is ·200) have standard calibre barrels.

Modern pneumatic rifles usually have the wooden fore-end of the weapon pivoted near the muzzle and forming the handle of a lever air pump. The chief advantages of such rifles lies in the fact that they can be pumped up to give far greater power than can be obtained from a spring-operated weapon, and also that they are very light in weight and very compact. They are ideal sporting weapons as they have a smoothness in shooting which is very pleasant indeed and they are easy to carry around. Another advantage is that they can be left fully pumped-up (but not cocked or loaded, please!) without any harm whatever.

There are also American gas-operated air-rifles, which are adjustable for power by means of a control screw, but which fill from a gas cylinder. These are to be preferred as they can be adjusted to give the same power as the pump-up types and, once filled with gas, will fire a great number of shots without, of course, the trouble or labour of multiple pumping.

There are many people who love antique weapons and who like to shoot with them. They would be especially delighted with the acquisition of an antique large-calibre air-rifle. These weapons have absolutely astounding power and if in good working order can be used with deadly effect against rabbits, hares, otters, and so forth, the enormous shocking power of the heavy bullet ensuring a certain kill even if your quarry is not hit in a vital spot. Even such large animals as deer have frequently been dispatched with a single well-placed shot from a large-calibre pump-up rifle. It has been estimated that the shocking power or impact of a bullet fired from one of these vintage pneumatic rifles is approximately fourteen times as great as that of the finest spring air-rifle ever produced. It is of course, dangerous to discharge such rifles in your back garden, unless you control their power by only partly filling the air-chamber, and even then it is essential to use a specially strong backstop. Outdoors, in the open country is the proper place to shoot these high-powered rifles and every care must be taken to ensure that the bullet cannot do any damage by travelling past the object you are aiming at.

If you kill a rabbit, the bullet will pass right through the animal and will travel quite a long way. I have on several occasions shot rabbits that were facing me head on, and in every instance the bullet passed clean through the rabbit, entering the head or chest and emerging near the tail.

Another type of vintage pneumatic is the air-shotgun. These were made on the same general lines as the antique rifles, but their barrels were smooth-bored and they were intended to be used with a charge of spread shot. I find that they are quite capable of bringing down birds on the wing, and are marvellous fun to shoot. All were made before the invention of choke boring and, as a result, the spread of the shot charge is very great at long ranges. Usually such old-time air-guns will give a sufficiently dense pattern at up to fifteen yards to ensure effective shooting against flying birds, but at distances much in excess of this, the spread of the shot is too great to be relied on, although the killing power is still there up to about thirty yards.

Many of these old weapons were arranged so that they could be used either as a rifle or as a shotgun. This was usually accomplished by having the rifled barrel in the form of a detachable tube, which when unscrewed and drawn out revealed the smooth-bored barrel. Some had the arrangement reversed by having a smaller smooth-bore tube sliding inside a large rifled barrel, but these are very rarely met with.

If you are interested in the possibilities of such weapons for actual use, rather than from a collector's point of view, I would strongly advise you not to purchase such a gun or rifle unless it is in perfect working order. It is extremely difficult to find anyone who has the skill, the knowledge and the inclination to repair these arms.

Modern pneumatics are principally of American manufacture and the owner of one can hardly send it to the United States to have it repaired, and unfortunately there are no agents in England for American pneumatic weapons. All this is very disappointing. As we have seen, the real reason why pump-up or gas-operated rifles are not produced in this country is because they are capable of far greater power than the authorities allow.

The penetrative power of air-rifles and air-pistols was investigated by the Bodkin Committee in 1934. This committee, under the chairmanship of Sir Archibald Bodkin, K.C.B., was appointed by Sir John Gilmour, Bt., D.S.O., M.P., on 2nd February 1934 to 'consider the various types of firearms and similar weapons capable of being used for the discharge of missiles or noxious substances, and ammunition therefor, and inquire and report whether, in the interests of public safety, any amendment of the law is necessary or desirable in respect of the definition or classification of such weapons and ammunition'.

The committee's report was published in December of the same year and the Firearms Act of 1937 was framed on the result of their findings.

It was found unnecessary to make any special rules declaring any particular type of air-gun or air-rifle to be specially dangerous, as no evidence had been furnished of the existence of any outstandingly powerful air-guns or rifles. Particular attention, however, was paid to air-pistols, because it had been decided in a law case in 1925 that an air-pistol must *legally* be considered to be an air-gun. The

Home Office were of the opinion that a degree of penetration should be fixed, and that if the power of any air-pistol should exceed this standard, the question of declaring it especially dangerous would arise.

The official test for air-pistols at present in force is based on one used in India to determine whether air-pistols of different types should be classed as toys or lethal weapons. The test consists in firing several shots from the pistol in question at a range of five feet at a number of strawboards each $\frac{3}{64}$ of an inch thick, packed closely together in a frame. The number of strawboards to be used is fixed at seven. If the pellets from the pistol do not completely penetrate the seven strawboards the weapon is not considered specially dangerous. The power of English-made air-pistols has been limited to comply with this test.

It has been rightly suggested that strawboards are not an ideal medium for such a purpose, as quality and density varies considerably, while atmospheric conditions cause differences in the moisture content and further affect the material. Many experiments were also carried out under the jurisdiction of the Bodkin Committee to determine the best material for such tests of penetration, and a number of different kinds of strawboards, and also different kinds of woods, were used.

It was found that the most satisfactory target material was 'selected white deal boards of even grain, free from knots and planed on both sides'. It was recommended that such a deal board half an inch thick should be used when testing air-pistols and a one-inch deal board for testing air-rifles and air-guns. In both cases the range specified was five feet and if pellets passed through the boards or the pellets could be seen from the back of the boards the weapons should be considered to exceed the standard laid down.

Further tests were also carried out, using several white deal boards as previously specified, but in these tests the boards were a quarter of an inch thick, and twenty of them were packed closely together in a frame. No air weapon which was tested was found capable of shooting a pellet through two of the quarter-inch thicknesses of board, the range as before being five feet.

The authorities consider that it would not be in the public interest to allow air weapons to be obtainable which exceed in power those already in general use, unless the sale of such weapons were subject to control.

These standards of penetration provide a good guide by which the power of any new type of air weapon can be assessed with regard to its legality. Such tests can of course be modified at any time by a Home Secretary, and the final decision as to whether or not any air weapon is specially dangerous is left entirely to his discretion.

These regulations may be for the good of the community, especially when one remembers that air-rifles can legally be possessed by lads of fourteen years of age; but manufacturing enterprise is strangled. It would be of little use for a maker of air-rifles to design and produce an outstandingly powerful rifle, knowing that it would immediately be classed as a lethal weapon. This would result in so many restrictions being put on its sale that only a handful of licensed enthusiasts would be able to purchase it.

These remarks should be of particular interest to anyone who is considering the commercial production of any such super-powerful pneumatic weapon. They are not intended to apply to the gunsmith, professional engineer, or amateur guncraftsman who is capable of constructing a special high-velocity air-rifle for his own use, neither do they apply to any type of old-time air weapon.

I once invented, patented, and constructed a gas-operated pistol which was designed to use a standard 'Sparklet' gas bulb. The pistol was orginally made and protected by Letters Patent as a single-shot weapon in that the slugs had to be inserted singly for each shot, although one gas bulb would provide the propelling force for up to forty shots. The pistol was later experimentally modified by fitting a magazine tube, and became, as far as

I know, the only fully automatic gas-operated 'air' pistol in the world. It definitely worked; but the consumption of carbon dioxide gas needed to operate the automatic feed device was infinitely greater than I had expected, and it could only be relied on to fire a very few shots on one gas bulb. The idea, although basically sound, was not a commercial proposition and my hopes of a fortune rapidly faded—but that's another story!

When purchasing an air-rifle or pistol, it is of course best to have a new one if you can afford it. You only get what you pay for, so buy the best you can afford. It is far better to wait until you can buy the weapon you fancy, rather than take the next best. If you have set your heart on a particular rifle you will only be discontented if you allow yourself to be persuaded into buying something inferior, and the longer you have it, the more you are going to wish that you had waited a little longer and bought the best one.

If a new one is out of your financial reach, then try to get a good second-hand one. A small advertisement can be inserted in your local paper, or very likely a chance word with a friend will do the trick. Some papers have a special column for shooting needs, and second-hand air-rifles and pistols are frequently advertised in their pages.

It must be remembered that second-hand goods, unless specifically guaranteed by a dealer or other advertiser. may prove faulty, in which case you have no redress. Also that weapons described by letter as being in fine condition may not come up to expectations, because the seller's idea of 'fine condition' may be more than somewhat exaggerated.

On many past occasions I have had air-rifles described to me as being in 'superb condition', 'excellent order', 'absolutely perfect', and so on, yet when inspected they proved to be rusty and generally dilapidated, with broken stocks, bent levers, and wood screws hammered in, in place of proper gun screws.

For these reasons it is always best to examine second-hand weapons before parting with your money. An external scrutiny will show whether there are any screws missing or parts which have been bent or broken, whilst damaged screwheads denote that it has been dismantled at some time by an inexperienced person. The stock should be examined to see if it is dented, nicked, or cracked, and all such blemishes taken into account when reckoning the value. If the weapon is a modern one, it can be sent to the makers to be reconditioned, but if it is an out-of-date rifle, any parts needed may have to be specially made, and this is a costly business. To test the accuracy, several shots should be fired at a target from the prone position, and the weapon rejected if it does not group the shots reasonably well.

The power is best tested by shooting a pellet at a smooth, flat piece of steel, such as the bottom of a flat-iron and comparing the flattening of the pellet with a pellet shot in the same way from a new rifle. This is a far better way of comparing the power of different air-rifles than by shooting at a piece of wood. This method only gives a very rough idea of power, because it is nearly impossible to find a piece of wood of a uniform hardness, and the smallest variations in the grain will cause differences in penetration.

A new, modern, underlever air-rifle, or a second-hand one in perfect order, should completely shatter a ·177 pellet into small pieces if fired at a steel plate at a range of one yard; and a ·22 calibre model should be capable of shattering the edge of the pellet, usually leaving the centre part as a small cone. This is the desirable standard of maximum power. If the rifle flattens the pellet completely without actually causing any lead fragments to fly off, it should be considered quite satisfactory, but if it only flattens the head of the pellet without any appreciable spreading taking place, it is obvious the rifle needs attention.

If you regard the comparison of the power of air-rifles as a fine art, then these methods will not satisfy you. Should you want to be able to compare with absolute accuracy the penetration of different rifles or pistols, this is the way to do it. You must arrange, one behind the other, a number of squares of cardboard, leaving a small space of, say, a quarter of an inch between each square. The easiest way to do this is to obtain a long wooden batten about two inches square and mark this off with pencil lines every quarter of an inch, saw cuts being made across the batten at each pencil line, to a depth of about three-quarters of an inch.

Square pieces of cardboard of uniform thickness and density must be inserted in these saw cuts so that the cards are one behind the other. This arrangement should be set up in front of a safe background with the first card facing you. All you now have to do is to shoot at this card so that the pellets will also pass through the other cards and by comparing the number of cards penetrated by different rifles, an absolutely exact test of penetration can be made. It is surprising how many cards you will need, especially if testing the power of underlever or pneumatic rifles.

If you have a rifle that you wish to dispose of, it can be sold to a dealer or part-exchanged for another weapon, or it can be advertised and sold privately.

Should you be selling privately, especially by means of an advertisement, you must be particularly careful to make sure that the purchaser is over seventeen years old. To safeguard yourself, if there is any doubt in the matter, it is best to ask for this information in writing. This is especially necessary when dealing by post with someone away from your locality as it is often almost impossible to tell from a letter whether the buyer is seventeen or seventy. Dealers usually have a small printed form in which the purchaser must write his name and address, his age and his purchases, and by such means the seller is completely safeguarded. The absence of such a precaution may lead you into trouble.

Selling privately usually means that you obtain a better price for your rifle than you would if you disposed of it to a dealer. Often, however, it is more convenient to go to a dealer, especially if he has a weapon that you want to buy since in this case your old rifle can be taken in part exchange for the one you are purchasing. It also saves much time and trouble spent in letter writing.

People are often upset, when disposing of their air-rifles, at the comparatively low prices offered by dealers, even if the rifle is in new condition. We must remember, however, that the dealer, who has his living to make has heavy overhead expenses, and also expensive stocks to maintain. It is no use expecting him to re-purchase your rifle at a price slightly less than the retail price of a new one, as this may exceed the trade price which the dealer pays for them in the first place.

Once an air-rifle has been used it *must* be sold as second-hand. Another point that is often overlooked is that the purchase tax of $36\frac{2}{3}$ per cent at present payable on all air weapons cannot be charged twice. This means that from the original retail price paid for the weapon must be deducted the purchase tax, the dealer's usual trade discount, and a further amount because the rifle is now second-hand and must be priced lower than a new one, and still provide a modest profit. The price you should expect is approximately half the original price paid when new, but a higher allowance may be made if you are exchanging the weapon for a more expensive one.

Collecting unusual air weapons is a fascinating hobby. At the time of writing, the collector has things pretty much his own way, because there are very few serious collectors and consequently prices are low. It is, therefore, an ideal time to look around for specimens of peculiar air-operated weapons which may well form the nucleus of an interesting collection.

The usual way to start such a collection is to buy any and every sort of air-rifle, gun, or pistol that comes along, provided they are all different and the price is reasonable. This certainly gives one a good insight into the collecting hobby, but as a rule one becomes more discriminating as time passes and the arsenal grows larger. At first, the condition of the different items may seem of no importance, provided one keeps on adding to the array, but later on, items in bad condition can be disposed of in favour of duplicates or near duplicates that are in better fettle. Antique air-arms are, of course, easily the most desirable pieces to try for and they may often be picked up in junk shops, country sales, or through advertisements, at quite modest prices.

Serious collectors are very particular people and their standards are high. As your collection and knowledge grows you will find yourself becoming more particular regarding condition, until eventually you will seek mainly arms that are quite flawless. These are described in the language of collectors as 'mint condition'.

Naturally, the older and weirder the arm, the more desirable it becomes, particularly if it is in good working order or can be put in good order.

Collections are usually started with the casual purchase of an unusual piece, which arouses one's interest and makes one want to learn more about such things. Often the weapon is shown to one's friends and eventually someone will remark, 'My father has an old air-gun at home that he has had for years.' This is produced and inspected and usually changes hands in due course.

From that moment you are sunk—you have caught the Collector's Fever and your symptoms will become more and more pronounced as you acquire more specimens.

It is queer how the acquisition of two or three old air-guns will so whet one's appetite for more that one seems to develop an uncanny knack of finding such things in the most unlikely places.

News soon gets around, and it will not be long before people you have never heard of start writing or calling and offering you what they describe as 'very rare pieces', and you must use great discrimination when buying such items. They may be valuable or they may not, but provided you can purchase cheaply, you cannot go far wrong.

Collectors generally manage to infuse some of their

enthusiasm into others, and as a result, items can be exchanged among fellow enthusiasts to their mutual advantage. One thing leads to another, and after a period of months or years, according to how quickly your armoury has grown, you will begin to specialize in a particular type of weapon. You may even decide to part with all weapons not conforming to the type in which you have the greatest interest. This is just the chance that another would-be collector is waiting for and you will have no difficulty in disposing of your surplus, probably at a good profit.

Most collectors do a certain amount of dealing. This helps to offset the cost of the items you intend to keep and, indeed, such buying and selling if judiciously carried out can quite easily pay the whole cost of your collection.

Specialist collectors may decide to collect air-pistols, air-guns, or air-rifles. They may narrow the field further by collecting, for example, only pump-up air-guns, or they may desire only a particular class of pump air-gun. I once knew a man who collected only walking-stick air-guns and rifles and he had over fifty different specimens in his private museum.

There is no real object in making a collection of modern weapons, unless they are just to shoot with. Of course, it is nice to have many different guns and rifles, but if you want to dispose of them, you will almost certainly lose money. Antique arms if acquired at reasonable prices, and if in 'mint' or 'good' condition, will always realize a good price and will generally make you a handsome profit if you keep them for a few years. For this reason, many collectors look on their purchases as an investment which can be turned into cash at any time.

There is no accepted standard of price. This depends purely on demand. If, for instance, air-gun collecting becomes popular, then prices will rise and such weapons will become increasingly scarce because so many will be seeking them. The rarest items are antique pneumatic pistols, because only a very few were ever made, and those mostly to special orders.

The standard of workmanship on the old guns was really wonderful, especially when we consider the primitive tools that the old-time craftsman had to use. Patience was indeed a virtue in those times, and a gunmaker would spend days or weeks making a complicated gun part entirely by hand. Every gunmaker was a true craftsman, and we may well marvel at their skill and ingenuity in producing work that cannot be equalled to-day.

If you collect vintage pneumatic guns, do not alter them in any way. I have seen many fine guns ruined by having their barrels cut down, by being 'converted' to smaller bores, and by having pieces cut off the stocks. Such damage is irreparable and reduces their value to a fraction of what it should be.

Another way in which such guns are often spoiled is by having them blacked, when the correct contemporary finish was brown. Happily this black finish can be removed and they can be restored by re-browning. An antique weapon that someone has 'modernized' is a travesty not to be tolerated. Missing screws should be replaced with old gun screws, and not by the insertion of modern engineers' metal screws.

One thing is certain. If you do start collecting, the more weapons you get, the more interested you will become in them, and the more you will marvel at the originality of the craftsmen who made them. It has often been said that there is nothing new under the sun. Gun collecting will bring home to you the truth of those words.

When the knowledge you will gain through your collecting has reached the point when you can immediately recognize an old weapon as an air-gun, and can say how it works, and when it was made, then you will have become an expert.

To revert to the questions about the most powerful air-guns, and the best air-gun. The most powerful air-guns that were ever made were the three tremendous pneumatic guns with which the United States Navy cruiser *Vesuvius* was equipped. They were used in 1898 to hurl enormous high-explosive shells at the shore fortifications around Santiago de Cuba in the Cuban war.

These colossal air-guns had barrels sixty feet long and eight inches bore and were exhaustively tested by Lieutenant Zalinski of the United States Army in 1886. They operated on a pressure of a thousand pounds to the square inch, and the air was stored in eight reservoirs each of which was a foot in diameter and twenty feet in length.

Similarly operated field-guns were also used by the Americans in the Cuban War, and these could throw very heavy shells filled with dynamite a distance of 3,600 yards!

The best air-gun, from the point of view of its costly and exquisite workmanship, is undoubtedly the gun made by Kolbe about the year 1750 and now on display at the Victoria and Albert Museum in London.

It is a true pneumatic although it is made to resemble a flintlock gun. This unique weapon has its air-reservoir arranged like a shell around the barrel and this shell is made of silver and richly chased. The stock alone is a work of art and is embellished with carvings and inlaid scroll work, and contains the air pump which is concealed by a plate. It was believed to have been made for George III, and may well be the actual gun with which George IV when Prince Regent, used to shoot for amusement in the grounds of the Brighton Pavilion. It is well worth a visit to the Museum to feast your eyes on this magnificent weapon.

CHAPTER 18

THE CARE, MAINTENANCE, AND REPAIR OF AIR WEAPONS

AIR-GUNNERS can, like the weapons they use, be divided into several groups.

Firstly, and I am glad to say easily in the majority, are those who obey the safety rules and do not take chances when shooting. They are to be commended on their good sense. Such persons invariably look after their weapons and give them the care and attention they deserve.

Next come the careless types, who take chances, shoot without satisfying themselves that there is a safe background, and often omit other essential precautions. These gentry are as careless with their guns as they are with their shooting, and it is common to find their guns rusty and dilapidated after only a short period of use. Their conduct is to be deplored.

Lastly we have the totally irresponsible members of the shooting fraternity, who discharge their rifles and pistols at anything and everything, ignore the most elementary safety rules, and are a positive menace to everyone.

These people treat their guns with the same utter disregard that they show to persons and property, and they are a public menace and general nuisance. Their behaviour cannot be too strongly condemned. I am glad to say that this type represents only a very small proportion of the grand total of responsible enthusiasts.

In wartime, a soldier's rifle is his best friend, and in

peacetime an air-rifle can easily be, for very different reasons, your best friend, or at least one of your most cherished possessions. It asks very little of you in the few minutes you should spend occasionally in keeping it in good order, and the enormous amount of enjoyment you will derive from its ownership will be out of all proportion to its trifling demands on your time. If you live in the country and you can shoot on your own land, then you are fortunate indeed.

Alternatively you may be a townsman, who has permission to shoot over land belonging to a farmer or other landowner. In this case, you will probably only be able to shoot at week-ends, but you will enjoy yourself just as much, when you do shoot, as your more favourably situated colleague. Although you may have only a small garden or backyard, great sport can be had with target practice, especially if one's friends are invited to compete.

Even a cellar, if of reasonable dimensions, can be easily rigged up as a shooting gallery. But the fact remains that whenever you shoot and wherever you shoot, you must give your air-rifle or pistol a little regular attention to maintain its appearance and efficiency.

The external black or blue-black finish is traditional and serves three main purposes:

It imparts a pleasing appearance to the arm, it acts as a deterrent against rust, and it materially lessens the reflection of light into the eyes of the shooter.

This black colour is obtained by means of various chemical processes which necessitate elaborate and costly equipment. This blacking is very durable and will normally last for a very long time before it eventually becomes worn with constant handling.

Therefore, if you take a pride in your air-rifle, it is essential to rub an oily rag over the metal parts, before laying it aside. This film of oil will keep the blacking in good condition and prevent corrosion. Every person's hands are, to a smaller or greater degree, moist, and it is most disconcerting to find your rifle has rusted overnight merely because you have not taken the trouble to wipe it over with an oily rag after use. If you live near the sea coast or in a district where the air is damp, this precaution is doubly important. It is a good idea to keep the oily rag in a closed tin or jar where dirt and grit cannot reach it.

Do not keep your rifle in a kitchen, outhouse, cellar, or other place that may be damp, as prolonged storage in damp places will, unless special precautions are taken, speedily cause rust and discoloration to steel and woodwork.

Neglect of these simple precautions will result in your weapon quickly losing its fine finish, and in my opinion nothing upsets the owner's pride of possession more than this. Moreover, such neglect, if allowed to continue, will cause rust to eat its way deeply into the metal, and also creep down the bore and attack the working parts, eventually ruining not only the external finish, but the whole weapon.

Assuming that the rifle or pistol you own has been allowed to become rusty through neglect or indifference on the part of yourself or a previous owner, it can of course be reblacked. I am assuming that the rust is only 'surface rust' which has not penetrated below the surface of the metal. If, however, the rust has eaten below the surface, causing deep pits, these cannot be removed and will show up badly even when reblacked.

Normally, this is not a very expensive job and such work may be entrusted to any good gunsmith. Alternatively, if the weapon is a modern one it can be returned to the makers, who have all the facilities and equipment on hand to make a first-class job. It necessitates dismantling the entire weapon, removing the rust and whatever remains of the original blacking, repolishing and degreasing the steel-work, and immersing for varying periods in a succession of tanks containing chemicals, until the desired finish is obtained.

I do not think there are many shooters, enthusiasts, or general gun cranks who have not at some time or other tried hard to reproduce the professional gun-black finish, which is so universally admired. Some have been partly successful inasmuch as they have obtained, by the use of one of the many known formulae, a black, or dark grey colour, which is certainly preferable to bright steel and, to a limited extent, acts as a rust inhibitor. But unless one is prepared to go the whole hog and install gas-heated tanks for stripping, degreasing, blacking and oiling, together with polishing motors and other costly equipment, it will be far cheaper and more convenient to send such work to specialists.

There are literally dozens of formulae claimed to produce a black finish on steel. I have tried most of them, some work after a fashion and others do not work at all. If you are of an experimental turn of mind, go right ahead. These recipes are to be found in books dealing with metals and metal finishes, and in books on gunsmithing and allied subjects. You will, no doubt, thoroughly enjoy yourself, but I do not think you will have much success.

There has recently come on the market, however, a cold gun bluer, eminently suitable for the home enthusiast who wants to refinish his gun or rifle. Stocked by many good gun dealers and sports shops, it costs 12s. 6d. for two ounces and can be relied on to produce professional results, even in inexperienced hands. It is most useful for touching up worn blueing and for colouring sights, screws and other small parts, but is equally good for a complete weapon.

I have never known anyone not to be delighted with this bluer, and use it myself for all small blueing work brought into the shop. It is called 'Magic Bluer', and certainly lives up to its name. The makers are Birchwood Casey Chemical Co., Inc., of Minnesota. An English importer supplies the trade with a complete range of Birchwood gun finishes, all of which are first-class products.

Antique weapons are usually 'browned' and such arms should under no circumstances be blued. From a collector's point of view, nothing looks worse than a fine vintage weapon which some evilly disposed person has had blued, probably under the impression that he has 'improved' it.

This brown finish is really the result of a carefully controlled process of rusting, produced by a mixture of acids. It looks really well, if expertly done, particularly so if the barrel is made of Damascus iron and has a nice twist pattern. Such pattern will show up handsomely if browned, but will be completely obliterated if blued.

There are nearly as many recipes for brown finishes on steel as there are for blue and black. The solutions used are all corrosive, and as the process takes several days and needs no small degree of skill and judgment, which can only be obtained by long experience, I do not think the amateur would be well advised to attempt it.

The stocks of good air-rifles call for little attention to keep them in condition. Gun and rifle stocks should be made of walnut, but to-day, owing to difficulties in obtaining suitable wood at a reasonable price, many stocks are made of beech and other hardwoods which, although not so desirable as walnut, will nevertheless give lasting service. Some stocks have a bright polished or varnished finish. These should be given an occasional rub with any of the proprietory brands of wax polishes. Walnut stocks are usually oil finished and have a dullish lustre. These are best kept in condition by a brisk rub with a clean rag, moistened with a little raw linseed oil.

Oil-finished stocks stand up well to rain or damp climatic conditions because each application of oil penetrates into the pores of the wood until eventually the stock becomes almost impervious to water absorption. Should an oiled stock become dented through rough usage (unless a piece of the wood has actually been gouged out) the surface will retain its water repellant properties. With a polished or varnished stock, however, the gloss does not penetrate more than a microscopic amount below the surface and thus any damage, however slight, will cause the surface finish to chip off, leaving the wood unprotected. In cases where this has occurred the wood usually becomes discoloured and the old varnish or polish must be removed by careful scraping and rubbing with fine glasspaper, and the stock refinished.

For those enthusiasts who wish to recondition the stocks of their air-rifles, or for that matter, the stocks of any rifles or guns, here is the procedure.

If the stock is oil-finished and has been dented, the dents can be raised by steaming, without the necessity of scraping the entire stock. The method of raising dents is to cause a very fine jet of steam to impinge on and around the dent. This makes the bruised fibres of the wood swell and eventually regain their original form.

If the dents are only shallow ones, try the following. Fold a piece of white cloth several times, wet it thoroughly, and wring it out. Place the folded cloth over the dent and apply a hot iron to it. Keep on wetting and ironing until the dent has been raised to the level of the surrounding wood. This method generally produces the desired result. If the dents are deep and will not respond to the above treatment, proceed as follows.

Get hold of a large lever-lid tin. This needs to be big enough to hold about half a gallon of water. Drill or punch a hole in the lid and solder in a small piece of copper or brass tube a few inches long. Now obtain a length of rubber tubing of such a size that it can be connected to the copper tube, and on the other end of the rubber tube fit a small nozzle. An ideal nozzle, and all ready-made into the bargain, is the spout sawn from an oil can.

You are now all ready to begin. Half-fill the tin with water and put on the gas. Bring it to the boil. When boiling, you should have quite a high pressure jet of steam issuing from the nozzle. This jet should be allowed to impinge on the centre of the dent and every now and then the wood surrounding the dent should be lightly tapped with a smooth-faced hammer. This process is slow and runs the gas bill up quite a bit, but if you persevere you will find that really deep dents that at first appear hopeless can be successfully raised, and will eventually be impossible to discover.

After steaming, the stock must be set aside for two or three days, or until such time as it is thoroughly dry. The original oil finish will be destroyed around the dent, but a thorough rubbing with oil will put matters right.

If, however, the damage consists not of dents or bruises but the wood itself has been badly torn or nicked, the professional method is to cut away the damage and inlet a piece of similar wood, being careful to match up the grain and colour as far as possible. This inlay is glued in position and allowed to set, and then glass-papered down level and stained and oiled with raw linseed oil. Such repairs, however well done, are usually discernible but they are less noticeable on a dark-coloured stock than on a light one.

Polished or varnished stocks can be treated in exactly the same way to remove dents but invariably the steaming so spoils the finish that the entire stock must be scraped and refinished.

The professional way to remove the polish is by means of a good swabbing with a strong, hot solution of caustic soda. I do not recommend this for amateur use, however, as unless it is used with extreme caution, it is liable to remove the skin from your hands as well as the finish from the gun stock. Another disadvantage (to the amateur) is that it removes the filler from the wood and leaves the grain open.

I suggest, therefore, that you use a cabinet-maker's scraper or a 'Skarsten' scraper to remove the bulk of the old finish, scraping carefully in the direction of the grain, afterwards using fine-grade glasspaper to give a smooth finish. It is advisable to use successively finer grades of glasspaper until a really super-smooth surface is obtained. If the stock has a chequered grip it is a good idea to cover this with adhesive tape which will minimize the risk of damaging the finely cut diamonds, as such damage is permanent and next to impossible for the amateur to repair.

The stock is now ready for polishing. French polish looks well, and its high gloss is much admired, but it does not stand up well to rain and is easily scratched. Varnish is more durable and is almost unaffected by weather conditions, but does not have such a high lustre.

It often improves the appearance of a stock to darken it slightly by the judicious use of a little stain before commencing polishing. I would recommend that a spirit stain be used rather than a water stain as this does not raise the grain unduly. Such stains can be bought at any ironmongers' and are usually sold in powder or crystal form and have only to be mixed with methylated spirit to make them ready for use.

It is hardly within the scope of this book to describe the processes of varnishing and polishing, and I would refer the reader to any one of the numerous books available on this subject.

If your stock has actually had wood gouged out of it and you do not feel qualified to build up the damage by inletting, an alternative method of repairing such damage is both simple and very effective. This is by using a preparation known as 'plastic wood', which is obtainable at hardware shops in handy and modestly priced lever-lid tins.

This plastic wood can be pressed straight into the crack or cavity, and when set, is extremely tough and durable. Very neat repairs can thus be made and it can be filed, cut, stained, and polished. I can thoroughly recommend its use. If you have occasion at any time to make use of this preparation, here are a few tips that are worth knowing. Firstly, plastic wood shrinks a little when setting, and therefore it is necessary, when filling the cavity, to leave the plastic wood slightly higher than the level of the stock and smooth down level with fine glasspaper when quite hard. Secondly, if the cavity is deep, the material will take a long time to set. It may appear hard on the surface, but give it plenty of time, because it hardens on the surface first, and may not have had time to set right through. It is useless to start trimming it while the centre is soft, so do not try to hurry matters, and if in doubt err on the side of allowing too much time rather than risk having to start all over again.

Thirdly, although this material can be stained after it has set, it is far better to work a little colouring into the plastic before filling the cavity. Do not use for this purpose any stain containing oil as this may prevent the plastic wood adhering.

The bore of your air-gun, rifle or pistol does not become fouled after shooting, like that of a shotgun or cartridge-rifle, and therefore the question of cleaning the bore after shooting does not really arise. Nor does the rifling suffer from 'leading' as does the cartridge-rifle. This is the term given to denote the presence of a film of lead throughout the length of the rifling. I have examined many thousands of air weapons and have never yet been able to find any measurable traces of lead, even in weapons that have been in constant use for forty years and have fired probably not far short of a million pellets through their barrels. In fact, provided you take reasonable care and do not deliberately misuse your weapon the barrel will last virtually for ever.

I do not intend to imply that a cleaning rod may be dispensed with. It is a very necessary accessory and has its uses, as follows:

1. To oil the bore if the weapon is laid aside and is not intended to be used again for a considerable time.
2. To clean out this oil before the weapon is used again.
3. To push out a defective pellet that may have become lodged in the barrel.
4. To scour out rust from a neglected barrel.

The best type of cleaning rod is one that has a celluloid covering. These are available for both ·177 and ·22 calibres, while if you possess a large-bore air-rifle or air-shotgun, an ordinary rifle or shotgun cleaning rod will serve admirably.

Various interchangeable brushes are available for these rods and the air-gunner will need a bristle brush, a jag or a loop and possibly a wire brush.

Oiling may be carried out either with the bristle brush or by the use of a flannelette patch wrapped round the jag or slipped through the loop. In either case, a little medium-grade good quality lubricating oil should be applied either to the patch or the bristle brush.

To remove this oil it is only necessary to use a clean patch round the jag or through the loop, and pull through, repeating once or twice with clean patches, until the bore is quite free from oil and the patches come away unsoiled.

In practice, I have found that it is not really necessary to oil the bore every time the weapon has been in use, as the action of shooting the rifle atomizes the oil that is, or should be, always present between the piston and cylinder. This oil vapour is constantly passing up the barrel and is deposited in minute particles, sufficient to keep the bore in good condition but not enough to have any adverse effect on one's shooting.

The wire scouring brush is intended to be used only to remove rust from barrels that have been neglected. If the rust is light and powdery, it can often be cleaned out, leaving no trace, but if the bore is deeply pitted it is doubtful whether the weapon will ever be of any real use. Such pitting destroys the accuracy and, in addition, increases friction between pellet and bore and results in a serious loss of power.

Do not under any circumstances shoot in your air weapon anything except the proper ammunition intended to be used in it, as anything else will certainly not do the weapon any good at all, and may do it plenty of harm. The cost of pellets is so little that one should always keep an ample supply in hand. If this is done, there should be no temptation to try out the possibilities (lethal or otherwise) of shooting matchheads, matchsticks, elderberries, or lumps of chewing gum!

All these and many other queer missiles have become lodged in the barrels of air-rifles brought to me for attention.

Two common obstructions are matchsticks and pieces of rag, both of which are usually packed in solid. The former is caused by two matchsticks jamming together and aggravated by a succession of match or other sticks being introduced in an effort to dislodge the first two. This usually results in a complete blockage of the barrel.

Pieces of cloth or rag, if pushed down the barrel without using a proper cleaning rod, will frequently pack up so tightly in the barrel that they cannot be pushed out. The harder you push the tighter they jam. Such obstructions should be removed as follows:

Obtain a fine-pointed, brass wood screw of such a size that it will easily enter the bore of your rifle. Cut the head off this screw and braze it to the end of an old cleaning rod. Alternatively, the shank of the screw may be drilled and tapped to screw on to the thread at the end of your cleaning rod.

Insert the rod in the bore until it meets the obstruction. Twist the rod until the screw gets a bite and withdraw it by pulling straight out. This will bring with it a portion of the 'foreign body'. Repeat this procedure until all matter has been removed. (N.B. If you are the type of person who likes to drag his overcoat through the bore of his air-rifle, it is best to remove the buttons first.)

Air-gunners often desire to replace a broken foresight or exchange the sights fitted by the makers for others more to their liking.

Foresights and backsights are usually dovetailed in to the barrel and are always driven in place from right to left. It is a simple matter to exchange such sights. Assuming you wish for example, to replace a blade foresight with a barley-corn, this is the way to do it. Grip the rifle barrel in a vice as near the foresight as possible, taking care to pad the vice jaws with stout leather or several thicknesses of stiff card-board. It is essential to do this to prevent the barrel becoming marked by the jaws of the vice. The stock of the rifle must be supported by nailing a board on your bench and allowing one end to project over the edge on which the stock can rest. Carefully scratch a fine line on the barrel as near the dovetail as possible and exactly in the centre of the existing foresight. The sight must now be driven out from left to right, using a short piece of hard fibre rod, or a piece of very hard wood, and a hammer. Tap gently at first, increasing the blows until the sight starts to move, when a further light tap will remove it. If, instead of doing this, you give it 'a fourpenny one' the sight will most likely shoot out and you may spend the rest of the day trying to find it! Keep sights and all such other oddments. They usually come in handy for other jobs.

The new foresight (which should be exactly the same height as the one it replaces) must be inserted from right to left and should be driven in nearly to the mark you have made on the barrel, using the hammer and fibre rod.

Now test the rifle for accuracy, and drive the sight in a little at a time, testing frequently until it is shooting correctly. The reason for not first driving the sight right up to the mark is that if it should have to be tapped back slightly to correct any shooting vagary, the dovetail may have been expanded enough to make the sight loose when moved the opposite way. The use of fibre or wood when removing or fitting sights obviates any possibility of the sights being marked, which they undoubtedly would if they were driven in place by the hammer alone.

Aperture sights can be fitted to air-rifles and several makers supply them to order. They call for a higher degree of skill in their fitting, and it is often necessary to drill and tap holes in the metal of the weapon. Such work needs tools probably not in possession of the reader. I suggest, therefore, that such fitting should be entrusted to a gunsmith who will be glad to supply and fix an aperture sight for a reasonable sum.

One English air-rifle that fitted a fully adjustable aperture sight as a standard and integral part of the rifle was the Webley and Scott 'Mark II' Service air-rifle, which was produced just prior to World War II. These particular weapons were unique in many respects and together with the earlier Webley 'Mark I' rifles were the only commercially produced air-rifles to have detachable and interchangeable barrels.

Although manufacture of these particular models has been discontinued, Messrs. Webley & Scott make a series of excellent spring-operated air-pistols with interchangeable barrels, which are very widely used to-day. These, indeed, are so well known that the words 'air-pistol' are practically synonymous with 'Webley'.

Well-known makes of British spring-operated air-rifles and pistols have been brought to such a state of mechanical efficiency that, like old soldiers, they never die. Faults in their construction are extremely rare because all such weapons must pass a very rigid inspection at every stage of their manufacture.

After prolonged use, however, their power gradually decreases and they no longer satisfy the demands of their critical owners. This falling-off in power is usually due to one of three things, and sometimes to a combination of all three.

1. The mainspring may have lost its strength or may even be broken.
2. The piston-head seal may be damaged or worn.
3. If the weapon is an air-pistol or a breakdown air-gun or rifle, the breech washer may be missing, worn, or otherwise defective.

The renewal of mainspring, leather piston head or piston ring, and breech washer are all jobs that can easily be tackled by the amateur gunsmith.

It would take a long time to describe in detail the exact procedure for dismantling every make of air-rifle and pistol for the purpose of replacing springs and other working parts. I am, therefore, treating the matter in a general way, which, while not quite so helpful for the owner of any one specific make of air weapon, will be, I hope, of general interest.

With most modern air-rifles, the stock must first be removed. Examine the stock carefully and decide how it is attached. Sometimes there are two screws in the forepart and a third screw near the trigger-guard. The screw is often one of the screws used for attaching the trigger-guard itself and goes right through the woodwork and is threaded into the steel of the breech. In other air weapons, the stock is secured by a long bolt passing lengthwise through the stock. This may be visible and accessible through a hole in the butt plate, but sometimes the butt plate must be removed to disclose this bolt. There are two difficulties that may be met with here—the bolt-head may be so deeply recessed into the stock that it is hard to reach. If the bolt-head is slotted it will need a very long screwdriver to reach it, but assuming you have, or can obtain, such a tool, your troubles are over.

If, however, the bolt-head is hexagonal it will need a specially long box spanner, to do the trick. You may be able to borrow such a thing from your local garage if they know you well enough. Alternatively, you may have the patience and skill to make one for yourself. A dodge that I have used very successfully on more than one occasion is to join two or three box spanners together by inserting them end to end, to give the necessary length.

It would be as well to mention that there are some types of weapons, for example, the Webley 'Mark II' air-rifle, where the stock does not have to be removed to gain access to the spring, because the spring and piston are inserted from the forward end of the rifle.

Also there are other types where the stock can be removed and the spring is directly accessible. In one such weapon, the B.S.A. pre-war underlever rifle, the three screws fastening the trigger-guard must be removed, and the stock complete with trigger-assembly can then be unscrewed and the spring extracted.

Assuming you have removed the stock and cannot yet get at the mainspring, the next step is to consider carefully whether the breech unit can now be removed or whether it is being held by a parallel pin, taper pin, or other screw or screws. This decision is best made after trying to unscrew the breech using hand pressure only. Never, under any circumstances, use force until you are quite positive that there are no pins or screws preventing the breech from being taken off. If there are, they must be removed first.

If the breech is secured by a lockpin, both ends of the pin should be examined. If one end of the pin is of a slightly larger diameter than the other end, it denotes that a taper pin is present and this must be punched out from the small end of the pin. Do not use a nail for this purpose. A properly made engineer's punch only costs about one and sixpence and will save you far more than that in spoiled blueing and hammered fingers.

After satisfying yourself that there is nothing to stop the breech being taken off, go right ahead.

Should the weapon have been neglected, the threads may be rusty, and it will be difficult or impossible to unscrew. The application of ordinary paraffin oil to the threads will assist matters, particularly if this is allowed to soak in overnight. There are on the market several proprietary makes of penetrating oils which are inexpensive to buy and are far more effective than paraffin in easing and freeing rusted threads. The efficiency of these oils can be still further increased by first heating the rusted part till it is just too hot to hold with the hand, and then applying the oil. This heating expels the air from in between the threads and the oil will be drawn in as the parts cool down.

If your rifle stock is attached by the 'screw through trigger-guard' method, you will find that this fixing screw is often threaded into a lug or projection which is itself screwed into the rifle. This lug must be unscrewed and will generally be found to have a left-handed thread, and must be removed by a wide-bladed screwdriver turned in a clockwise direction. The reason for this left-hand thread is to prevent the lug from being unscrewed when the screw that attaches the stock is tightened. (An enthusiast of my acquaintance was not aware of the left-handed thread business, and thought the screw was just being awkward. He applied a very large pipe wrench and, giving a mighty heave, stripped the thread. I arrived just as this happened and timed him as he swore for five minutes without stopping!)

By now the breech unit should be off and the spring removed. The spring may be broken, but usually it is just weak from constant usage. It should be replaced with a new one of exactly the same dimensions. By this I mean that not only should the length and the internal and external diameters be identical with the old spring, but the coil thickness should be the same as well.

If you try and fit a spring that is too long, you will generally find that it will not be possible to compress the spring sufficiently to screw the breech back in position. If, on the other hand, you use a spring of the correct length, but made of much thicker wire, you will very likely manage to screw the breech on again, but will probably find that the rifle cannot be cocked. This is because the spring, when fully compressed, will be longer than the original one and this extra length will prevent the piston being pushed back far enough for the sear to engage. The amount of extra length will of course be represented by the number of turns of the spring multiplied by the amount by which the spring wire thickness exceeds the diameter of the original wire.

It is of the utmost importance, too, that the spring slides freely into the hollow piston. It is not generally appreciated that when a coil spring is compressed, its diameter slightly increases. If, therefore, you attempt to use a spring that is a tight fit in the piston, you will find that when you attempt to cock the weapon, the action will be accompanied by horrible noises, and the result will be one of three things:

(*a*) Great friction between outside of spring and inside of piston, resulting in loss of power.

(*b*) Spring becoming partly jammed inside piston.

(*c*) Broken spring.

It is usually just as well, before assembling the rifle, to inspect the piston-head. On some rifles the piston-head seal takes the form of a metal piston-ring. If this appears worn, or is damaged, it should be replaced by a new one.

To remove such ring, gently expand it and slip it off over the piston-head. Replace by easing the new ring over the piston-head when it will snap into place on reaching the groove made to receive it. One air-rifle using a metal piston-ring is the Webley 'Mark II'.

The majority of air-guns and rifles, however, use the leather piston-head. On the older weapons this was a plain, thick leather disc, screwed to the head of the piston by means of a large-headed steel screw. Modern weapons which are fitted with a leather piston-head usually use a cup-shaped leather washer similar to an ordinary cycle pump washer. When these are used in an air weapon, a thick leather or metal disc is fitted inside the cup washer and the securing screw passes through both the disc and the cup washer and into the piston-head.

The renewal of a cup washer entails only removing this screw and replacing it when the old washer has been taken off and replaced by a new one.

Before replacing the piston and spring, look into the cylinder and, if dirty or very oily, clean out thoroughly with a clean rag wrapped round a wooden rod and oil the piston-head and the cylinder walls sparingly with a light grade lubricating oil.

Underlever air-rifles must have the lower arm of the cocking lever removed before the piston can be slid out. Breakdown air-rifles and guns can be treated in the same way, but it is often convenient to take out the barrel pivot screw, when the barrel and cocking arm can be removed intact. If this is done, it facilitates the removal and replacement of the breech-joint washer. This can be gently prised out with a scriber or some similar instrument and the new washer inserted into place and pressed home with the fingers.

Piston-washers, breech-washers, springs and all replacement parts should at all times be obtained from a recognized dealer or purchased direct from the makers. With vintage weapons, of course, the position is rather different and breech-washers must be trimmed down from standard ones or made specially. From the variety of springs available, one can generally be found very near to the original, which will answer quite well. Cup-washers are also available in a variety of sizes and can often be bought at hardware and cycle shops. If the correct size cup-washer cannot be found, it is best to get one a shade too small than one too large. In the first case, the washer will rapidly conform to the diameter of the cylinder when the weapon has been discharged a few times. In the latter case, the washer will most likely be damaged in the struggle to insert it in the cylinder and the very tight fit will provide unwanted friction which will lessen the weapon's power.

In spring-operated air-pistols, the replacement of springs, piston-head seals and breech-washers follows much the same procedure, except that it is simpler as there are no stocks to remove and the weapons themselves are less awkward to handle.

We come now to a matter of the utmost importance, and this is 'oiling'. I have already dealt with external oiling for the purpose of preservation, and we must now consider the question of internal oiling for lubrication.

Air-operated weapons of all types are generally either over-oiled or not oiled at all. The enthusiast lubricates his rifle until it literally drips oil from every part of it. The careless man never gives it a drop. Both extremes are bad for the weapon.

An air-rifle is a precision-made machine and naturally needs lubricating, but not to excess. If it is literally starved of oil and the working parts are dry, abnormal wear will be created which can only be remedied by the replacement of the worn parts. Also, of course, the rifle will not be developing its full power. This is because, no matter how strong a spring your weapon contains, unless you have a film of oil to provide a seal between the piston-head and the cylinder, air will by-pass the piston and much of the compression will be lost.

Excess lubrication of external levers, etc., to such a degree that oil actually runs from the part will actually cause dryness of the part. This may seem strange but it is, nevertheless, a fact that any oil running down from a joint will cause, by capillary attraction, all the oil to be drawn from that joint, leaving the part dry.

Internal lubrication of the piston, trigger mechanism, etc., should also be done very sparingly. I would suggest that the oil applied to the piston should not exceed two or three drops for every thousand slugs fired. If oil appreciably in excess of this amount is used, it will result in a loss, not a gain, in the power. This loss of power will last until the weapon has had sufficient use to disperse the excess oil. Another argument against the too liberal oiling of the piston is that until the excess oil has been shot out of the rifle, its shooting will be inaccurate, due to the surplus oil being carried down the barrel.

With underlever tap-loading rifles, the oil is best applied by opening the tap, dropping the oil in, and closing the tap again. When the rifle is cocked, this oil will be drawn into the cylinder. Breakdown rifles and pistols should have the oil dropped into the hole in the breech-washer, and allowed to run in. It does not matter at this stage, whether the oil reaches the cylinder walls or not, because the first time the weapon is fired, the oil will be atomized and deposited all over the working surface of the cylinder.

If the makers recommend a special oil, it is as well to use it. Such recommendations are not made without good reason, but if no special oil is advocated, then any good quality light lubricating oil may be used.

You will notice I have not had a great deal to say about air-guns. This is because their care, repair, and maintenance is, for all practical purposes, the same as for air-rifles and pistols. Air-guns with smooth-bore barrels are a thing of the past, and are not manufactured to-day except as toys, with the single exception of the American air-shotgun, known as the 'Plainsman'. There are, however, many thousands of smooth-bore spring air-guns still in existence and many are still in use. They were made in No. 1, No. 2, and No. 3 bore and were mostly of the breakdown type. I have never seen an *underlever* air-*gun* with smooth-bore barrel, but it is possible that there is such a thing.

Pneumatic or pump-up air-guns, rifles, and pistols should have the same care externally as spring weapons. If the pump is built into the arm and the weapon is therefore self-contained like the Crosman, Benjamin, or Sheridan rifles, a very occasional spot of oil should be applied through the air inlet which will be found a short distance down the pump tube. This will lubricate not only the piston of the air-pump, but some oil will penetrate to the air pressure chamber and will keep both the inlet and exhaust valves working freely. Similar oiling is needed on the Crosman and Benjamin and other pneumatic air-pistols. Gas-operated pistols, such as the Benjamin, 'Plainsman', Schimel, etc., should have one drop of oil put into the filling orifice for approximately every 250 shots, and the Crosman gas-rifle, one drop for every complete charge of gas, firing about seventy shots. Antique 'pump-up' weapons usually have a separate pump and this pump piston should be lightly lubricated and a very occasional spot of oil dropped on the valve before pumping-up the air reservoir.

Pneumatics are far more complicated in construction than spring weapons and, moreover, their mechanisms are much more difficult for the amateur to understand and to repair.

I can assure you that it is a losing bet to try and repair a pump-up weapon unless you have the necessary highly specialized knowledge. Usually far more harm than good results in any such attempt, and I would strongly advise you to leave them alone. Pneumatic weapons have not been made in this country for very many years, but they are a standard product in some countries, and notably in the U.S.A. English gunsmiths seem to take the view that they are an invention of the devil and are specifically guaranteed to send any self-respecting dealer to perdition. I have heard of gunsmiths spending a week trying to make a valve air-tight and then running amok and heaping curses on its maker.

Pneumatic repairs are a very specialized business indeed, and it would be quite impossible without writing another book on the subject, to convey sufficient knowledge to the amateur to enable him to do his own repairs and I can, therefore, only recommend that you take all pneumatic repairs to a specialist who is competent to carry out such work successfully.

Before we leave the subject of repairs, it would be advisable to say something about screwdrivers. The ordinary carpenter's screwdriver, such as is in general use, is totally unfit to be used in any gun work. When removing screws from any rifle, gun, or pistol, it is of the utmost importance that only screwdrivers of the correct size, and ones that have been ground in a special way, should be used. If you like tinkering with your rifles, I strongly advise that you provide yourself with a set of properly ground screwdrivers and keep them for this work only. The screwdriver blade should exactly fit the slot in the screw you wish to remove and, more important still, must be ground in such a way that the sides are parallel at the tip, and not tapered. This will ensure that the driver will do its work efficiently, and will not slip out of the slot when pressure is brought to bear on it. If the ordinary household screwdriver with its tapering point is used, it will most definitely slip out of the screw slot causing damage to both the screw and the weapon. Damaged screw heads show badly and knock pounds off the value of any sort of weapon, and also convey at a glance the fact that the arm has been dismantled by an inexperienced person.

Lastly, if you own a good air-rifle, please do your best to obtain a cover for it. Rifle covers can be purchased in various qualities and they are the ideal way to keep out dirt, grit, and damp.

CHAPTER 19

BALLISTICS

THERE are many enthusiasts and experimenters who would like to know something about the ballistics of their weapons.

This is indeed a very specialized and complicated subject if we consider it in all its aspects; and many highly technical books have been written which deal fully with it.

Nevertheless there is no reason why the air-gunner should not be able to make use of known principles and formulæ which will enable him accurately to work out problems which will in turn help him to understand better the mysteries of his air-rifle and its performance.

The study of ballistics covers the whole flight of the pellet from the instant it is set in motion by means of the compression of the air behind it until such motion eventually ceases.

Part of the time the pellet is in motion it is travelling from the breech of the weapon and through the bore, and the study of this particular branch of the subject is known as 'internal ballistics'.

The study of the movement or motion of the pellet from the instant it *leaves* the muzzle until its flight is over is known as external ballistics, and it is this particular part of the whole subject that I feel sure will be the most interesting to the enthusiast.

Any object which is set in motion becomes possessed of a certain force or energy known as kinetic energy, or the energy of motion, and when we refer to the energy possessed by a pellet or bullet leaving the muzzle of a weapon we call this force muzzle energy.

A bullet, pellet or any other missile fired from any type of weapon will continue to travel until this energy has been expended by either:

1. The missile being stopped by its impact with some other object.

or

2. The initial energy becoming less and less, due to the continued friction of the air or other media through which it passes, until its flight ceases altogether.

Pellets fired from air-rifles or air-pistols behave in exactly the same way as bullets fired from any other type of weapon.

The heavier the bullet or pellet is, and the faster it travels, the harder it will be to stop and the farther it will travel through the air; thus the heavier the pellet, the more effective it will be as a weapon and the longer its range, but the greater the force that will be needed to set it in motion in the first place.

Muzzle energy varies *directly* as to the weight of the pellet. For example an air-rifle pellet weighing 15 grains will possess twice the muzzle energy of a pellet weighing only 7½ grains *provided both pellets are projected at the same speed or velocity.*

This is the reason why the ·22 air-rifle pellet has a longer effective range and greater killing power than the lighter ·177 pellet.

There are other factors too, which cause slight variations, the principal one being the shape of the pellet itself, but to avoid unnecessary complications we must neglect these factors which do not greatly affect us in our consideration of air operated arms.

Muzzle energy is measured in 'foot pounds', one foot pound being the amount of energy that would be needed to raise a weight of one pound, a distance of one foot. Alternatively a weight of one pound dropped a distance of one foot would acquire the same kinetic energy.

Three foot pounds energy would mean the amount of

energy that would be needed to raise three pounds through a distance of one foot or one pound through a distance of three feet.

When a pellet or bullet is set in motion it moves against opposing forces which offer considerable resistance to its progress.

Thus anything through which the pellet passes will slow down its speed and will stop it completely when the resistance becomes equal to the initial energy of the pellet.

This 'work' done by the pellet is in theory equal to the force in pounds multiplied by the distance in feet. If, for instance, a 1 pound weight was suspended just in front of the muzzle of a rifle which was pointing vertically upwards, and you fired at it a bullet having a muzzle energy of 10 foot pounds, the 1 pound weight would be driven upwards a distance of 10 feet before it stopped the pellet, or alternatively a 10 pound weight would only move 1 foot.

We must now consider muzzle velocity. This denotes the speed at which the pellet is travelling immediately it leaves the muzzle, and it is always expressed in terms of feet per second.

The energy possessed by the moving pellet varies not directly, but as to the *square* of its velocity.

For example if we shoot a ·22 pellet from an air-rifle at a muzzle velocity of 700 feet per second it will be not twice but 4 times as hard to stop, and will have 4 times the muzzle energy of an identical pellet fired from an air-rifle giving a muzzle velocity of 350 feet per second.

Similarly if the muzzle velocity is trebled, then the pellet will have 9 times its former energy.

The muzzle energy in foot pounds for any particular pellet can be calculated quite easily provided the muzzle velocity of the weapon is known.

To find the muzzle energy we must multiply the square of the muzzle velocity by half the weight of the pellet (expressed in pounds), and divide the result by the acceleration of gravity, which is 32·16 feet per second per second.

Thus the formula is

$$E = \frac{WV^2}{2x\ 32{\cdot}16}$$ where E is the muzzle energy W the weight of the pellet in pounds and V the muzzle velocity in feet per second.

For example if we wish to find the muzzle energy possessed by an air-rifle pellet weighing 15 grains and fired from an air-rifle at a known muzzle velocity of 500 feet per second the calculation would be

$$\frac{15 \times 500 \times 500}{2 \times 7000 \times 32{\cdot}16} = 8{\cdot}3 \text{ foot pounds}$$

It will be noticed that the factor 7000 is used to convert the weight of the pellet from grains to pounds, and as the other factors 2 and 32·16 also always occur in calculations of this nature it saves time and trouble to remember that their product is 450240, and that it is therefore only necessary to multiply together the pellet weight in grains and the velocity squared and divide the result by 450240 to give the answer in foot pounds.

We shall now consider another matter which comes under the heading of ballistics, and that is amount that the pellet drops during its flight.

We have already seen in another chapter that an air-rifle pellet does *not* travel in a straight line, but follows a curved path which is known as its trajectory, and we also know that this curved path is caused by the force of gravity acting on the pellet and pulling it towards the ground.

Many enthusiasts may like to know more about the amount the pellet drops so that they can make their own calculations and draw graphs to illustrate the trajectory of a pellet shot from their own particular air weapon.

The drop of the pellet in feet is expressed by the formula $D = \frac{1}{2} At^2$ where D is the distance the pellet drops A is the acceleration of gravity and t is the time in seconds that the pellet has been travelling.

The acceleration of gravity is 32·16 feet per second per second, but it is usually convenient for easy calculation to neglect the decimal places as this will give the answer with reasonable accuracy.

If for instance our air-rifle pellet takes $\frac{1}{2}$ second to reach the target, then the amount the pellet has dropped during this time will be

$$\frac{1}{2} \times 32 \times (\frac{1}{2})^2 = 4 \text{ feet.}$$

It will be obvious that in any calculation to find the drop of a pellet in a given time the factor 32·16 or (if we disregard the decimals) 32 occurs. Thus the formula can be conveniently expressed as $D = 16\ t^2$. We must also remember that the weight of the pellet in no way affects its drop, as the pull of gravity is exerted equally on everything irrespective of its weight. Thus we can see that the only one factor affecting bullet drop is the *time* during which the force of gravity has been at work on the pellet, or in other words the length of time that the pellet has been travelling.

It is regrettable that the air-gunner cannot determine the muzzle velocity of his air-rifle without complicated apparatus which would be beyond the capabilities of the average enthusiast to construct for himself.

Muzzle velocity is measured with an instrument called a chronograph which is constructed in such a way that the time taken by the passage of the pellet over a definite measured distance is recorded. From this information the muzzle velocity in feet per second can easily be calculated.

There are various methods employed in the operation of such chronographs, but the principle is, of course, the same in every case. One such instrument in general use is known as the Potter Chronograph, and is operated electrically by the pellet passing through two 'screens' each containing a photo-electric cell. These 'screens' are like hollow frames, and the time taken between the pellet passing through the first and second screen is automatically recorded by means of electrically energized solenoids. Such instruments are extremely accurate, but are bulky and very expensive and these factors alone are sufficient to prohibit their acquisition by the air-gunner.

All modern air weapons are tested by their makers and their muzzle velocities are recorded, and this information can usually be obtained from the manufacturers. Often, too, the muzzle velocities of obsolete weapons can also be obtained, providing the firms that made them are still in existence. In the case of vintage weapons, however, the position is rather different, as such weapons were made long before anyone thought of checking the muzzle velocity of an air operated weapon, and with very early weapons, before the invention of the chronograph.

Therefore the muzzle velocity of such weapons can only be obtained by submitting them to a firm possessing a chronograph, unless you are one of those fortunate persons who have access to such instruments and can carry out the test yourself.

It is hardly within the scope of this book to attempt to delve deeply into such a complex subject as ballistics, and as books are available for those who want to study the matter at greater length I make no apology for mentioning only those facts which I feel sure are of particular interest to owners of air weapons.

CHAPTER 20

INTERESTING DATA ABOUT SPRING AIR-RIFLES

IN Chapter 6, I stated that for all practical purposes the whole of the energy stored in a spring under compression is given out again when the spring is allowed to expand to its full length. It has occurred to me that this statement may be misconstrued by readers, who may wrongly assume that the whole of such energy is therefore available for the projection of the pellet from a spring operated air-rifle or pistol.

Nothing is farther from the truth. An air-rifle or air-pistol is in reality a type of engine, and in common with any and every other type of engine, cannot give one hundred per cent efficiency.

A reciprocating steam engine for example is only about 9 per cent efficient, which means that approximately only this amount of the total energy developed is available for doing work, while the rest is wasted in thermal and frictional losses.

An air-rifle also suffers serious losses in efficiency and in fact more than two thirds of the theoretically available energy is wasted, leaving approximately only thirty per cent of the total energy for actually doing work, which in this case means projecting the pellet from the barrel.

At first sight, this appears to be a very poor performance, but if we delve deeper into the relative efficiency of many other types of engines we shall find that the air-rifle does not compare at all unfavourably with them.

An air-rifle reduced to its bare essentials is simply a glorified pop-gun and it operates in the same way. A child's pop-gun expels its cork at the exact moment when the air behind the cork is at its highest compression and the pressure is able to overcome the frictional grip of the cork in the muzzle.

An air-rifle behaves in exactly the same way, but in this case the compressed air is utilized by causing it to expand against the base of the pellet, thus causing the pellet to travel through the barrel, and at the same time having a rotary motion imparted to it due to its close contact with the rifling of the barrel.

As in the case of the toy pop-gun, the projectile does not start moving until the air behind it has a degree of compression sufficient to overcome the frictional grip between pellet and rifling.

All this is simple enough, but there are scientific aspects of the matter which are far more complex than one would imagine.

We must stop for a moment and consider Boyle's Law of Compression, which states that the pressure or tension of air or gases is inversely proportional to the space into which they are compressed.

This means for example, that if any stated volume of air or gases at ordinary atmospheric pressure is compressed into half the space it previously occupied, then its pressure will have doubled.

This is perfectly true provided that we add an important qualification, namely, that the compressed air or gas remains under compression long enough for the surplus heat created by such compression to be dissipated. As we have seen in Chapter 6, when air is compressed its temperature materially rises, and as long as such heat is retained, the resultant pressure is considerably greater than is indicated by Boyle's Law. This law must therefore be interpreted to apply only to air or gases which have remained under compression long enough for the heat to have passed away. The old time Pneumatic air-rifle is a perfect example of the application of Boyle's Law, as the air pumped into the reservoir of such a weapon is not generally used for some time afterwards and may in fact, be used days, weeks, or even months, later.

With the spring operated air-rifle, the position is vastly different, because the air compression takes place almost instantaneously and therefore for all practical purposes no heat is lost.

Theoretically of course, a thermal loss must occur, but as maximum compression is reached in approximately a hundredth part of a second, the heat loss is so infinitesimal that we may well disregard it altogether.

We may assume that in all good air-rifles the base flange or skirt of the pellet fits tightly into the rifling and the pellet has therefore sufficient grip to prevent any air escaping past it.

We must also assume for the moment that no air escapes past the piston head, although in practice, small losses of air do occur at both these points.

It is a simple matter to measure accurately the energy that the spring develops during the several stages of its compression and some years ago, I carried out experiments with a pre-war ·177 German Underlever air-rifle in order to find out the exact relation between the energy delivered by the spring and the final muzzle energy of the pellet.

It was first necessary to measure the distance from the face of the piston to the end of the cylinder when the rifle was cocked and the spring therefore fully compressed. This was found to be 2·5 inches, and this measurement also represents the total length of travel of the piston.

The next step was to ascertain the actual strength of the spring, and this was done by means of a length of ¼ inch diameter steel rod, one end of which was threaded and provided with a large washer and nut, and the other end bent into the form of a large hook. The spring was then slipped on to the rod, the washer and nut replaced and the whole arrangement set upright in the vice, the jaws of which were closed just enough to allow the rod to slide freely between them without allowing the spring to follow.

Weights were next loaded on the hooked end of the rod and notes made of the weighting needed to produce various degrees of compression up to the point when the spring was fully compressed. The average was found to be 96·5 pounds and this represents the mean force of the spring over its 2·5 inches of travel. The energy in foot pounds was therefore 96·5 x ·208 (the latter being the decimal equivalent of 2·5 inches expressed in feet) and the product of this is 20.

We can therefore say that the spring of this particular air-rifle, when compressed, represents an energy of 20 foot pounds, and this energy is available for compressing the air in front of the piston head, propelling the slug, imparting a rotary motion to it, overcoming friction and so forth.

The muzzle velocity of the air-rifle under discussion was tested by means of a chronograph and found to be 516 feet per second, and this represents a muzzle energy of 5·9 foot pounds.

This can be calculated by means of the formula given in Chapter 19, and was arrived at by multiplying the weight of the pellet expressed in pounds by the velocity squared and dividing by 64·4, viz.

$$\frac{10}{7000} \times \frac{516^2}{64 \cdot 4}$$

It may thus be seen that of the original 20 foot pounds of available energy generated by the spring, only 5·9 foot pounds of energy is possessed by the pellet. This gives the rifle an efficiency of 29 per cent.

These are many factors that account for this loss of efficiency. The length of air-rifle barrels is such, that an appreciable amount of air is vented from the muzzle *after* the pellet has left the rifle. This is unavoidable if air-rifles are to be kept compact and easily handled, although it is an established fact that a longer barrel does result in greater efficiency, and therefore increased power.

We must not lose sight, however, of the fact that by increasing the length of the barrel we also increase friction between pellet and rifling and it is this very friction that contributes its share to loss of efficiency.

Another factor which is responsible for a certain amount of lost power is the spin imparted to the pellet by the rifling, but this is necessary for accurate shooting and cannot be dispensed with, although muzzle velocity would be slightly greater if the pellet travelled straight through the barrel without turning.

Another frictional loss occurs between the piston and the cylinder, and although we have seen that the spring developed 20 foot pounds of energy, when tested on the bench, this was reduced to 18 foot pounds when the piston was working in contact with the walls of the cylinder.

We will now turn our attention to the air pressure generated inside the rifle.

The diameter of the piston head was 1·1 inches giving an area of ·95 square inches. The bore diameter was ·177 inches making the area of the bore ·0246 square inches.

Maximum compression in spring air-rifles is reached when the piston is within ¼ inch of the limit of its travel and it is at this point that the pellet starts moving.

The total air capacity of the cylinder at ordinary atmospheric pressure (·95 x 2·5 cubic inches) is suddenly compressed into a space measuring ·95 x ·25 inches and as the pellet starts to move, this volume of compressed air is driven into the barrel, causing the pellet to travel about 10 inches (·95 x ·25) ÷ ·0246. After the pellet has travelled approximately 10 inches, the mass of compressed air expands and continues its thrust against the base of the pellet for the remaining 9 or 10 inches of barrel length.

The remaining pressure will be lost when the pellet leaves the muzzle.

It has been calculated that in an air-rifle of these dimensions, the air acts on the base of the ·177 pellet with a pressure of approximately 100 pounds to the square inch.

It is interesting to consider the progressive rise in air pressure from the moment the spring is released until maximum compression is attained.

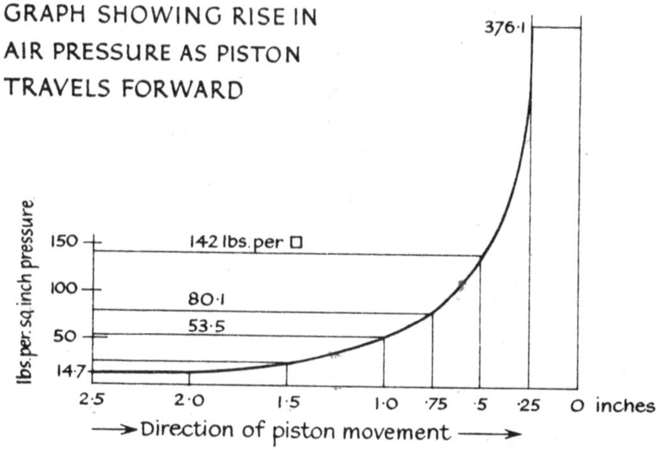

This can best be seen by means of the graph which I have drawn, showing clearly how the air pressure rises slowly at first and then more rapidly, building up very rapidly to a climax when the piston is $\frac{1}{4}$ of an inch from the end of its travel.

From this position the presssure drops, and the piston eventually stops when it is $\frac{1}{8}$ inch from the end of the cylinder, *and not until the pellet has left the muzzle does the piston complete its travel.* It is for this very reason that shooters are advised not to discharge their air-rifles unless loaded with a pellet, as if this is not done, the air is vented from the muzzle without being appreciably compressed and there is nothing to stop the smashing blow of the spring driven piston from causing fracture and breakage.

CHAPTER 21

LATER DEVELOPMENTS

THIS chapter has been added to keep readers informed of the principal developments in the field of air and gas weapons and to describe the latest types of such arms.

Many new models are now in production by established manufacturers, in most instances taking the place of their forerunners. This is all by way of progress; although manufacturers who frequently produce new designs create a problem for the supply of spares for the older models.

Spare parts thus become difficult to obtain quickly, and usually within a year or two no spare parts are available; any enthusiast wanting to replace a broken part may have to have it especially made, which can be very expensive.

There have been no major changes in the size and shape of pellets, and the well-known waisted shape still hold sway. Experiments are in progress on pellets made of aluminium, different alloys, and various plastics.

Triumph Brand air-rifle pellets are no longer available and will not be produced again.

The 'Triumph' heavyweight double flanged pellets were originally intended for use in the older types of smooth-bored air-guns, as they gave a better air-seal between pellet and bore, and they did perform very well in such weapons. The valid argument against their use was that the double flanged head increased friction between the pellet and the bore of the gun.

The advantage of such pellets used in modern high-velocity air-rifles is the considerably greater shocking power or muzzle energy resulting by the increased weight; whilst the improved sealing reduces air losses to a minimum; always assuming that such pellets are only used in rifles of sufficient power to overcome the additional friction created. Another loss is that of the old ·25 or No. 3 bore waisted pellet. No air-rifles of this calibre have been made for many years, although formerly there were several makes of air-rifles that fired ·25 pellets.

The demand for this pellet has therefore become very small and for some years only Lanes Ltd., and Webley and Scott Ltd., have manufactured them. Recently Lanes have discontinued their ·25 'Beatall' pellet, and in 1960 Webley and Scott have followed suit; neither firm will make them again. If these ·25 pellets are pushed through a small and easily made die, the result is a heavyweight ·22 pellet. This die need only consist of a small block of brass or steel through which a hole has been drilled and tapered with a taper brooch or reamer. This hole would need to be about ¾ inch long and slightly larger than ·25 inches at its largest end. The small end should be exactly the diameter of your air-rifle bore, so that the finished pellet will be exactly the size required.

Since the last edition I have had so many requests for the old ·25 air-rifle pellets that, after negotiations with various pellet manufacturers, I have found one willing to co-operate with me on supplies. This pellet maker has agreed to make ·25 pellets exclusively for me, and if any reader unable to obtain these pellets cares to write to me, I can supply his needs. Future supplies will depend entirely on demand, so if you own a ·25 air-rifle and want to be able to buy pellets in the future, you must use your weapon as much as possible to ensure a continuance of the availability of pellets.

A brand of pellets now available is the 'R.W.S. Diabolo' (often called 'Squirrel Brand'). These pellets are of the popular waisted shape but have a perfectly flat head, and are manufactured to a very high standard of precision. They are made in both ·177 and ·22 calibre and are also available for target shooters in small plastic containers holding 100 ·177 size. These containers are flat in shape, and each pellet fits snugly into its own cavity in the plastic, whilst a metal cover can be slid back exposing in turn each row of 5 pellets. Pellets cannot rub against one another and become deformed, as they often do when packed loosely in a tin; there is the added advantage of it being quick and easy to tip out 5 pellets at a time for club shooting.

'R.W.S. Diabolo' pellets are dearer than other brands, but appear to be growing in popularity with air-rifle club-men. I consider them very good; and when used in some air-rifles they give a higher muzzle velocity than other brands. It's well worth trying *many different brands of pellets* in order to find those that best suit your own air- or gas-rifle or pistol. My own experiments have shown that this can increase muzzle velocity by as much as 12 per cent.

Several arms described and illustrated in this book are now no longer made. Both the Schimel and the Plainsman gas-pistols are now obsolete, and the latter was only in production for a few months. The Schimel gas-pistol suffered a similar fate, although the weapon was redesigned as a 6-shot repeater using ball ammunition. It was again marketed, but under the name of Carbo-Jet. After a few months' production it again ceased, and it is now a rarity.

The Schimel used a type of gas release quite unlike anything that has been utilized before or since. It consisted of a sliding seal shaped like a double cup, the centre of which fitted closely over the breech-end of the barrel tube whilst the outer cup flanges made close contact with the inner walls of the pressure chamber. The charging lever released a charge of gas in front of this seal, and when the trigger was pressed the disengagement of the sear allowed the cup seal to be blown backwards away from the breech-end of the barrel by the gas pressure, thus exposing the pellet, to the instantaneous blast of gas which drove it up the barrel.

Other gas-operated weapons now out of production are

the Crosman models filling from a separate CO_2 cylinder.

All Crosman gas weapons now in production are charged with either one or two Crosman 'Powerlets'. The majority of shooters prefer this system, as these small gas bulbs are very convenient to use; are easily carried in one's pocket; and, being expendable, are simply thrown away when empty.

Crosman make an adaptor which is interchangeable with the normal gas cap of their gas-rifles and pistols. It contains a shuttle-type valve and is screwed to suit the threads of a 10 oz. gas cylinder, so that the weapons can be charged from one of these cylinders. This system gives more shots per filling and much cheaper shooting, because one only pays for the gas used and not for the cost of making and marketing the powerlets. The disadvantages are that the larger cylinder must be carried around on shooting expeditions, and if the cylinder runs out unexpectedly no more shooting can be done unless a spare is carried. This should not happen if the shooter weighs his cylinder occasionally and thereby keeps a check on the gas content.

The Hahn Model 166 Lever Action BB Repeater (Weight 3 lb., Overall Length 24 inches, Barrel Length 17 inches) is a junior-type magazine air-gun of lower power, ideal for the young shooter. It is powered by one Crosman powerlet and fires up to 100 shots on one charge of gas. The barrel is not rifled, the weapon shoots either steel or lead ·177 BB shot. The triggerguard lever has a space for the fingers and a very short stroke of only 2 inches. To operate the gun the knurled gas cap is unscrewed, a powerlet dropped in (small-end first) and the cap replaced. The lever is moved downwards and back again and the trigger is pressed. This pierces the gas bulb seal and releases the gas into the expansion chamber. The tube magazine is filled with shot by drawing back the magazine feed slide and dropping BB shot into the loading hole until full. It is now only necessary to move the lever down and up again to cock and load the gun ready for shooting; repeating the movement for each successive shot. The cocking is effortless and the gun can be fired very rapidly. When using steel shot in any air- or gas-powered arm, it is dangerous to shoot at a steel-backed target or at any very solid substance, as the steel shot will rebound with considerable force and could easily cause injury to the shooter.

The Hahn '45' single-action gas-operated revolver is a very cleverly designed weapon built on the lines of the old ·45 Peacemaker 6 shooter. It has the same overall length of 10 $\frac{5}{16}$ inches and the same feel and balance, and the hammer can be 'fanned' and shots ripped off at lightning speed. The revolver has a smooth-bored barrel and is of low power. The cylinder holds 6 shots and the tube magazine a further 12, giving 18 in all. To operate the weapon a powerlet is placed underneath the barrel and pushed backwards so that the neck of the powerlet enters the cylinder. The knurled nut in front of the powerlet is turned until the gas bulb is held securely in place. The hammer is cocked and the trigger pressed to pierce the gas bulb seal. The hammer is pulled back to half cock and the tube magazine filled by drawing back the feed slide, dropping 12 shot in the loading hole, and releasing the feed slide again. The cylinder must be revolved by hand one complete turn, which results in 6 shots being deposited in the cylinder from the tube magazine, which can now be topped up with a further 6 shots. The hammer is pulled back to full cock and the revolver is ready to fire. Either lead or steel BB shot can be used, and as one powerlet will fire about 80 shots, shooting is very economical.

The Crosman Single Six Revolver is a gas-operated revolver identical to the Hahn '45', except that the calibre is ·22, the barrel is rifled, and there is no tube magazine.

The weapon is more powerful and more accurate owing to its rifled barrel. The Single Six is operated in the same way, except that the six ·22 pellets are loaded directly into the front of the cylinder. This is accomplished by drawing back the hammer to half cock and revolving the cylinder by hand as each pellet is pushed backwards, tail-end first, into each chamber. The hammer can be 'fanned' and all six shots are then capable of being rattled off at top speed.

The Crosman Model 130 ·22 calibre pneumatic pistol (Model 137 ·177 calibre) has been modified slightly. Instead of a wooden pump handle it is made of pressed steel, and the wooden grip plates have been replaced by plastic ones which fit the hand better. The pistol is self-cocking and as soon as it has been pumped and loaded with a pellet it is ready to shoot.

The Crosman Models 150 ·22 calibre and 157 ·177 calibre gas-pistols have also been modified by fitting larger and more robust front and rear sights, but the hand-fitting plastic grips have been replaced by straight ones. For high power the cocking knob is pulled back as far as possible, but for low power only half-way, until a click is heard. When released, the cocking knob returns to fit closely against the pistol body. The internal hammer has two grooves in which the sear can engage, and the strength of the hammer blow on the valve stem is determined by whether the hammer spring is fully or only partly compressed: hence the two cocking positions.

The Crosman Models 140 and 147 pneumatic rifles (·22 and ·177 respectively) are basically the same, but do not have to be cocked before pumping. The bolt handle has been dispensed with, the breech is enclosed with a sliding cover like the Crosman pneumatic pistol.

Crosman Model 180 ·22 calibre gas-rifle (Weight 4 lb., Overall Length 34 inches—and Model 187 ·177 calibre) is a bolt-action single-shot gas-rifle cocked by means of the knurled knob at the breech-end of the gas chamber. It is charged by a single powerlet gas bulb, which gives approximately 40 shots at a muzzle velocity of 450 feet per second. Groups of ¾ inch can be shot at 25 feet, and the killing range is 35 yards with an extreme carrying range of 100 yards. It is fitted with a cross-lock positive safety catch, an open adjustable vee backsight and a ramp-type front sight. Construction is of blued steel throughout and the stock is detachable by means of a knurled thumb nut.

The Crosman Model 160 ·22 calibre single-shot gas-rifle (Weight 5 lb. 10 oz., Overall Length 39¼ inches—and Model 167 ·177 calibre) is built on the same lines as the 180 and 187, but is a more powerful weapon charged with 2 powerlets, which give approximately 50 shots at 600 feet per second. Further refinements are a really good micrometer aperture backsight and a safety catch automatically applied when the bolt is pulled back, whilst the closing of the bolt automatically cocks the rifle. The rifle is operated by unscrewing the gas cap and inserting 1 powerlet (neck first) followed by the second one, round-end first, and replacing the gas cap. The rifle is cocked and fired once, and this automatically pierces both gas bulbs simultaneously; the rifle is then ready for use. The killing range is 40 yards and the extreme range 100 yards.

The Crosman Model 400 Repeating gas-rifle ·22 calibre is fitted with a 10-shot detachable tube magazine, and each opening and closing of the bolt automatically carries a pellet from the tube magazine to the breech. Two powerlets are used in charging the rifle and it is cocked by pulling back a knurled knob similar to the Model 180 gas-rifle. The pellet feed is designed for Crosman Brand pellets, which are slightly longer than other makes; the operation of the bolt is smooth and effortless and the pellets feed perfectly in any position. 'Marksman' pellets will work successfully provided, of course, that the shooter closes the bolt in one quick smart movement without hesitation or fumbling. Failure to do this will result in the pellets turning sideways and jamming, necessitating removal of the magazine and pushing out the jammed pellets with a cleaning rod.

One of the latest additions to the Crosman range of gas-operated weapons is the Model 99 gas rifle. This is a fine-looking *lever*-action arm, closely resembling the well-known Marlin series of lever-action cartridge rifles.

It is powered by a Crosman gas powerlet inserted in the underside of the receiver and held tightly in place by a few turns of a circular slotted nut. The Crosman 99 gas rifle is made in ·22 calibre only and is unique in being the first *lever*-action repeating gas rifle to feed and fire waisted pellets. The magazine, located within the receiver on the left side, holds 14 ·22 pellets which are kept pressed against the feed cam by a light spring loading.

The cocking lever forms the trigger guard, and the extension of this forms a loop for the fingers. The lever stroke is short and effortless and automatically feeds a pellet from the magazine to the breech, whilst at the same time cocking the external hammer. This 'one-stroke operation' gives the rifle a very high rate of firing, and in fact it is quite easy to fire all 14 shots in 14 seconds.

Up to 60 shots can be fired from one Crosman gas powerlet; whilst if higher power is desired the lever is operated and the hammer manually pulled back to a second-notch position, which gives approximately 40 high-velocity shots from one gas bulb.

The rifle is 39 inches in overall length, with a 10-inch rifled barrel, and weighs about 6 lb. The foresight, a hooded blade set on a ramp, and the open backsight are fully adjustable both vertically and laterally.

The rifle's receiver is drilled and tapped ready for attaching the Crosman pressed steel telescopic sight mount; and if this is fitted, then either the Crosman Superscope or any other telescope with a similar tube diameter can be speedily mounted on the rifle.

Perhaps the most remarkable weapon in the Crosman range is the Model 600 Semi-automatic gas-pistol. This is the product of four years of experimental work by the designers and engineers and is years ahead of all other gas-operated arms. The sight base is $8\frac{3}{4}$ inches and the barrel length $5\frac{1}{16}$ ins.: Weight 2 lb. 10 oz., Overall Length $9\frac{5}{8}$ inches.

The rifling of the barrel is the usual right-hand twist, one turn in 16 inches with 6 lands. The rear sight is fully adjustable and the trigger pull short and crisp. Each pistol is factory-tested to group in $\frac{3}{4}$ inch at 25 feet, which is better than the majority of shooters can hold. One powerlet provides the gas charge and fires approximately 40 shots at an average velocity of 340 feet per second.

To charge the pistol with gas the knurled slide on the left side is pushed rearwards and then moved to its forward position. This cocks the internal hammer and allows the outlet valve to close. The gas cap is unscrewed and a powerlet inserted, round-end first. The gas cap is screwed on fully to pierce the seal and then quickly backed off a fraction of a turn to release the gas from the bulb. The pellet magazine is filled by drawing back the magazine feed slide into a notch, dropping in 10 pellets through the loading gap, and gently releasing the feed slide again. Although the feed is designed to operate with Crosman pellets and holds 10 of these, it will work perfectly with several other brands of English pellets and will hold 12 of some makes.

The pistol is now ready for use; each time the trigger is pressed to shoot the pistol will re-cock and re-load entirely automatically. One charging of gas will fire 40 shots at an average muzzle velocity of 340 feet per second. The pistol is fitted with plastic grip plates which fit the hand very well; a safety-catch is also provided. The backsight is fully adjustable. This pistol should be handled with extreme care and the safety-catch applied immediately shooting is stopped, because as long as there is gas in the chamber and pellets in the magazine, the pistol will remain fully cocked and loaded.

Crosman are now producing a slide-action repeater air-gun. This is the model V350, a low-priced junior-type firing BB shot, giving a muzzle velocity of approximately 350 feet per second. It can be used either as a single-shot weapon or a ·22 repeater; at a glance it can be seen whether the arm is cocked or loaded and if the magazine is filled or empty. The gun is cocked and loaded by merely sliding back the barrel with the left hand and pulling it forward again. It is then ready to shoot.

The Crosman Arms Co., Inc., now manufactures two new ·22 gas-operated revolvers, which are beautifully styled and extremely well designed and are a considerable advance on the company's original 'Single Six' gas revolver. These two weapons are known as the 'Target' Model H.38T with 6-inch barrel and the 'Combat' Model H.38C with $3\frac{1}{2}$-inch barrel; apart from the barrel lengths they are identical.

These revolvers can be used with either single or double action and have fully adjustable sights. Loading has been considerably simplified and improved, as the pellets can now be loaded from the rear of the revolving magazine instead of having to be pushed in backwards from the front as in the 'Single Six'.

Another improvement is that the gas 'powerlet' is now housed inside the butt of the revolver and is not visible. Charging is accomplished by lifting off the left-hand grip plate, inserting the gas bulb and replacing the grip again. The bulb seal is pierced by tightening a screw, located at the heel of the butt and provided with a suitable coin slot. I particularly like the way in which the weapon is constructed, with a removable cover plate, so that the mechanism can be inspected without fear of everything flying apart as it does on many mass-produced weapons. The overall length of the 'Target' model is 11 inches and the weight 2 lb. 12 oz.; the 'Combat' is $8\frac{1}{2}$ inches long, weight 2 lb. $8\frac{1}{2}$ oz.

Other additions to Crosman's comprehensive range of air and gas weapons include the 'Powermaster' Model 760 180-Shot BB repeater, which strongly resembles a normal ·22 pump-action firearm. The fore-end is actually operated as a pump to build up compression, and the power varies according to the number of strokes. The magazine holds 180 ·177 BB shot. The arm also shoots ·177 pellets. Maximum velocity is over 550 f.p.s. The stock is hardwood, the sights are fully adjustable, and provision is made for fitting a telescopic sight. Length is 35 inches and weight 4 lb. 2 oz.

The 'Slidemaster' Model 3500 is a 22-shot BB repeater which is spring operated, the barrel sliding back into the body to cock the gun, whilst a BB shot is fed in automatically at each cocking. The overall length is 36 inches and the weight 4 lb. Provision is made for 'scope mounting, and the gun is well made and finished and ideal for the younger shooter, for whom high power is not required.

The 'Carbine' Model M.1 is basically the same as the Slidemaster in power, capacity, calibre and operation, but the woodwork has been modified and a tommy-gun type of magazine added to give it the authentic carbine appearance. Overall length is $35\frac{5}{8}$ inches and weight $4\frac{1}{2}$ lb.

The Model 166 BB repeater is a 30-shot lever-action CO_2-powered arm resembling a Marlin ·22 lever-action firearm. The lever cocks the hammer, and feeds and loads the BB shot from the tube magazine to the breech. It is charged with one CO_2 powerlet, which is more than sufficient to fire a full magazine. Overall length is 34 inches and weight 3 lb. 8 oz.

The 'Pumpmaster' Model 1400 is a modified and improved version of the old Model 140 pneumatic rifle, which it replaces. Noteworthy features are the provision of a positive safety-catch which is interchangeable from right to left hand, and an adjustable trigger. Maximum muzzle velocity is in excess of 575 f.p.s., and the calibre is ·22 only. Dimensions are the same as the old Models 140 and 147.

The old Model 130 pneumatic pistol has been given a new look with a much improved hand-fitting grip in place of the two separate grip plates, and a much better rearsight and foresight. A further improvement is the fitting of a larger pump lever grip, which is designed not only to improve the appearance but to make pumping easier—and it certainly does both! General dimensions are the same as the Model 130 pneumatic pistol.

The 'Pellmaster' Model 700 ·22 calibre and 707 ·177 calibre CO_2 repeating rifle has been developed particularly for the American N.R.A. 10-metre air-rifle competitions, has a quick-loading rotary-type magazine and high comb 'Monte Carlo' type stock, and is powered by a single Crosman CO_2 gas bulb; it produces steady muzzle velocities of approximately 500 f.p.s. in ·22 calibre and 550 f.p.s. in ·177. The gas powerlet is pierced by a simple push-button, once the bulb has been inserted and the gas cap replaced. Overall length is 36¾ inches and weight approximately 4 lb.

The 'Powermatic' Model 500 is a 100-shot semi-automatic CO_2 repeater using BB shot, and can be fired as fast as one can press and release the trigger. It will fire 100 shots from one powerlet at approximately 350 f.p.s., which makes it remarkably inexpensive to shoot. It has a tubular spring-loaded magazine and the usual elevating open rearsight and blade foresight, and is a well designed, robust, and good-looking arm. Overall length is 37¾ inches and weight 4½ lb.

The Mk I ·22 calibre and Mk II ·177 calibre CO_2 target pistols look, feel, and handle like fine match pistols, and are the most accurate Crosman pistols so far produced. Both have micro-type rearsights which are fully adjustable for windage and elevation, finely adjustable triggers and chequered grips with thumb-rest. Power is variable, from 300 to 400 f.p.s. for the Mk I and 320 to 420 f.p.s. for the Mk II; and 120 shots at low power or 55 at the high power setting may be expected from one Crosman CO_2 powerlet (slightly less from a standard Sparklet CO_2 bulb, although the same muzzle velocity is produced). Barrel length is 7¼ inches and the weight 43 oz.

The 'Frontier 36' CO_2 BB revolver is, as one would expect, a replica of the Colt Frontier single-action revolver, and is charged with a single powerlet. When the hammer is cocked the cylinder revolves, and as the BB shot are fired from the revolving cylinder the spring-loaded magazine automatically refills the chambers. As the filled cylinder holds 6 BB shot and the magazine a further 12, a total of 18 shots can be fired without reloading. Overall length is 10⅜ inches and weight 34 oz. Great fun for Western enthusiasts!

The 'Peacemaker 44' is a revolver similar in operation

and mechanism to the Frontier, but is modelled as a replica of the old Colt Peacemaker with long spur hammer. It is a straightforward 6-shot BB CO_2-operated arm without the spring-loaded feed magazine, and has a revolving cylinder holding one BB shot in each of its 6 chambers. Like the Frontier BB revolver it is very cleverly designed, and once again is great fun for budding cowboys of all ages from nine to ninety!

Last, but by no means least, is one of the most remarkable of CO_2 Arms, the 'Trapmaster' 1100 skeet shotgun.

This weapon has been evolved by Crosman engineers to bring low-cost skeet shooting within the reach of all. It is quite true to say that Crosman Arms Co. not only have invented the new American sport of miniature clay shooting but have designed and are producing the guns and all the necessary accessories as well.

The 'Trapmaster' is a single shot CO_2 gun of ·380 gauge 46½ inches long with a 28-inch barrel, weighing 6¼ lb. and making very little noise when discharged. As its range and power are much less than those of a conventional powder arm it can be used safely in quite small areas such as back gardens. With the special miniature clays and the specially made trap really grand and inexpensive sport is assured.

The Model 50 trap throws the clays up to 60 feet at any angle, and is fitted with a foot-actuated release which can be put at a distance to give remote control. The clays are everlasting, being in fact made of moulded plastic, shaped like normal clays, but with an outer ring that breaks away when hit and can be snapped on again and used indefinitely. The shot shells are small plastic tubes with a projecting rim at one end, filled with shot and closed with a wad at each end. As the shot shells are very cheap and easily obtainable in the U.S.A., once one has acquired the outfit the cost of shooting the gun is reduced to the base cost of the gas powerlets, the shot, and the wads.

The cartridges normally hold 55 No. 8 shot, but of course any other size shot can be used. In fact these shells are available in different colours to distinguish shot size loading, and the shells, shot, wads, and simple loading tool are sold as an outfit complete with a box large enough to carry the equipment plus powerlets and clays.

Coming back to the gun itself, this is charged with two powerlets at once, and has a power control for high or low setting. On high power 30-shot shells can be fired; on low power 40. The range is up to 60 feet, and although the shot will travel farther, the pattern thins out at anything over this range and is not effective. The extreme carrying range of the shot (*not* the effective range) if the gun is elevated 30° is 300 feet.

The bore is not choked, and using No. 8 shot the pattern size is: at 10 feet, 3 inches; at 20 feet, 5 inches; at 30 feet, 8 inches; and at 60 feet, 18 inches. The gun can also be used like any other small-bore shotgun for the destruction of small birds and vermin, provided it is used at close ranges only.

Since Crosman have now been making and filling their own gas bulb 'powerlets' for some time, they have modified their gas weapons so that they can only be used with their own powerlets. The Crosman powerlet has a smaller neck than the standard type CO_2 soda bulbs and a new type of gas seal is used. The gas cap, as fitted to their gas-rifles and pistols, is now made with a smaller diameter recess where the piercing-pin is located, and this only accommodates the small neck of their own powerlets, not the standard size neck of an ordinary gas bulb. To operate a Crosman 600 auto-gas pistol using an English 'sparklet' gas bulb, it is now necessary (as well as using a metal spacer behind the bulb to bring the bulb length up to the length of a powerlet), to modify the gas cap as follows:

Set the gas cap up in a lathe chuck, using a brass or dural split collar to hold the cap in front of the knurled grip, and carefully turn out the diameter of the recess to approximately ·350 inches, sufficiently to accommodate the neck of the sparklet. The pistol will then operate perfectly.

English sparklets contain the same gas under the same pressure as the American powerlets and therefore give exactly the same muzzle velocity, but being shorter in length *they will not fire as many shots*. A pistol such as the Model 600 which will give 40 shots from a powerlet will give only 30 from a sparklet bulb and if this is taken as a comparison ratio the number of shots any Crosman weapon will fire on a sparklet can be easily estimated.

All other American or European gas-rifles and pistols (except those made by Crosman) that use the gas bulb system for charging operate on standard gas bulbs, of the same size as the normal English sparklets.

The Hämmerli Target gas-pistol (Weight 2 lb. 10 oz., Overall Length just over 13 inches) Model R.D. is the most accurate gas-pistol that has ever been commercially produced. It has several unique features. The barrel is $5\frac{1}{2}$ inches long, rifled 1 turn per 18 inches and the backsight is micrometrically adjustable both laterally and vertically. The sight base is $11\frac{1}{8}$ inches. The grip is solid and massive and fits the hand perfectly, and the adjustable trigger pull is extremely fine. The pistol is made only in ·177 calibre and can be used as a single-shot weapon by loading pellets singly through the breech-loading tap, or as a repeater by dropping 6 ·177 precision ball-shot in the loading hole just behind the loading tap. To operate the pistol, unscrew the knurled gas cap, insert a standard gas bulb small-end first and replace the gas cap cock by pulling back the knurled cap; then press the trigger to pierce the bulb seal. The pistol is now ready for use. If used as a repeater it is only necessary to re-cock for each shot as the balls feed in by gravity. It will fire about 70 shots on one charge of gas and is designed solely as a high-grade super-accurate target pistol. It is not a powerful weapon and is not suitable for any other type of shooting.

Hämmerli also manufacture a single-shot precision gas-pistol similar to their model R.D. gas-pistol but with the following differences: the pistol is cocked by pulling back with finger and thumb the two cocking knobs located on each side of the pistol immediately above the trigger. It has a patented spring-loader, simple, safe and positive, which will load either a ·177 waisted pellet or a ·177 ball shot; and a blow-off device which empties the pressure chamber.

Hämmerli also make two precision gas-rifles, the 'Match' and the 'Junior' in calibre ·177, which are ideal for target and competition shooting as they are absolutely free from recoil or vibration, and both have the famous Hämmerli 'split hair' accuracy.

Hämmerli have recently developed a precision air-rifle especially for competition shooters. This is called the Hämmerli Puma, is produced in ·177 calibre only, and sets a high standard of quality. Special features include a rotary breech-loading block, removable barrel weight, adjustable trigger, fully adjustable micrometer sights, side cocking lever for easy cocking from the prone shooting position, and massive hardwood stock with cheekpiece.

The receiver is grooved to take a stand and telescopic sight, and the rifle is designed to give a high degree of accuracy and penetration with negligible recoil. Removal of barrel weight, and adjustment to trigger pressure, can only be carried out when the stock has been removed, and this, I feel, is unnecessarily irksome and could be improved.

The world-famous German Haenel air-rifles are available again in England, and represent really amazing value for money, being almost half the price of other air-rifles of comparable power, size, and quality.

The standard model is available in both ·22 and ·177 calibres and is a full-size adult weapon producing the maximum power legally allowed without a firearm certificate (approximately 550 f.p.s. for the ·22 and 600 f.p.s. for the ·177). Special features include an adjustable trigger, elevating open rearsight, hooded foresight, steel butt plate, grooved receiver for attaching 'scope sight, and an automatic safety-catch located at the extreme rear of the spring chamber. The rifle is a standard break-barrel cocking type, with an extra link on the cocking arm for easier operation. The safety-catch knob must be pushed forwards after each cocking before the rifle can be discharged. Dimensions are: barrel length 14 inches, overall length 43½ inches, weight 6¾ lb. The Haenel match rifle is a lower-powered precision weapon with massive pistol-grip stock, micrometer-type aperture sight with 6-hole eyepiece and rubber eyecup. The rifle is cocked and loaded by means of a bolt, the trigger is adjustable and the foresight is the tunnel type with interchangeable sight elements. The weapon is available in ·177 calibre only. Dimensions are: barrel length 16½ inches, overall length 43¾ inches, and weight 7½ lb.

The Walther Model LP2 pneumatic pistol is undoubtedly the Rolls-Royce of air-pistols, and the finest target air-pistol I have ever handled; moreover it is the only *pneumatic* pistol so far produced that does not come within the scope of the latest legislation and therefore does *not* need a firearm certificate. Dimensions are: barrel length 9½ inches, overall length 13 inches, weight 2 lb. 14 oz. The pistol is fitted with a micrometer backsight, which is provided with click adjustments for both vertical and lateral adjustment; the foresight is matted to eliminate glare, and the sight base is 11½ inches. The end of the pump lever is shaped to fit neatly round the outside of the trigger guard, and one stroke only of the pump charges the pistol. It is, in fact, impossible to use more than one stroke as no inlet valve is used; and, the air chamber being an extension of the pump cylinder, the air is merely held compressed in front of the pump piston.

The barrel, which is fitted with a really hermetic 'O' ring instead of the usual leather breech washer, pivots slightly downwards for loading, and the locking catch is located underneath. Four separate trigger adjustments are provided: length of pull before release; exact release point; trigger travel after release; and weight of pull. In common with other pneumatic arms it produces no movement or recoil whatever on discharge. It is produced in ·177 calibre only and the pump mechanism is self-lubricating.

The Heathways Plainsman Model 9401 semi-automatic gas-pistol (Weight 1 lb. 12 oz., Length 9¼ inches, Height 6¼ inches—not to be confused with the obsolete 'Plainsman' single-shot gas-pistol) is a cleverly designed weapon built to resemble the Colt Woodsman. It shoots BB steel shot and can be fired as fast as one can pull the trigger. The trigger has a light but very long pull, because the first part of the pull operates the slide which feeds the steel shot to the breech. The magazine is located within the body of the pistol and is filled by sliding up the cover which carries the backsight and pouring in up to 100 balls.

There is a power controller, giving three separate power stages, at the heel of the butt near the gas plug, operated by inserting a coin into a slotted spigot and turning to the desired power. To charge the pistol with gas the gas plug is unscrewed, a standard gas bulb inserted round-end first and the plug replaced. The small lever in the plug head is pulled upwards to pierce the bulb seal, and as soon as the magazine has been filled the pistol is ready for use. A safety-catch is provided, which disconnects the trigger mechanism and prevents discharge. The safety-catch should always be applied if shooting is stopped, as the pistol remains loaded as long as there are shots in the magazine; and with this weapon, even if the shots are tipped out of the magazine, one will still remain in the feed slide. It is designed expressly as a plinking pistol, and although accurate enough for vermin shooting it is not a target pistol.

A small round magnet is set into the vertical feed slide. This holds each shot successively in the breech after it has been fed by gravity from the magazine, and for this reason only steel shot can be used in the pistol. Approximately 60, 45 and 35 shots can be fired on low, medium and high power respectively, and the penetration on high power is astonishing. High power shooting penetrates right through both sides of the average tin can; but steel shot does not spread on impact like lead pellets do and penetration is therefore much greater.

Another Plainsman CO_2 pistol made by the same firm and looking the same is Model 9400. This pistol has a rifled barrel and fires nickel-plated ·177 round lead balls; it is much more accurate and is well worth the small extra cost.

The Western CO_2 is available in America in three models. Model 9404 fires ordinary No. 1 BB shot, either lead or steel, and is a single-action weapon, with a capacity of 20 shots. A power adjustment allows the choice of medium or high power at will, and the makers claim that, using the high power setting, steel BB shot will easily penetrate the average tin can. Another feature is the removable barrel, allowing ·177 calibre darts to be fired.

Available also are: the Model 9406, basically the same weapon except that the barrel is rifled and it is designed to fire ·177 nickel- or copper-plated round lead balls, with much greater precision; the Model 9405 again looks the same as the Model 9404 and 9406, but the arm is operated by spring power like an ordinary spring air-pistol, and is intended solely for short-range indoor practice.

The Daisy Manufacturing Co. of America have entered the CO_2 field and they are now manufacturing a good-looking repeating gas-pistol. This is the 'Daisy Model 200 gas-pistol' and closely resembles the Colt and Hi-standard range of ·22 cartridge pistols.

The Daisy 200 is not a powerful pistol, but is designed to provide a lot of shooting on very little gas. The pistol will accept either the standard CO_2 sparklets type of gas bulb, or the larger bulbs which they also market; using the larger bulb, approximately the same size as a Crosman Powerlet, up to 160 shots can be obtained. The pistol fires ordinary ·177 BB shot and the magazine has a capacity of 175 BBs. The backsight is fully adjustable for elevation and windage.

I consider the Daisy CO_2 one of the nicest-looking of the inexpensive ·177 BB Guns. I particularly like its streamlined appearance, its simplicity of construction in having a minimum of moving parts, and the fact that, although the pistol holds 175 BB Shot and either lead or steel can be used, only 5 shots can be fired rapid. To replenish the magazine for a further 5 shots it is only necessary to push the spring-loaded feeder forward, repeating the movement every fifth shot until all the BBs have been used.

Other Daisy products include the Model 300 CO_2-operated 200-shot semi-automatic BB gun. This is a most unorthodox-looking weapon, but is a joy to shoot and can be held very firmly and steadily, thanks to the unusual but practical grip. The gas bulb is inserted into the grip itself, and the same 5-shot device is employed as on the Model 200 pistol, although in this case the gun actually holds approximately 200 BBs. The stock and fore-end are moulded plastic grained to resemble wood. Dimensions are: overall length 38 inches, sight base 18¼ inches, and weight approximately 4 lb.

The Daisy Model 26 BB gun is a replica of the well-known Remington 'Fieldmaster' ·22 rifle, and is a 45-shot pump-action repeater of lower power, but nevertheless ideal for a youngster, and good fun for adults too.

The Model 1894 BB gun is a replica of the Winchester lever-action 44–40 saddle carbine, and is a 40-shot repeater, cocking and loading by the underlever. The Model 96 is a 700-shot lever-action shooting type BB repeater, and can be supplied with or without telescope sight.

The Model 95 is basically the same, but with differently shaped stock and fore-end. The Model 94 is a cheaper and smaller 500-shot carbine-type repeater, and the Model 102, the smallest of the BB repeaters, is also a lever-action 500-shot-capacity gun.

We next come to the Daisy series of pellet guns and rifles, of which there are 6 separate models, becoming progressively larger, heavier and more powerful.

Model 160 is a junior smooth-bore gun shooting pellets or darts, and produces a remarkable 450 f.p.s. velocity. All are reliable, well-made weapons with ample power. The 440 and the 460 have fully adjustable micrometer target-type aperture sights, with rubber eyecups and hooded

Model	*Calibre*	*Bore*	*Overall Length* (in.)
160	·177	smooth	33
220	·177	rifled	36
230	·22	rifled	38
250	·22	rifled	39
440	·177	rifled	39
460	·22	rifled	42

foresights. The complete series all have beechwood stocks. An unusual feature on both the 440 and 460 is the safety-catch. Personally, I am not keen on safety catches on spring-operated air-rifles, as shooters tend to cock the rifles, apply the safety catches, and then forget to discharge them; this compression of the spring for lengthy periods completely ruins the power of the rifles, and spring replacements are needed frequently.

The Daisy Model 179 'Spittin' Image' is a spring-operated BB revolver modelled as a replica of the Colt Peacemaker. A 12-shot repeater with spring-loaded tube magazine, it gives remarkable accuracy at 10 feet range, although the power is of course rather low, as one would expect for this type of arm.

There is also a low-powered spring-operated Daisy target pistol, which is a 150-shot BB repeater resembling an orthodox type of automatic pistol, and this also gives accurate shooting at 10 feet only.

Lastly in the Daisy series of weapons is a rifle so completely new in concept that it could well revolutionize the manufacture of sporting rifles. This is the V/L Model 0002 ·22-calibre single-shot rifle, and it is the first production rifle to use caseless ammunition. It is a true *firearm*, but I have included it here as it is so interesting, because it uses the principle of air compression to ignite the propellent. The rifle is of handsome appearance and looks very much like an ordinary single-shot ·22 cartridge firearm, but here the resemblance ends.

The rifle contains a piston (driven by a very powerful spring) and working in a cylinder exactly like a spring-operated air rifle. This spring is cocked by a lever positioned underneath the rifle. When the lever is operated the piston is forced rearwards against the spring pressure and held in this position by the trigger and sear mechanism, whilst at the same time the breech opening is exposed and a V/L bullet is inserted. Closing the lever against the rifle hermetically seals the breech.

Each V/L projectile is actually a 29-grain lead bullet having the V/L propellent attached to it. They are packed conveniently in plastic tubes each holding ten rounds.

What actually happens when the rifle is fired is that the air in front of the piston is compressed and forced through a small hole and around a ball-check valve. The rapid compression of air causes an extreme rise in the temperature, and this jet of heated air ignites the propellent attached to the bullet. Some idea of the rifle's potency can be imagined from the fact that the 29-grain bullet is projected from the muzzle at 1150 f.p.s. Many advantages are apparent: the propellent is very clean-burning, and there are no corrosive primer fumes, no primer at all, no hammer, no firing-pin, no extractor and no ejector.

The V/L ·22 Rifle is fitted with a safety-catch, and also has a safety device to prevent the trigger's being pressed until the cocking lever is returned to its normal position against the rifle. It is available in a luxury version (Model 0003) with selected walnut stock and complete in presentation case. Both models are well-made, practical weapons and should have a big future.

Benjamin pneumatic pistols all have the same dimensions: length 11 inches, barrel length 8 inches, and sight base 10 inches, with adjustable backsight.

Model 132 is a single-shot pistol with a ·22 rifled barrel; Model 137 the same with a ·177 rifled barrel, and Model 160 has an 8-shot magazine and a smooth-bore barrel for shooting steel shot. Each pistol is well made and of good design with a turned wood pump handle, a positive cross-lock safety-catch and plastic grips which fit the hand very well. The makers claim a maximum muzzle velocity of 500 feet per second, and all will penetrate ⅜ inch of soft pine. The maximum killing range is 50 feet. The 1300 and 1320 are basically the same, but are fitted with tube magazines located along the top of the barrels. Model 1300 has a magazine holding 50 BB lead shot and Model 1320 a 35-shot magazine for ·22 calibre lead shot.

To operate these pistols the knurled bolt head is turned slightly to unlock the breech, and the bolt pulled back to cock the internal hammer. The single-shot models are loaded with a pellet and the bolt closed and locked by twisting the bolt head, but on the models fitted with a magazine the shot is gravity-fed to the breech and the balls drop in one at a time on each operation of the bolt. The pistol is pumped and then ready to use.

Model 160 will group only 4 inches at 50 feet but the others will give groups of 1¼ inches.

Benjamin gas-pistols are all 9¼ inches in length with 5¾-inch barrels and a sight base of 7¾ inches. All operate on one standard soda bulb and fire about 50 shots at 450 feet per second from one charge of gas. All have very light trigger pulls and safety-catches.

Model 260 fires BB shot through a smooth-bore barrel and will group its shot 1¼ inches. Model 262 has a rifled ·22 calibre barrel and will shoot ¾-inch groups, and Model 267 a ·177 rifled barrel and will group in ⅝-inch. All three pistols have two-stage power adjustment. Model 2600 is the same as Model 260 except for the addition of a 35-shot tube magazine mounted on top of the barrel, and Model 2620 is the same as Model 262, except for the additional tube magazine. They are operated in the same way as the Benjamin gas-rifles and will penetrate ⅜ inch of soft pine. Maximum killing range is 50 feet.

Benjamin pneumatic guns and rifles are available in many

models, both as single-shot and repeaters. They are built on the same lines as the pneumatic pistols and the following specifications are common to all models: length 35 inches, weight approximately 5 lb., gun-metal finished bronze barrels 23 inches long, walnut stocks and very light trigger pulls. All will penetrate up to 1 inch of soft pine. Maximum killing range is 40 yards. The makers claim a muzzle velocity of 700 feet per second at full power. Model 310 single-shot smooth-bore ·177 calibre; Model 312 single-shot ·22 rifled-bore; Model 317 rifled ·177 barrel. These three are also available with a custom-type stock which adds about half a pound to the weight. All have safety-catches fitted. Model 317 will group its shots in a ⅝-inch circle at 20 yards, whilst the smooth-bore pistols will group 1 inch.

The Model 720 has a 25-shot magazine, fires steel BB shot and will give groups of 3 inches; the Model 3100 has a 100-shot magazine and fires BB lead shot, and the Model 3120 is ·22 calibre and has an 85-shot tube magazine. These three models are also available with custom stocks.

Benjamin gas-rifles all operate from a single-standard gas bulb and have a two-stage power controller. About 35 shots can be fired from a sparklet-type gas bulb at an average muzzle velocity of up to 600 feet per second. Penetration is ¾ inch of soft pine, maximum killing range 35 yards.

All are operated as follows: unscrew the gas plug from the muzzle-end of the pressure chamber, insert the gas bulb neck first and replace the gas plug; then cock and fire the rifle once to pierce the gas bulb seal.

Overall length is 35 inches, bronze barrels 23 inches; they also have walnut stocks, safety-catches, and sheave-type adjustable backsights.

Model 360 ·177 calibre smooth-bore for lead shot groups 1 inch. Model 362 ·22 single-shot, with rifled barrel for shooting lead pellets, groups ¾ inch, and Model 367 ·177 single-shot rifled barrel groups ⅝ inch. All three are available with custom stock if desired.

Finally there are the repeater gas-rifles with 'Piggy Back'

tube magazines along the top of the barrels. Dimensions are the same as before. Model 3600 is a 100-shot gas carbine for shooting ·177 lead shot, and will shoot 1-inch groups. Model 3620 is similar to Model 3600 but is ·22 calibre, has an 85-shot magazine and will group in 1 inch. Both are available with or without custom stocks.

The English-made 'Cadet' and 'Cadet Major' air-rifles manufactured by B.S.A. Guns Ltd. have been replaced by a new B.S.A. rifle, the 'Meteor'. (Overall Length 41 inches, Weight 5¼ lb., Barrel 18 inches and precision rifled.) This is a very robustly made and well designed breakdown rifle roughly midway between a junior and an adult size weapon. It is available in ·177 and ·22 calibres and is surprisingly powerful, giving muzzle velocities of 550 and 500 feet per second respectively. The sight base is 16¾ inches, both sights being mounted on the barrel, as is standard practice on breakdown air-rifles. Provision is made for the attachment of a plastic telescope sight above the spring chamber, and this is available at small extra cost, and may be attached and detached by means of two knurled clamping nuts.

The B.S.A. ·22 'Airsporter' air-rifle has been improved by the cutting of two dovetail slots on either side of the spring chamber, so that the same telescopic sight can be used on this rifle. The 'Airsporter' is worthy of a better scope, and it is easy to mount a really good quality optical sight with standard mounts, using the dovetail slots already provided.

The American Hyscore single-shot air-pistol is now available in England in both ·177 and ·22 calibres and is an extremely well-designed and exceptionally powerful weapon. If a pellet from the ·177 calibre model is fired at a steel plate the pellet is completely shattered on impact, while the ·22 calibre pellet is well and truly flattened. The pistol develops its remarkable power from four important factors. Firstly the central barrel design, in which the barrel runs through the centre of the air chamber and by which means the barrel is only ¼ inch less that the overall length of the pistol. Secondly the use of a high-quality mainspring, carefully heat-treated to give maximum life and efficiency. Thirdly by the use of a neoprene air seal on the piston, completely eliminating the use of leather washers and metal piston rings; and lastly by a clever and positive breech seal at the loading hole. Loading a pellet is simply a matter of twisting the knurled breech knob to expose the loading hole, dropping a pellet in the hole and twisting the knob again. This opens and closes a shutter, which has a ground face and slides across the breech-end of the barrel and results in a very positive and hermetic seal. The pistol has a very light trigger pull comparable to a high-grade target arm, and is cocked by using the butt as a lever. By partly starting the cocking stroke the trigger is 'set' and the pistol can be aimed and snapped without harm, as unless the cocking stroke is fully completed the pistol remains uncocked and only the trigger is set. The trigger disconnects from the sear until the pistol butt is locked against the body in the firing position. The overall length of the weapon is 10¼ inches, the barrel length is 10 inches and the weight 2 lb. The pistol is manufactured mainly from steel pressings and the finish is the regulation gun-blue. The backsight is adjustable for elevation. The weapon is very accurate indeed, very reliable and extremely powerful, and is designed to function perfectly with the absolute minimum of maintenance.

Webley and Scott have discontinued the MK 1 air-pistol, although spare parts will be available for many years. The famous Webley 'Senior' air-pistol has now been discontinued and replaced by the Webley 'Premier', which is an air-pistol of similar size, weight, and power, but has the advantage of an adjustable trigger. The piston ring has been replaced by a P.T.F.E. plastic piston washer which needs no maintenance and is extremely long lasting. The Webley Junior air-rifle has been superseded by a new Junior air-rifle, the 'Jaguar'. (Weight 3 lb. 12 oz.) Further additions to the Webley air-rifle range are the 'Ranger' (Weight 3 lb. 12 oz.) and the 'Falcon'. The

Ranger is available in ·177 calibre only with smooth or rifled barrel, and is suitable for the older boy who wants something better than the Jaguar. It has a lighter trigger pull, wheel adjustable backsight and 14-inch barrel. The Falcon is available in ·177 and ·22. (Weight 6 lb., Overall Length 41½ inches, Barrel Length 17¼ inches.) The weapon is very robustly made of high-quality materials. Muzzle velocity of the ·177 calibre is 550 feet per second, and of the ·22 calibre, 500 feet per second. All Webley air-rifles now incorporate a dovetailed block on top of the breech-end of the spring chamber, so that a telescopic sight can be attached without fitting costs. Webley and Scott manufacture a low-priced telescope which fits on all their models, or there are many other makes of telescopic sights of higher power quality and price that can also be fitted.

The Webley MK 3 air-rifle remains unchanged, but for club shooters there is the Webley Super Target Club air-rifle. This is basically the same as the Mark 3 air-rifle except for a heavier barrel, a micrometer aperture sight with 6-hole eyepiece, a tunnel foresight with interchangeable sight elements and an attachment to the stock to hold the spare elements. The Super Target air-rifle is available in ·177 calibre only.

The German firm of Anschutz have now entered the very specialized field of the air-rifle marksmen, by producing a Top Grade Match air-rifle. Model 220 (Overall length 45 inches, Weight 9½ lb.) is available in ·177 calibre only. The rifle is equipped with a fully adjustable micrometer peepsight with graduated scale plate numbered dials, and tunnel foresight with interchangeable elements.

A wealth of accessories are available as extras, including an adjustable iris-type eyepiece, colour fitters, rubber eyecup, adjustable palm rest, adjustable sling, special foresight spirit level, and many others.

The rifle is an entirely new concept in weapons, and incorporates many new ideas. The rifle is cocked by a lever positioned *on the right hand side of the arm*, and this is a great advantage when shooting from the prone position. Operating the cocking lever exposes a loading platform upon which a pellet is placed and pushed into the breech of the barrel.

The piston head is fitted with a new material to provide the necessary air seal, and this material is virtually self-lubricating, which entirely eliminates the need for oiling the air chamber or the piston. The mainspring is especially heat-treated to give a durability far in excess of the life of a normal air-rifle spring, and the trigger mechanism is of the highest quality and precision. No recoil is felt on firing, due to the new system of compensating compression; and only after the pellet has left the barrel can the piston be felt to strike the end of the air cylinder. The sight base is 31½ inches and the oiled walnut stock has a chequered pistol grip and cheek piece.

This rifle is also available with cocking lever and stock especially for left-handed shooters, whilst the general feel, balance and appearance of the weapon sets a high standard of quality, ingenuity and workmanship.

The makers of the 'Original' series of air-rifles also make two spring-operated air-pistols, the Model 5 and Model 6. The former is a very large air-pistol 16 inches long, has a tunnel foresight with interchangeable elements and a fully adjustable vee backsight; because of its length it has an exceptionally long sight base. The grip is of plastic material nicely shaped to fit the hand and the pistol is made in both ·177 and ·22 calibre with nicely rifled barrels. It is virtually a breakdown air-rifle cut down to large pistol size. It is powerful and accurate and weighs 2¾ lb.

The 'Original' Model 6 air-pistol looks like the Model 5, the overall length being also 16 inches; but the weight is 3 lb., and the weapon is made in ·177 calibre only. There is one very big difference. This is the first spring-operated air-pistol without recoil or rebound. This is cleverly accomplished by utilizing two mainsprings and two pistons which are automatically pushed together and held by the sear when the pistol is cocked and are driven apart when it is fired. The original Model 6 makes use of a really revolutionary system by which one piston compresses air whilst the second one is a dummy exactly counter-balancing the thrust of the air piston. The pistol stays perfectly still during discharge and after the slug has left the barrel; no perceptible movement, no recoil and no rebound is felt at any time during shooting. The sights have also been improved by the fitting of a fully adjustable, micrometer-type vee backsight. Extremely accurate shooting is possible. The original Model 6 is made specially for target and competition shooting in calibre ·177 only.

The 'Original' series of air-rifles has an important addition in the new Model 60 Precision air-rifle. This rifle is manufactured expressly for Match and Competition shooting, and is available in ·177 calibre only. It employs the same principles, and a similar mechanism as the original Model 6 air-pistol; this results in a spring air-rifle with positively no kick, recoil or rebound whatever. The weapon weighs 9½ lb. and is 44 inches in overall length, with a barrel 19¼ inches long. It has a micrometer-type dioptric rear-sight, fully adjustable, capable of the very finest variations; and a tunnel fore-sight with interchangeable sight elements. The trigger is extremely sensitive and capable of adjustment from a pull of 3½ oz. to 14 oz.; the stock is of polished walnut with chequered pistol grip and cheek piece. The weapon possesses an air of distinction and quality. Muzzle velocity is 580 feet per second.

One of the finest (if not the finest) target air-rifle ever produced is the Feinwerkbau Model 300. This is a top grade match rifle designed to give the ultimate in precision shooting. It is of superb quality throughout; the compression cylinder is ground and honed internally, with a similarly treated piston fitted with a piston ring, and is designed to give absolutely recoil-free shooting. The cocking lever is on the *side* of the rifle, to facilitate cocking from the prone position; this lever also exposes the loading chamber when the rifle is cocked and produces an airtight breech seal when the lever is closed against the rifle. The micrometer rearsight is of course fully adjustable, and the tunnel foresight has interchangeable sight elements. The trigger is adjustable from 3 to 10 oz. and can be increased to 50 oz. by fitting an extra spring. The actual release point is also adjustable, and so is the initial trigger travel. The Feinwerkbau rifle is made in ·177 competition calibre only, and can be supplied with every conceivable accessory that one could desire. Barrel length is 22 inches and sight line 32–3 inches. Weight is 4·5 kg., or with barrel sleeve fitted 4·9 kg.

Contemporary with the above is the Feinwerkbau Model 65 match air-pistol, which is also a weapon of exceedingly high quality and built to give the ultimate in precision shooting. The cocking lever is positioned on the left side of the pistol. A similarly honed piston with piston ring working in a honed cylinder gives the compression; and the weapon is again designed to have no recoil whatever; but the recoil-eliminating device can be blocked at will to produce a recoil if preferred. Calibre is ·177 only. The trigger pull can be adjusted from 17⅜ oz. to 48 oz. The barrel length is 7½ inches, and the sight line an exceptionally long 14 inches.

The sights are of course fully adjustable with micromatric settings, and the pistol weighs 42 oz.

When this book was first published, American and other foreign pneumatic and gas-operated weapons were being imported into England in very limited quantities.

Their popularity and novelty appeal resulted in a rapidly increasing demand, until eventually the trickle of imports became a flood. Indulgent and misguided adults frequently bought these weapons for children of tender years, and needless to say many accidents were reported. With the advent of the semi-automatic gas pistol the accident rate for both youngsters and adults rose alarmingly, and it became obvious that some control on sales was necessary. (See Chapter 14.) It must be stressed that the very high accident rate was not due to any faults in the weapons in question—

only to inexperience or negligence on the part of their owners.

I would particularly ask readers to handle all air and gas weapons very carefully, and to take every possible precaution against accidents. If the accident rate rises then there is every likelihood that imports will be stopped and further restrictions placed on home sales.

One final request to all owners of pneumatic and gas-operated rifles and pistols. Please do not dismantle these to 'see how they work'. The repair and adjustment of all such weapons requires special tools and very specialized expert knowledge, and considerable harm can be done them unless you have both. Do not attempt any such work or you will almost certainly double the repair bill.

APPROXIMATE MUZZLE VELOCITIES

The muzzle velocities given on the following page are only approximate for the following reason:

1. A new spring air weapon does not usually develop its full power until it has been in use for a sufficient time for the initial stiffness of the working parts to become free, and more particularly to allow the piston to bed exactly to the cylinder.

   For this reason the spring air weapons selected were old enough to have had some use, but not sufficiently worn to have adversely affected their power.
2. To save unnecessary complications the same brand of pellets was used for tests of ·177 and ·22 weapons, but it is an undisputed fact that other makes of pellets would produce higher velocities in some weapons and lower in others.
3. The performance of all air operated arms varies appreciably with atmospheric temperature and humidity, whilst the power or gas operated weapons can vary by as much as 40 per cent from a cold winter day to a summer heatwave.

The gas-rifle and pistol velocities shown in this table were produced at a test temperature of 72°F.

TABLE OF APPROXIMATE MUZZLE VELOCITIES OF VARIOUS AIR WEAPONS

Make	Calibre	Muzzle velocity in ft. per sec.
B.S.A. Underlever Air-Rifle, 1909 (now obsolete)	·177	685
Britannia Air-Rifle, 1914 ... (now obsolete)	·177	690
Webley Mark II Air-Rifle, 1932 (now obsolete)	·177	685
Warrior Air-Pistol, 1933... ... (now obsolete)	·177	350
Webley Mark II Air-Rifle, 1937 (now obsolete)	·177	508
Greener Air-Rifle, 1939	·177	650
Abas Major Air-Pistol, 1951 ... (now obsolete)	·177	410
Acvoke Air-Pistol, 1954	·177	360
Webley Mark II Air-Rifle, 1932 (now obsolete)	·22	546
Webley Mark II Air-Rifle, 1937 (now obsolete)	·22	487
Greener Air-Rifle, 1939 ... ... (now obsolete)	·22	590
Crosman Gas-Pistol, 1954 ...	·22	600 (at full power)
Schimel Gas-Pistol, 1954 ...	·22	580
Crosman Gas-Rifle, 1954 ...	·22	700 (at full power)
Webley Mark II Air-Rifle, 1937 (now obsolete)	·25	420
Austrian Army Air-Rifle, 1780...	·44	500
Crosman Single Six Gas-Revolver	·22	330
Crosman Model 180 Gas-Rifle ..		450
Crosman Model 160 Gas-Rifle ..		600
Crosman Model 400 Gas-Rifle ..		450
Crosman Model 150 Gas-Pistol..		370
Crosman Model 130 Pneumatic-Pistol		300
Crosman Model 140 Pneumatic-Rifle (at maximum power) ..		500
Crosman Model 600 semi automatic Gas-Pistol		355
B.S.A. Airsporter	·22	550
B.S.A. Club	·177	600
B.S.A. Meteor	·177	550
B.S.A. Meteor	·22	500

COMPARATIVE DATA OF WEBLEY AIR-RIFLES AND PISTOLS

	Senior Air-Pistol ·177	Senior Air-Pistol ·22	Mark I Air-Pistol ·177	Mark I Air-Pistol ·22	Junior Air-Pistol ·177	Junior Air-Rifle ·177	Mark III Air-Rifle ·177	Mark III Air-Rifle ·22
Number of strawboards $\frac{3}{64}$" thick placed $\frac{1}{2}$" apart penetrated at 20 feet	11	13	10	11	7	12	16	18
Velocity in feet per second	360	330	350	314	290	405	600	540
Range	20 feet					30 feet		

Table Showing Dimensions of Pre-War Haenel Air Weapons

		Mod. X	Mod. XX	Mod. XXX	Mod. XXXX	Mod. I	Mod. VIII	Mod. II	Mod. III	Mod. VJ	Mod. VRJ	Mod. IV	Mod. V	Mod. VI	Mod. VII	Mod. IV R	Mod. V R	Mod. 28	Mod. 28 R	Mod. 26	Mod. 50	Mod. 51
Bore		·177	·177	·177	·177	·177 ·22	·177 ·22	·177 ·22	·177 ·22	·177	·177	·177 ·22	·177 ·22	·177 ·22	·177 ·22	·177 ·22	·177 ·22	·177 ·22	·177 ·22	·177	·177	·177
Weight . . .	oz.	31	50	56	60	74	100	106	106	82	85	114	114	130	130	122	128	40	40	24	10	10
Length overall . .	in.	31½	34½	35½	36	38¼	42	42½	42½	38	38	43	43	45½	45½	42½	42½	10	10½	10	8¾	7¾
,, of stock from trigger to butt-end .	in.	13¾	12½	12½	12½	13½	14¼	14¼	14¼	13½	13½	14¼	14¼	14¼	14¼	14¼	14¼	—	—	—	—	—
,, of barrel . .	in.	8½	14¼	14¼	14½	15¾	18½	19	19	15¾	15¾	19	19	19¼	19¼	19	19	4⅛	4	4⅛	3½	3½
Distance between sights .	in.	13¾	20⅞	13⅜	13⅜	14½	17⅝	17¾	17¾	14½	13	17	17	17¼	17¼	15¾	15¾	8¾	8¾	8¾	6¾	5¼
Rifling (inches per complete turn)		—	—	—	12	12	12	12	12	12	12	12	12	12	12	12	12	12	12	—	—	—

INDEX